Sustainable Revenue for Museums

A Guide

Sustainable Revenue for Museums

A Guide

Edited by Samantha Chmelik

ROWMAN & LITTLEFIELD
Lanham • Boulder • New York • London

Published by Rowman & Littlefield
A wholly owned subsidiary of The Rowman & Littlefield Publishing Group, Inc.
4501 Forbes Boulevard, Suite 200, Lanham, Maryland 20706
www.rowman.com

6 Tinworth Street, London SE11 5AL, United Kingdom

British Library Cataloguing in Publication Information Available

Library of Congress Cataloging-in-Publication Data Available

ISBN 978-1-5381-1298-4 (cloth: alk. paper)
ISBN 978-1-5381-1299-1 (electronic)

♾™ The paper used in this publication meets the minimum requirements of American National Standard for Information Sciences—Permanence of Paper for Printed Library Materials, ANSI/NISO Z39.48-1992.

For the volunteers, staff, and board members at museums, historic sites, zoos, aquaria, botanical gardens, and nature parks

Contents

List of Figures, Tables, and Textboxes

FIGURES

TABLES

TEXTBOXES

Acknowledgments

This idea for this book came from my editor, Charles Harmon. After multiple discussions, we honed his vision and then developed a methodology to maximize the amount of knowledge to be shared.

The over fifty museum professionals, funders, and experts who graciously contributed to this book are appreciated and humbly thanked by this editor. Their expertise and knowledge have created a unique and valuable book. New learnings unfurl each time one rereads their words. I hope that they will consider expanding their chapters into books for the benefit of the profession.

Preface

Understanding revenue strategies and tactics is vital to ensuring the long-term stability and sustainability of museums, historic sites, zoos, planetariums, aquariums, and botanical gardens. Revenue is, obviously, the lifeblood of an institution. Without it, an institution has failed its responsibility to preserve, protect, and share the stories and artifacts that the public has entrusted to it. Yet discussions, strategies, and data about revenue are difficult to find—especially in one source.

Sustainable Revenue for Museums examines how institutions balance diverse funding sources to provide sustainable revenue within the parameters of their nonprofit status. Museum professionals, consultants, and subject matter experts have come together to share their professional expertise and to build a body of knowledge that will benefit all their colleagues. They represent institutions of all budget sizes and types. You may recognize their names from their conference presentations, webinars, articles, or books. These contributors delve into the strategies and tactics that they have used in their institutions or practices to generate and manage revenue. Because the data sources used in chapter 1 are freely and publicly available, you can download future updates to maintain currency. (Note: Given the significant impact of governance structure and institution discipline on financial management strategies and tactics, this book does not directly address financial management, budget, or cost/expense reduction as holistic topics.)

Finding data and statistics about museum revenue categories and subcategories can be challenging. The latest data and expert opinions presented here can be used immediately in any department for multiple purposes with staff of all experience levels. The data provide parameters for revenue mixes, set expectations for the relative contribution of different revenue streams, and show rates of change over time. (Note: The terms "revenue" and "income" have different meanings according to their context, that is, finance, accounting, or taxation. For the purposes of this book, our contributors use revenue and income interchangeably to describe incoming monies.)

ABOUT THE CONTRIBUTORS

Why are museum professionals, consultants, and subject matter experts contributors to this book? That diversity of viewpoints offers a more holistic understanding of a topic. For example, are you considering applying for your first grant? Have you ever wondered how a foundation or grantor evaluates your grant application? After receiving a grant, how do you manage the grant funds and the relationship with the grantor? The authors in the "Contributed Income: Grants" section represent all those perspectives.

In addition to the regular chapters, the book contains mini-chapters titled "Expert Opinion" or "Roundtable." Those sections, culled from interviews with other museum professionals, consultants, and subject matter experts, delve into specific topics like endowment investing, special events fundraising, pricing, crowdfunding, and program development.

While you may be tempted to read the sections relevant to your daily roles and responsibilities, the learnings in one section are transferable. Have you considered completely restructuring your program development process or your fundraising benefits? Unsure about using recommendations from a consultant? Chapter 8, "Simplicity, Flexibility, Loyalty, and Profitability: Revamping the Longwood Gardens Membership Program," discusses how the Longwood Gardens completely rebuilt their membership program, understanding that they would lose some members and selectively implementing recommendations from a consultant. Discouraged about fundraising rejections? Searching for different tactics to establish a relationship with grantors and donors? Zinia Willits guides us through her roller coaster journey to obtain grant funding for new storage units. If your institution is considering community engagement initiatives, Marie Berlin's discussion of the YAA ArtHouse, established by the Young At Art Museum, provides an example of such an initiative. Trying to expand the audience for your collections? Concerned about managing culturally sensitive collections? Balancing curatorial and retail points of view for disseminating your collections? Our rights and reproductions authors present examples and practices that address those issues; Michael Guajardo also discusses sensitive collections in his chapter on product development for museum stores. Looking to build more constructive relationships with colleagues? Managing multiple vendors? The contributors in our museum store subsection share their expertise on those issues, as well as their tactical approaches to pricing and revenue maximization.

BOOK STRUCTURE

Sustainable Revenue for Museums begins by sharing the most recent publicly available revenue data in chapter 1, which you can use for comparison purposes. Chapter 2 reviews revenue impact factors like pricing, attendance, and governance structure, as well as including a roundtable discussion on these topics from our institutional professionals.

The book contains five main sections that cover different categories of revenue:

- Passive Income
- Contributed Income: Fundraising
- Contributed Income: Grants
- Earned Income: Museum Services
- Earned Income: Retail Services

"Passive Income" discusses revenue sources that an institution's staff or board do not actively or materially manage, like investment income or municipal bonds. "Contributed Income: Fundraising" includes membership, general fundraising, and major gifts. "Contributed Income: Grants" encompasses state and federal government grants and foundation grants. "Earned Income: Museums Services" examines revenue from programs, education, and collections. "Earned Income: Retail Services" covers food services, facility rentals, and the museum store.

Sustainable Revenue for Museums closes with a section about the future of revenue. Can the current revenue business model evolve via a maximization of earned income? Or should institutions consider an alternative model based on the concept of shared authority? How can institutions respond to broader macroeconomic and community participation changes? Both questions and chapters could be used to spark discussions at your institution.

The resources recommended by the contributors are included in their individual chapters and collected into the "Resource List" at the end of the book; additional resources relevant to the topics covered in this book have been added.

Sustainable Revenue for Museums is a book that you can reread as you progress throughout your career or as you need inspiration for your current role and responsibilities. There is no magic formula or perfect revenue mix that works for all institutions. You can use the information in this book to craft and implement the optimal revenue mix, strategies, and tactics for your institution at any particular point in time. Most importantly, your institution's sustainability will improve, allowing you to focus on fulfilling your mission and maintaining the public's trust.

INTRODUCTION

Before we can discuss revenue mixes, strategies, and tactics, we must first understand revenue trends, the impact of individual revenue streams on the different disciplines and sizes of institutions, and other factors that affect revenue.

Finding data and statistics about revenue categories and subcategories can be difficult. Associations and consulting firms collect data intermittently, specifically, and privately. Federal government departments do collect data consistently and broadly and publish it freely. As you will read in chapter 1, there are issues with that data, but the value and accessibility of the data outweigh those issues. The statistics on the contributions of different revenue streams are particular noteworthy and detailed. You can see the percentage contribution of facility rentals versus investment income versus government grants versus admissions to total revenue, for example.

Revenue doesn't exist in a vacuum. Simply having a state-of-the-art point-of-sales system or a rigorously detailed fundraising protocol is not a guarantee of revenue success. Institutions exist in a broader environment and have competitors for visitors' attention. Attendance is an obvious factor that affects revenue. Chapter 2 reviews other impact factors and contains the first roundtable discussion from our institutional professionals, who share their thoughts on these issues.

The context established in chapters 1 and 2 forms the background for the rest of the book. As you read the other chapters, you can consider how the individual impact factors affect strategies, tactics, and processes and how the contributors incorporate data into strategies, tactics, and processes.

1

Revenue Data

Multiple sources for different types and categories of museum revenue exist. Access to those sources can depend on memberships in associations, like the Museum Store Association or the Association of Art Museum Directors, or subscriptions to data services, like GuideStar. The "Resource List" at the end of the book lists the various associations and subscription services for your consideration. The Institute of Museum and Library Services (IMLS) also occasionally publishes a Museum Universe Data File that does not include retrospective or annual data; FY 2015 Q3 was the last version published. In 2016, the American Alliance of Museums (AAM) and BoardSource partnered to conduct a governance survey with the intent to facilitate benchmarking among museums and versus other nonprofit organizations. BoardSource published "Museum Board Leadership 2017: A National Report," which includes revenue source and investment asset management data. The sample size was only 715 institutions, and retrospective data were not published. The link to this publication is included in the "Resource List" at the end of this chapter and the master "Resource List" at the end of the book. For this book, we will utilize two sources of free and publicly available data: the US Census Bureau (the Census Bureau) and the Urban Institute's National Center for Charitable Statistics (NCCS). Links to these data sets are included in the "Resource List" at the end of this chapter and the master "Resource List" at the end of the book. To improve table and chart readability, some category names in both datasets have been shortened or reordered. Otherwise, this book uses the original category or code names to facilitate your use of the original data sources.

In general, data are only as relevant as their collection and quality control policies. When using a data source, read the scope or methodology notes to understand what data are collected, how the data are processed, and how the data are categorized or coded. Miscategorizations, inconsistencies, rounding rules, and reporting policies also affect the dataset. Over time, data categories may be redefined to accurately capture current conditions. For example, the Internal Revenue Service (IRS) completely revised the Form 990 and filing requirements in 1979 and 2009, which impacted the NCCS database categories. In those circumstances, the data vendor may automatically convert the old data into the new categories or simply note the changes in the database scope notes and let the users make any necessary conversions.

Data can also be purposefully omitted. The US Census Bureau chooses not to publish specific data points in data subcategories in which only a few institutions exist to protect the confidentiality of organizations—a policy more relevant in the for-profit world. However, those data are included in the category total. If you add the subcategory totals, your total may not match the official Census Bureau category total. The Census Bureau does note in the data tables when it has purposefully excluded data. We will see such examples in this book.

In order to interpret the data provided by these sources, we must first understand how each source collects data, the inconsistencies in those collection processes, and the source's purpose in collecting data. The Census Bureau collects museum revenue data for the Bureau of Economic Statistics as part of its five-year Economic Censuses. Revenue data from all industries in the US economy are collected, aggregated, and processed in the same manner. The data and data categories are constructed for for-profit businesses. Not all museums submit data to the Census Bureau. The data is only collected and published every five years. The last data set is from 2012 and was published in 2015. The 2017 data set should then be theoretically published in 2020.

NCCS culls data from the Form 990 tax statement that nonprofit organizations file with the IRS and publishes several databases with that information. This book uses the NCCS Core Files, which are published annually. There is a lag time between collection and publication; the 2015 data is currently available for this book's publication in 2019. The data and data categories conform to IRS rules and regulations for the Form 990. Nonprofit organizations that do not file Form 990s or Form 990s-EZ are not included. The amount of income generated in different categories and the governance structure of an institution may also determine how an accountant reports that income on the Form 990.

Each database also creates its own groupings of like institutions. The Census Bureau has one category for all museum disciplines, while NCCS has seven categories. The

Table 1.1   Data Source Comparison

US Census Bureau	NCCS
Number of Institutions (Most Recent Year): 7,319 (2012)	Number of Institutions (Most Recent Year): 11,500 (2015)
Institution Discipline Subcategories: <ul><li>Museums</li><li>Historical sites</li><li>Zoos and botanical gardens</li><li>Nature parks and similar institutions</li></ul>	Institution Discipline Subcategories: <ul><li>Museums</li><li>Art museums</li><li>Children's museums</li><li>Folk arts museums</li><li>History museums</li><li>Natural history and natural science museums</li><li>Science and technology museums</li><li>Historical organizations</li><li>Historical societies and historic preservation</li><li>Botanical gardens and arboreta</li><li>Zoos and aquariums</li></ul>

table 1.1 compares the total number of institutions included in the most recent dataset for each source and the institution discipline subcategories used.

Because direct comparisons between these datasets and their subcategories would be problematic, we will review the highest levels of data from each dataset and the unique information provided by each set in this chapter. In the section introductions, additional details specific to those sections will be provided. Income category names have also been adjusted to mirror the sections in this book.

We will also focus on the most recent sets of data for each source to provide up-to-date information and rates of change. For the Census Bureau, we will look at the data for 2002, 2007, and 2012. For NCCS, we will look at the data for 2011, 2012, 2013, 2014, and 2015. The Census Bureau data provides a pre-2008 to post-2008 perspective; NCCS reflects contemporary conditions.

GENERAL REVENUE TRENDS

We will look at revenue growth/loss and rates of change at the main category level (all institutions) for each data source and then at the institution discipline subcategory levels.

Census Bureau

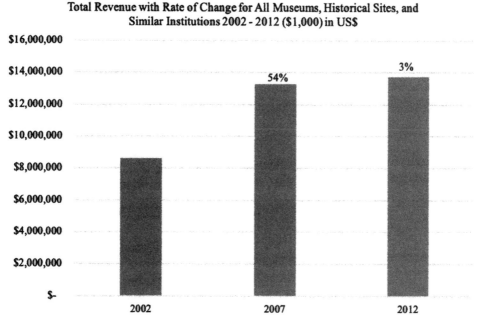

Figure 1.1 Total Revenue with Rate of Change for All Museums, Historical Sites, and Similar Institutions 2002–2012 ($1,000) in US$

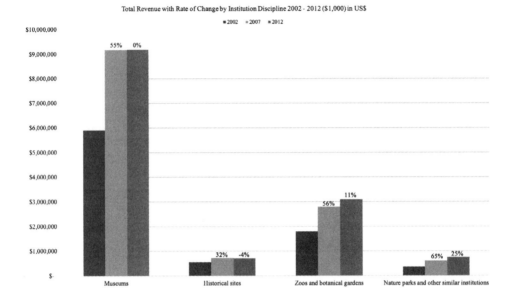

Figure 1.2 Total Revenue with Rate of Change by Institution Discipline 2002–2012 ($1,000) in US$

NCCS

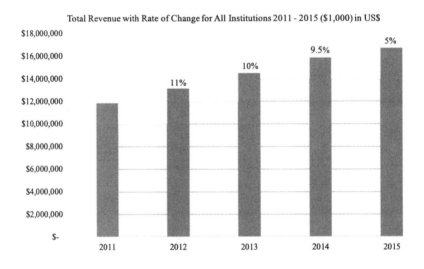

Figure 1.3 Total Revenue with Rate of Change for All Institutions 2011–2015 ($1,000) in US$

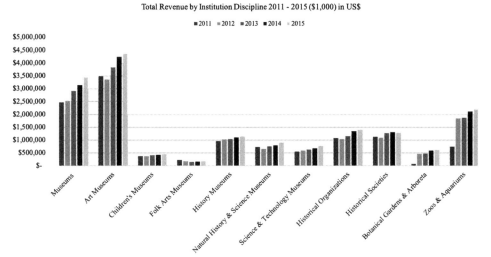

Total Revenue by Institution Discipline 2011 - 2015 ($1,000) in US$

Figure 1.4   Total Revenue by Institution Discipline 2011–2015 ($1,000) in US$

Table 1.2   Rates of Change of Revenue by Institution Discipline 2011–2015

	2011–2012	*2012–2013*	*2013–2014*	*2014–2015*
Museums	2.5%	15.1%	8.0%	9.6%
Art museums	−3.6%	14.2%	10.4%	3.1%
Children's museums	−0.8%	10.2%	2.5%	6.7%
Folk arts museums	−23.7%	−14.3%	9.6%	10.2%
History museums	6.1%	1.8%	5.5%	3.9%
Natural history and science museums	−10.5%	15.1%	4.9%	12.3%
Science and technology museums	5.6%	6.6%	9.2%	11.9%
Historical organizations	−3.2%	9.8%	16.7%	3.8%
Historical societies	−3.6%	16.2%	2.5%	−1.8%
Botanical gardens and arboreta	571.1%	2.7%	22.0%	4.5%
Zoos and aquariums	147.6%	0.9%	13.0%	4.3%

Inconsistent fluctuation best describes institutional revenue writ large and small. Despite the significant increases in the sheer number of institutions over time, those increases have not translated into revenue expansion that hides or mitigates revenue changes for longer-established institutions. The effects of the 2008 recession may be continuing but also do not explain the positive and negative growth swings or the year-on-year disparities in growth rates. Deeper dives into each category of institution discipline would be required to uncover the relevant hows and whys. For our more general purposes, these inconsistent fluctuations underscore the importance of understanding revenue sources and the importance of crafting a multisource revenue mix strategy to improve your institution's sustainability.

Revenue by Number of Employees

The Census Bureau also provides revenue breakdowns by number of employees at an institution and by number of employees for each institution discipline. These breakdowns may be more helpful to you because you can more easily compare your institution against a comparably sized peer with the same institution discipline. However, number of employees does not necessarily correlate with budget size—a key number in the nonprofit world. Because the Census Bureau is primarily concerned with for-profit businesses, it does not collect budget information and therefore cannot included that information in any analyses. Collecting information from all-volunteer institutions will also not be a priority. Nonetheless, these data do provide some parameters or benchmarks for your analytical purposes.

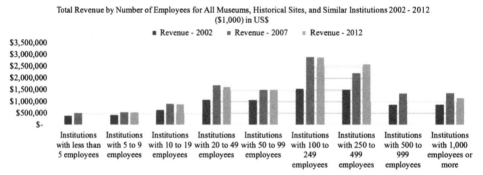

Figure 1.5   Total Revenue by Number of Employees for All Museums, Historical Sites, and Similar Institutions 2002–2012 ($1,000) in US$

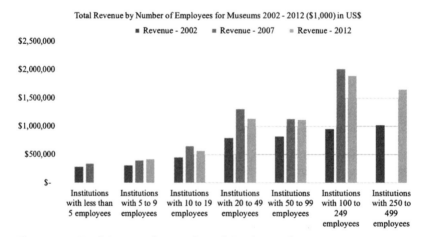

Figure 1.6   Total Revenue by Number of Employees for Museums 2002–2012 ($1,000) in US$

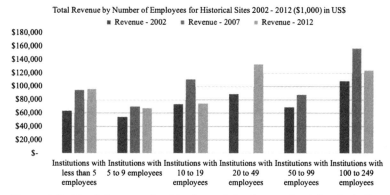

Figure 1.7   Total Revenue by Number of Employees for Historical Sites 2002–2012 ($1,000) in US$

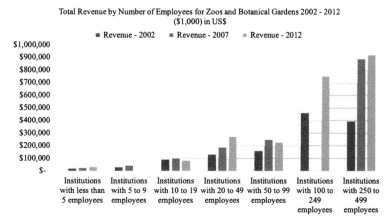

Figure 1.8   Total Revenue by Number of Employees for Zoos and Botanical Gardens 2002–2012 ($1,000) in US$

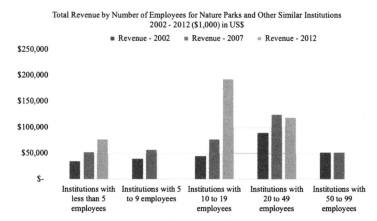

Figure 1.9   Total Revenue by Number of Employees for Nature Parks and Other Similar Institutions 2002–2012 ($1,000) in US$

Please note: Some categories lack data. As previously discussed, the US Census Bureau chooses not to publish specific data points in data subcategories in which only a few institutions exist to protect the confidentiality of those institutions. The nature parks data were particularly impacted, with data redacted for institutions with more than one hundred employees. The zoo and botanical garden and museums data for institutions with more than five hundred employees were redacted; the historic site data for institutions with more than five hundred employees were redacted or nonexistent.

Revenue by Type

In 2012, the Census Bureau calculated revenue by type (product line), which explicates how different revenue types contribute to total revenue. The Census Bureau also computed the percent of contribution for those institutions that did earn that particular type of revenue and the total percent of contribution for all institutions, regardless of whether or not they earned that type of revenue. Here are the top ten revenue sources for both circumstances and broken out by institution discipline.

Table 1.3   Top 10 Revenue Sources for Institutions with that Type of Revenue (Percent of Total Revenue)

	All Institutions	Museums	Historical Sites	Zoos and Botanical Gardens	Nature Parks and Similar Institutions
1	Private contributions, gifts, and grants (30.1%)	Private contributions, gifts, and grants (31.9%)	Private contributions, gifts, and grants (35.3%)	Admissions (37.1%)	Private contributions, gifts, and grants (50.1%)
2	Admissions (22.3%)	Admissions (18.1%)	Admissions (27.2%)	Private contributions, gifts, and grants (18.9%)	Guided tours and educative services (32%)
3	All other receipts and revenue (17.5%)	All other receipts and revenue (17.8%)	All other receipts and revenue (20.4%)	All other receipts and revenue (15.3%)	All other receipts and revenue (29.8%)
4	Government contributions, gifts, and grants (13.5%)	Government contributions, gifts, and grants (12.6%)	Facility rentals (19.8%)	Government contributions, gifts, and grants (14%)	Admissions (29.1%)
5	Investment income (11.3%)	Investment income (12.5%)	Government contributions, gifts, and grants (15.1%)	Membership (9.2%)	Government contributions, gifts, and grants (26.2%)

	All Institutions	Museums	Historical Sites	Zoos and Botanical Gardens	Nature Parks and Similar Institutions
6	Gains (losses) from assets sold (10.5%)	Gains (losses) from assets sold (11.8%)	Resale of merchandise (14%)	Meals and beverages services and merchandise sales (8.7%)	Overnight recreational camps (15.2%)
7	Merchandise sales (9.1%)	Recreational vehicle and tent sites for travelers (9.5%)	Investment income (13.7%)	Gains (losses) from assets sold (8.6%)	School visits, children's parties, and similar children's programs (14.7%)
8	Membership (7.2%)	Merchandise sales (8.8%)	Overnight recreational camps and parking services (12.8%)	Investment income (7.2%)	Facility rentals (12.3%)
9	Meals and beverages services (6.8%)	Facility rentals (7.3%)	Conservation services (10.9%)	Facility rentals (6.5%)	Meals and beverages services (11.8%)
10	Recreational vehicle and tent sites for travelers (6.2%)	Membership (6.6%)	Meals and beverages services (9.3%)	Admissions to live performing arts performances (4.4%)	Rental or lease of goods and/or equipment (11.4%)

Table 1.4   Top 10 Revenue Sources for Institutions (Percent of Total Revenue)

	All Institutions	Museums	Historical Sites	Zoos and Botanical Gardens	Nature Parks and Similar Institutions
1	Private contributions, gifts, and grants (26.5%)	Private contributions, gifts, and grants (29.2%)	Private contributions, gifts, and grants (28.5%)	Admissions (33.7%)	Private contributions, gifts, and grants (36.3%)
2	Admissions (19.1%)	Admissions (15.4%)	Admissions (17.7%)	Private contributions, gifts, and grants (15.6%)	Government contributions, gifts, and grants (13.2%)
3	Government contributions, gifts, and grants (9.2%)	All other receipts and revenue (9.8%)	Merchandise sales (10.9%)	Government contributions, gifts, and grants (9.2%)	Guided tours and educative services (9.7%)

Table 1.4   (continued)

	All Institutions	Museums	Historical Sites	Zoos and Botanical Gardens	Nature Parks and Similar Institutions
4	All other receipts and revenue (9.1%)	Investment income (9.6%)	Facility rentals (10.7%)	All other receipts and revenue (7.3%)	All other receipts and revenue (9.4%)
5	Investment income (8.3%)	Government contributions, gifts, and grants (9.1%)	Investment income (8.7%)	Membership (5.9%)	Admissions (6.1%)
6	Merchandise sales (6.9%)	Merchandise sales (7%)	All other receipts and revenue (8.3%)	Meals and beverages services (5.4%)	Merchandise sales (6%)
7	Membership (4.9%)	Membership (5%)	Government contributions, gifts, and grants (7.4%)	Investment income (4.9%)	Investment income (5.7%)
8	Gains (losses) from assets sold (3.5%)	Facility rentals (4.5%)	Guided tours and educative services (3.5%)	Facility rentals (3.1%)	Facility rentals (3.2%)
9	Meals and beverages services (2.8%)	Gains (losses) from assets sold (4.2%)	Meals and beverages services (2.7%)	Guided tours and educative services (2.5%)	Membership (2.9%)
10	Facility rentals (2.6%)	Meals and beverages services (2.1%)	Membership (2.2%)	Gains (losses) from assets sold (2.4%)	School visits, children's parties, and similar children's programs (2.5%)

Each of the main sections of this book are represented in these tables, along with some of the specific subcategories, that is, facility rentals. Section V, "Earned Income: Museum Services" will present additional product line breakdowns, for example, traveling exhibits, academic trips and tours, and packaged tours. You can use these numbers to compare your institution against your discipline and all institutions. Remember: These numbers do not represent optimal revenue mixes; they represent the reality of revenue mixes in 2012. Hopefully, the Census Bureau will calculate these data again for the 2017 dataset, which should be released in 2020. For now, the 2012 data offer a useful snapshot in time of how different revenue types contribute to an institution's total revenue.

Understanding revenue sources and crafting a multisource revenue mix strategy are critical first steps in the process of improving your institution's sustainability. When you understand from where your revenue is derived, you can adjust or expand your strategies to achieve the optimal mix customized for your institution.

DATA SOURCE LIST

US Census Bureau. 2002, 2007, and 2012 Economic Censuses. https://www.census.gov/programs-surveys/economic-census/data/tables.html. Accessed January–November 2018.

The Urban Institute. NCCS Core Files, 2011–2015. https://nccs-data.urban.org/data.php?ds=core. Accessed January–November 2018.

RESOURCE LIST

BoardSource. Museum Board Leadership 2017: A National Report. Washington, DC: Board-Source, 2017. https://www.aam-us.org/wp-content/uploads/2018/01/eyizzp-download-the-report.pdf. Accessed June 2018.

Institute of Museum and Library Services. Museum Universe Data File. https://data.imls.gov/Museum-Universe-Data-File/Museum-Universe-Data-File-FY-2015-Q3/ku5e-zr2b.

2

Impact Factors

Revenue does not exist in a vacuum. Its generation and effectiveness directly depend on the people who are managing and staffing those products and services. Revenue is also affected by other indirect impact factors. For example, if a retail store doesn't advertise or make quality products or price its products fairly, that store won't have customers—regardless of managers and staff. In this chapter, we will look at those impact factors that affect an institution's ability to generate revenue or effectiveness at maximizing revenue.

GOVERNANCE AND ORGANIZATIONAL STRUCTURES

The governance structure of your institution is a critical factor in crafting your revenue strategy. Institutions that are government departments, receiving the majority of their annual budget, may have restrictions on their fundraising or pricing abilities. Private nonprofit institutions might overemphasize major gifts or grants, expending time and energy on pursuing large dollars that could be more productively spent efficiently managing earned income revenue streams.

The constitution of your board and staff, as well as staff size, are considerations as well. Board members who are not comfortable with fundraising will need that training. All volunteer staffs may not have the time or experience to create, implement, and maintain a revenue strategy. Conversely, institutions with large staffs and siloed departments may each be pursuing independent revenue strategies that could negatively impact other departments.

The organizational chart can also affect your revenue strategies. In 2009, the Rubin Museum of Art, faced with budget reductions, restructured its separate education and admissions departments. Using an outside consultant, the museum discovered that visitors were unimpressed with the admissions staff's lack of knowledge about the museum, but were happy with the museum guides. Instead of cutting the education budget by 25 percent, the Rubin combined the education and admissions departments and replaced the admissions desk staff with the museum guides. An admissions coordinator trained the guides and managed the overall admissions operations. As a result, the new admissions desk staff were able to process more visitors without increasing staff levels and sold 18 percent more museum memberships than the previous year (Stafne 2010). Restructuring departments, of course, has myriad consequences, but it might also yield untold benefits.

DISCIPLINE

Type or discipline of institution also impacts revenue—typically the level of need thereof. Zoos and aquaria care for living creatures, who require food, shelter, and medical care. Art museums with large collections of highly valued objects have specialized preservation, insurance, and security requirements. Museums located in historic buildings have unique maintenance and repair considerations. In accounting terms, museums and related institutions have high fixed costs, which are expenses that are constant regardless of factors like visitation. Reducing fixed costs, for example, electricity or collection storage, is typically difficult because it entails reducing the collection or square footage. Preparing a detailed budget based on past income and expenses lays the groundwork for your revenue strategy. If you are not realistic about your expenses, you will never generate enough matching revenue.

ATTENDANCE

Attendance is the underlying critical factor in revenue. Earned income, contributed income, and even passive income depend on your institution's ability to connect with people and to invite them into your institution. Articles, studies, and books about attendance trends and strategies regularly appear in the museum literature. Well-known attendance or community participation studies, available via the internet, include

- Art by the Numbers—Association of Art Museum Directors
- CultureTrack—LaPlaca Cohen
- Humanities Indicators—American Academy of Arts and Sciences
- US Trends in Arts Attendance and Literary Reading—National Endowment for the Arts

The "Resource List" at the end of the book shows you where to access these studies.

Your local, regional, and state tourism boards may also have useful data; your local situation may differ from national trends. You can then compare your institution's data with these other sources to understand how your institution's attendance trends compare. Members of the American Association of State and Local History may also participate in the association's visitors count! The visitor research program, which creates a custom survey for your institution, analyzes the results and benchmarks your institution against similar institutions. Once you understand why people visit your institution, you can adjust your marketing and engagement strategies accordingly.

PRICING

Pricing is another topic that has generated numerous articles and books. Admissions software, especially online ticket sale software, has given institutions more data, more control, and more ability to experiment with pricing strategies. The software can generate instant reports that facilitate variable pricing and dynamic pricing of admissions and programs. Variable pricing is defined as setting different prices based on time of day, day of the week, location, or other criteria before the event goes on sale; dynamic pricing is the practice of changing prices after an event goes on sale in response to demand (Grzanowski 2018). Institutions like the Children's Museum of Atlanta have successfully utilized variable pricing to increase revenue and capture visitor behavior data (Lucas 2018). Software can also be used to itemize and calculate cross-departmental expenses to accurately compute program costs. The Wyckoff Farmhouse Museum employed that technique to understand and streamline its school program price—moving from a per student fee to a flat fee rate. That change increased the number of student visitors by 50 percent in the first year of implementation (Alleyne 2010).

In the roundtable in this chapter, our institutional professionals discuss their pricing strategies for admissions and programs, including how governance, visitor behavior, and benchmarking data impact final pricing. Some of our contributors also discuss pricing vis-à-vis their area of expertise.

SOFTWARE TOOLS

Throughout this book, contributors share the software tools that they use to store, manage, and analyze their data. Depending on the size of your institution and the amount of data you have, your institution may be able to obtain free or low-fee versions of these and other tools. For example, Salesforce has a nonprofit customer relationship management product: CRM for Nonprofits. Your existing software may have reporting features or new modules too. Periodically asking your customer service representative about new features or discounts for bundling modules may yield actionable information from your existing data.

This chapter closes with a roundtable discussion with institution professionals sharing their techniques for managing these impact factors.

ROUNDTABLE: IMPACT FACTORS

How do you balance the financial needs for programs, exhibitions, collection management, and strategic planning?

Dorothy Asher, Director, Lizzadro Museum of Lapidary Art

The budgeting process is an important part of the plan for the upcoming year. The majority of operating income goes into programs and exhibitions. Improvements in collection management and strategic planning may have increased funding if a special project is on the horizon, but generally the funds going into collection management and strategic planning are minimal in comparison to the overall budget.

Lauren Malloy, Program Director, Historic Congressional Cemetery

That's one of the most difficult parts of my job, to be honest. As with all museums, especially small organizations, there is a constant pressure to create successful programs that make money and bring in visitors, but also adhere to mission. Congressional Cemetery has a repertoire of over fifty programs that include tours, lectures, and larger events such as 5ks and festivals. Our mission is to "preserve and protect our historic yet active burial ground while interpreting the heritage represented by those interred here through education, historic preservation, community engagement, and environmental stewardship." Quite a lot can be justified—and rightly so—with the community engagement aspect of our mission. Not all of our programs need to be strictly educational, but we make certain that most of our efforts are directed towards a few larger programs that engage the community and fundraise for the cemetery, rather than spreading out our efforts and losing sight of mission.

Barbara Hogue, Executive Director, Christ Church Preservation Trust

It's a tricky balance. As a historic site, much of the revenue that we need for "special programs" like exhibitions, collections management, and strategic planning does not come from our operating budget. As a result, we have to find special funding opportunities to undertake any of these projects. For example, we recently received a $385,000 grant from the Council for Libraries and Information Resources to digitize our archival records along with records from eleven other historic congregations in Philadelphia. And, we received a $295,000 grant from the Pew Center for Arts and Humanities to present a commission of a new work for our pipe organ by composers Nathan Davis and Phyllis Chen, who are members of the New York-based, highly acclaimed International Contemporary Ensemble (ICE). As a historic site and not a museum per se, the majority of our operating costs are related to guide staff and preservation of our historic campus. But, we've been highly successful in planning for the implementation of special projects from year to year. We use a pretty simple plan that allows us to fundraise for the project one year in advance and then implement the following year. Using this framework enables us to always have a series of special campaigns to both fund and implement each year.

Christina H. Arseneau, Director, Niles History Center

Our mission is to connect the past, present, and future—fairly broad for a local history museum. We stick to local history for our collections policy. For our programs and exhibits, we are a bit more flexible. We collaborate with other community organizations to host events, such as a Renaissance Faire, Holiday events, and Wizarding Night for Halloween. In this way we broaden our audience and, in turn, our funding base.

Our budget is set by the city of Niles, which is governed by an elected city council. As the history center director, I submit a budget plan, which is approved first by the city administrator and then by the city council. Our budget from the city's general fund has remained about the same for the last 10 years or so. We follow the city's guidelines for other depts (i.e., if everyone has to cut 5% we do the same).

How do you determine admission and program pricing?

Christina H. Arseneau, Director, Niles History Center
I recommend pricing and it is approved by the city council [of the city of Niles].

Dorothy Asher, Director, Lizzadro Museum of Lapidary Art
The cost to bring in a visitor is not equal to the admission we charge. Admission is based on age (i.e., child, student, senior, adult) and relevant to our geographic area. Every couple of years we survey all area museums to see if we are within the range the general public will pay for a similar experience. Free admission days are always better attended. In the case of free admission, usually more people equals more sales in the Museum Shop. Most of the time this is the case. Program fees are charged based on the cost to provide the program. For example bringing in a speaker or securing a bus for a field trip, the minimum number needed to cover the cost will set the fee. A successful program will exceed the minimum number and make money.

Lauren Malloy, Program Director, Historic Congressional Cemetery
Typically I set the prices as program director, but for bigger programs I run them by my boss, President Paul Williams. I also present yearly to the board about our schedule of events, and they provide feedback on prices, especially for our bigger fundraisers. Personally, I feel strongly about continuing to offer a diverse set of prices for our programs—everywhere from free admission (many tours, concerts) to a $60 VIP ticket for our annual Soul Strolls fundraiser.

Thaisa Bell, School Programs Manager, Nashville Zoo
Prices for our education programs are usually determined by each program manager after calculating the current admission prices as well as the value of the particular activity for each program participant. The final prices/fees are ultimately set by our education director and chief operating officer.

Barbara Hogue, Executive Director, Christ Church Preservation Trust
Prices are usually set after we do careful planning and research. This research includes looking at what other institutions are paying for the same service or program. Many of our programs are free or on a "suggested donation" system. Keeping programs free and open to a diverse group of people is important and central to our mission. However, we are looking at other ways of increasing revenue in the future. For example, we may experiment with charging admission to see the church during the day. This is very controversial. Many churches are open during the day for people to visit and conduct quiet prayer and contemplation. We are trying to think of inno-vative ways to charge tourists for their visit without turning away individuals who are seeking solace in the historic church. Traditionally, the model we have relied on

was getting the maximum number of tourists into the church with the hope that they would leave a contribution for more than the "suggested donation." According to our research, this behavior rarely happens. Moving to a pay-to-visit model would also reduce the number of people who visit the church, which taxes the historic structure enormously.

How do current attendance numbers and attendance goals impact pricing decisions?

Christina H. Arseneau, Director, Niles History Center

Because we are funded by a municipality, most of our programs and attendance are free of charge, though we do request donations.

Thaisa Bell, School Programs Manager, Nashville Zoo

As our goal is always to increase the number of visitors in the park annually, if current attendance is lower than projected, we may consider boosting advertising and offering incentives to encourage more visitors to enter the park. Conversely, if current attendance numbers have exceeded our projected goals, that may indicate that we can consider a slight increase in admission prices in the upcoming year.

Barbara Hogue, Executive Director, Christ Church Preservation Trust

According to our research, the "suggested donation" model rarely yields the kinds of revenue needed to sustain an education program with paid and professional tour guides. Each year, we have over 200,000 individuals who visit the church and only $115,000 is collected in donation boxes placed around the church, which represents 57 cents per person. The suggested donation price is $7 per person. If we implemented a small fee, even a nominal one such as $3, then attendance could drop dramatically with an increase in revenue. The pay-to-visit model is a paradigm shifting model for a historic church and it is not where we are at the moment, but I believe that it is an important conversation that needs to be had. There is a lot of wear and tear associated with 200,000 visitors through a historic structure.

BIBLIOGRAPHY

Alleyne, Shirley Brown. "Making Programs Self-Sustaining at a Small Historic House Museum." *The Journal of Museum Education* 35, no. 2 (2010): 201–5.

Grzanowski, Cindy. "The Art and Science of Pricing: Maximizing Earned Revenue for the Performing Arts." *Arts Insights* 18, no. 1 (2018): 1–3.

Lucas, Stacey. "Variable Pricing—Increase Revenue While Capturing Data." Audience Round-table Blog, May 14, 2018. https://www.audiencebuildingroundtable.org/knowledgebase-group/2018/05/14/2018-5-14-variable-pricing-increase-revenue-while-capturing-data. Accessed June 2018.

Stafne, Marcos. "Integrating Service and Experience: When Education Meets Admissions." *The Journal of Museum Education* 35, no. 2, part 2 (Fall 2010): 257–65.

Section II

PASSIVE INCOME

Passive income refers to revenue sources that the institution's staff or board do not actively or materially manage. Examples of passive income include investment income (for example, interest income or dividends or bond coupons) and municipal funding (for example, tax revenue or municipal bond proceeds). Endowments could be the source of investment income. Local, regional, or state governments are the sources of tax revenue or bond proceeds used to fund museums; we are not referring to grants provided by government entities in this section.

Municipal funding is provided to institutions that are effectively departments of local, regional, state, or federal governments. That funding includes direct appropriations of tax dollars and proceeds from municipal bonds. While proceeds from municipal bonds is a separate line item on 990s, uncovering the number of institutions that receive all types of municipal funding or the breakdowns of those municipal dollars is incredibly difficult. The Securities Industry and Financial Markets Association (SIFMA) tracks the general use of municipal bond proceeds, but libraries and museums are included in the same category; parks, zoos, and beaches are combined into another category. Bonds can be issued for the benefit of one institution or for the benefit of multiple institutions in unrelated industries. Bonds can be issued by private institutions too. (Note: Bonds are loans, and as such they require collateral and must be repaid with interest to investors.)

The last, most comprehensive discussion of public financing of museums appears to be the *Exhibiting Public Value: Government Funding for Museums in the United States* report, published by the Institute for Museum and Library Services (IMLS) in 2008. For that report, IMLS surveyed a representative selection of institutions and reported the government funding data shown in tables II.1 and II.2.

In addition to the small sample sizes, neither table breaks down the type of funding supplied, that is, tax dollars, grants, or bond proceeds. IMLS itself notes both the general lack of data and the more specific lack of reliable data in its report (Manjarrez et al. 2008). Nevertheless, the data provide a general understanding of municipal funding at this point in time.

The National Center for Charitable Statistics (NCCS) has a tax revenues levied category, which includes the tax revenues levied for an organization's benefit and tax

Table II.1 Museums Reporting Government Contributions by Source and Type

	Some Federal Support	Some State Support	Some Local Support	Some Tribal Support	Some Gov't Support (any source)	N Total = 733
Art museums	42%	72%	52%	5%	63%	129
Children's museums	52%	74%	81%	0%	65%	41
History museums	30%	50%	68%	1%	59%	235
Natural history and science museums	36%	64%	70%	3%	60%	39
Science and technology museums	63%	49%	39%	0%	73%	41
Historical societies	21%	45%	72%	1%	47%	132
Arboretums and botanical gardens	53%	63%	58%	0%	56%	29
Zoos, aquariums, and zoological societies	19%	23%	21%	0%	70%	39
Hybrid and other	31%	64%	42%	11%	43%	48

Table II.2 Percentage of Government Revenue by Type and Source, FY 2006

	Federal	State	Local	Tribal	N Total = 582
Art museums	16%	30%	53%	1%	115
Children's museums	18%	24%	58%	0%	31
History museums	18%	43%	39%	0%	191
Natural history and science museums	18%	42%	39%	0%	33
Science and technology museums	52%	22%	26%	0%	35
Historical societies	46%	27%	27%	0%	85
Arboretums and botanical gardens	19%	13%	69%	0%	19
Zoos, aquariums, and zoological societies	9%	15%	76%	0%	37
Hybrid and other	7%	68%	24%	2%	36

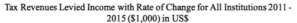

Tax Revenues Levied Income with Rate of Change for All Institutions 2011 - 2015 ($1,000) in US$

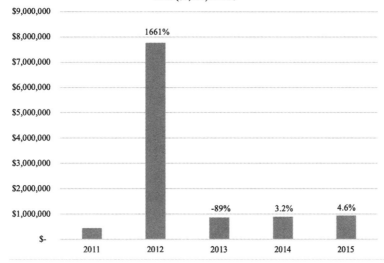

Figure II.1 Tax Revenues Levied Income with Rate of Change for All Institutions 2011–2015 ($1,000) in US$

Tax Revenues Levied by Institution Discipline 2013 - 2015 ($1,000) in US$

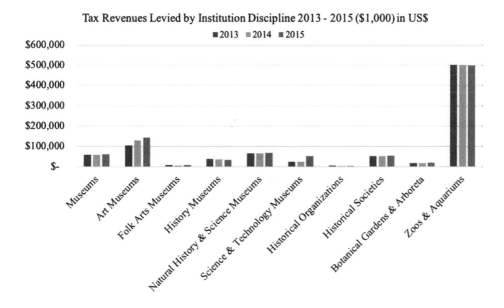

Figure II.2 Tax Revenues Levied by Institution Discipline 2013–2015 ($1,000) in US$

Table II.3   Rates of Change of Tax Revenues Levied by Institution Discipline 2013–2015

	2013–2014	2014–2015
Museums	2.2%	2.6%
Art museums	25.1%	10.9%
Folk arts museums	−8.9%	9.1%
History museums	−10.1%	−1.5%
Natural history and science museums	2.2%	2.8%
Science and technology museums	3.3%	118.1%
Historical organizations	−6.5%	−6.8%
Historical societies	3.0%	1.5%
Botanical gardens and arboreta	6.4%	6.1%
Zoos and aquariums	0.1%	−0.7%

revenues spent on its behalf. Figures II.1 and II.2 and table II.3 report those figures and the rates of change computed therefrom.

Due to extreme anomalies or lack of data in the 2011, 2012, and certain institution discipline subcategories, that information has been excluded.

Similar to municipal funding, not all institutions have investment income. Additionally, the use of that income can also be restricted per the original terms of a donor or governing body. Investment income can provide a steady stream of dollars that can act as a bulwark against the loss of grants or fundraising fluctuations. As mentioned in chapter 1, the US Census Bureau calculated the revenue by type (product line) in 2012. Table II.4 shows the contribution of investment income to the total revenue of institutions that earn investment income.

The NCCS reports the actual revenue generated from investment income, and rates of change can be computed therefrom.

The theme of inconsistent fluctuation continues with these graphs and tables. Some fluctuation will occur due to macroeconomic and investment conditions. Investment income does come with a special set of legal responsibilities for the boards and institutional staff members who are guiding the investment decisions. The legal obligations of the Uniform Prudent Management of Institutional Funds Act (UPMIFA) should prompt boards and institutional staff members to select conservative investment vehicles with steady rates of return. Consequently, the variability seen in these graphs and tables is disquieting.

Table II.4   Investment Income as Percent of Total Revenue by Institution Discipline— US Census Bureau 2012

All institutions	*11.3%*
Museums	12.5%
Historical sites	13.7%
Zoos and botanical gardens	7.2%
Nature parks and other similar institutions	9.2%

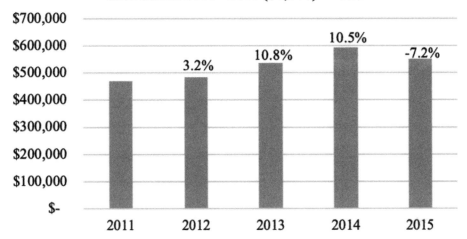

Investment Income with Rate of Change for All Institutions 2011 - 2015 ($1,000) in US$

Figure II.3   Investment Income with Rate of Change for All Institutions 2011–2015 ($1,000) in US$

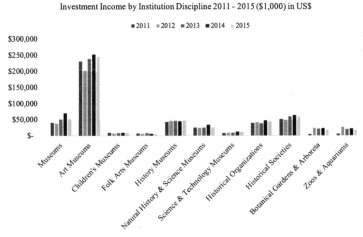

Investment Income by Institution Discipline 2011 - 2015 ($1,000) in US$

Figure II.4   Investment Income by Institution Discipline 2011–2015 ($1,000) in US$

Table II.5   Rates of Change of Investment Income by Institution Discipline 2011–2015

	2011–2012	*2012–2013*	*2013–2014*	*2014–2015*
Museums	−4.26%	31.69%	36.33%	−22.48%
Art museums	−12.35%	18.44%	5.50%	−2.17%
Children's museums	−14.83%	10.06%	9.32%	6.01%
Folk arts museums	−8.15%	28.75%	−22.69%	−16.15%
History museums	8.12%	−0.09%	−2.07%	6.33%
Natural history and science museums	−2.39%	2.90%	33.99%	−26.50%
Science and technology museums	7.95%	6.22%	30.59%	−11.52%
Historical organizations	6.17%	−7.61%	21.81%	−6.33%
Historical societies	−2.76%	21.53%	5.82%	−5.19%
Botanical gardens and arboreta	403.27%	−10.34%	2.94%	−13.28%
Zoos and aquariums	370.24%	−23.14%	6.52%	−14.97%

CHAPTERS PREVIEW

To establish a baseline understanding of the legal obligations for investing institutional dollars, this section begins with an "Expert Opinion." Valerie Newell, a registered investment advisor and the managing director of Mariner Wealth Advisors, outlines the key responsibilities and tasks of nonprofit investment management, including an introduction of UPMIFA. Susan N. Gary, professor of law and reporter for UPMIFA, reviews the act's history and delves into the obligations it imposes on boards, staffs, and organizations. This section closes with Heather McClenahan's chapter on how the Los Alamos Historical Society created and managed the six different campaigns used to establish endowments and other funds that would support the society's then-new designation as part of the Manhattan Project Historical Park. Heather describes how the society evolved from an institution with three part-time staff members and a budget of less than $100,000 in the early 2000s to an institution with a $250,000 budget, $200,000 endowment, and multiple multimillion-dollar capital campaigns within a decade. Underscoring the information shared in the first two chapters, Heather discusses the practical aspects and ramifications of understanding the legal and fiduciary responsibilities involved in endowments and capital campaigns. All three contributors underscore the importance of employing qualified and knowledgeable advisors to guide you through the legal and financial consequences of your investment decisions.

RESOURCE LIST

Manjarrez, Carlos, Carole Rosenstein, Celeste Colgan, and Erica Pastore. *Exhibiting Public Value: Museum Public Finance In the United States* (IMLS-2008-RES-02). Washington, DC: Institute of Museum and Library Services, 2008.
Rosensteil, Paul. *An Overlooked Financing Tool: How Non-Profits Can Issue Tax-Exempt Bonds*. San Francisco: California Association of Non-Profits, July 2016.

SIFMA. *Municipal Bond Credit Report First Quarter 2018*. Washington, DC: SIFMA, May 2018.

The Urban Institute. NCCS Core Files, 2011–2015. https://nccs-data.urban.org/data.php?ds=core. Accessed January–November 2018.

US Census Bureau. 2002, 2007, and 2012 Economic Censuses. https://www.census.gov/programs-surveys/economic-census/data/tables.html. Accessed January–November 2018.

3

Expert Opinion: Investment Management

Valerie Newell, Registered Investment Advisor and Managing Director, Mariner Wealth Advisors

What are the endowment management roles of board members and museum staff?

Board members should concentrate on the long-term strategies and long-term institutional success and survival. They represent past board members and donors. Board members must have a fiduciary orientation to their board service and the selection of investments.

Museum directors/[chief executive officers] CEOs and department heads, especially the [chief financial officer] CFO, should have a good understanding of investments and finances. They should know the legal responsibilities under the Uniform Prudent Management of Institutional Funds Act (UPMIFA) and their ethical responsibilities as museum professionals.

If your museum has a CFO, that person may or may not have an investment background and therefore be unable to advise on investment strategy. However, that person should still contribute their knowledge about the museum's revenue streams and day-to-day financial management. The CFO can help facilitate the connection between monthly finances and asset management.

How should finance and investment committees be organized?

The board's finance committee and investment committees should be separate. Both committees should have regular meeting schedules and agenda items, as delineated by UPMIFA.

While the finance committee should meet monthly in order to retain a firm understanding of the museum's finances, the investment committee can meet less—approximately three times per year usually is sufficient. If the portfolio needs to be rebuilt or refocused, additional meetings may be necessary.

The investment committee should have an annual work document that outlines meeting schedules and major agenda items for each meeting, including a review of the investment policy, the portfolio, investment fees, and the endowment spending policy.

What is the main goal for portfolio management?

Long-term success should be the cornerstone of a museum's portfolio management. The board is responsible for ensuring the current and future financial stability of the museum. Using professional investment advisors assists the board in best fulfilling their fiduciary duty.

What qualifications should your investment advisor have? Where can such a person be found?

Your investment advisor should have experience with and knowledge of UPMIFA. The advisor should be a registered investment advisor and should have a fiduciary orientation to their service and selection of investments.

Finding such an advisor can be challenging. Barron's publishes an annual list of Top Independent Financial Advisors, which can be used to identify potential candidates and their firms. Other nonprofits in your locality may also be able to suggest prospective candidates.

How should long-term and short-term goals and needs be balanced?

Both museum boards and museums staffs must recognize and acknowledge the inherent tension between long-term and short-term responsibilities. The museum staff sometimes has a focus on short-term finances, due to their responsibilities for the daily management of the institution, and their own career aspirations.

Museum boards are entrusted with respecting the wishes and interests of donors, past and present, and with protecting long-term institutional survival. Board members must have the strength and bravery to respect those past donors and the institution. Since they typically hired the museum director to enact certain strategies and tactics, the board also wants the museum director to succeed. Balancing that tension between the short-term interests and long-term success is key.

4

The Uniform Prudent Management of Institutional Funds Act

Susan N. Gary, Orlando J. and Marian H. Hollis
Professor of Law, University of Oregon

INTRODUCTION AND BACKGROUND

The National Conference of Commissioners of Uniform State Laws (also known as the Uniform Law Commission) promulgated the Uniform Management of Institutional Funds Act (UMIFA) in 1972. The act reflected concerns about how universities, in particular, were investing their funds. Restrictive interpretations of spending restrictions on endowment funds had skewed investment decision making. The foundations were investing in bonds to generate "income," which could be spent, and avoiding or minimizing investments in stocks that produced capital gains, which under the trust accounting rules in effect at the time could not be spent because they were treated as principal and not income.

UMIFA did three things: (1) provided guidance on investment authority; (2) authorized expenditure of appreciation of endowment funds; and (3) provided rules for the release of restrictions on the use or investment of funds. Forty-seven jurisdictions adopted the act.

In 2000 or so the Uniform Law Commission (ULC) began thinking about revising UMIFA and in 2002 the ULC appointed a drafting committee. After four years of committee work, with input from charity regulators, lawyers with donors as clients, lawyers working with charities, bankers and their lawyers, and others, the ULC approved the revised act, known as the Uniform Prudent Management of Institutional Funds Act, in 2006. Adoptions followed rapidly, and by 2018 every state except Pennsylvania had adopted the act.

The Uniform Prudent Management of Institutional Funds Act (UPMIFA), with an emphasis on prudence, updated guidance on investment authority by adopting language from the Uniform Prudent Investor Act. The new act changed the rules on spending from endowment funds, increasing flexibility while providing better guidance with the goal of protecting donors' intent. UPMIFA also added rules for modification of restrictions on the use or investment of funds, importing language from the Uniform Trust Code.

WHO AND WHAT DOES UNIFORM PRUDENT MANAGEMENT OF INSTITUTIONAL FUNDS ACT COVER?

Institution and Institutional Fund

The definitions of "institution" and "institutional fund" provide the scope of UPMIFA. Both of these terms come from UMIFA and have the same meanings they had under that act. An institution, for UPMIFA purposes, is an entity organized and operated exclusively for charitable purposes. In essence, UPMIFA applies to "charities," but by creating a defined term in the act, the drafters could be more specific about what they meant and what the act covered. The definition includes various types of entities, and also includes a trust with exclusively charitable interests. Charitable purposes is given the definition from the Uniform Trust Code, a definition that ties in the legal history of "charitable purpose." The exclusions from UPMIFA coverage come in the definition of institutional fund. An institutional fund is a fund held by an institution, with several important exclusions.

UPMIFA does not apply to program-related assets. Program-related assets are assets held "primarily to accomplish a charitable purpose and not primarily for investment." All assets held by a charity eventually serve a charitable purpose, including investment assets that generate income to use for the charity's activities. The exclusion for program-related assets, however, does not include investment assets, even if the income produced by those assets will be used for charitable purposes. The exclusion is intended to exclude bricks and mortar—the university classrooms, the building used by a soup kitchen, and the paintings displayed by a museum. The exclusion also covers assets with a mixed purpose, such as a fund used to make below-market loans to revitalize an inner-city neighborhood. As the comments explain, the institution should still be prudent about making these loans, even if the primary purpose of the activity is not investment.

UPMIFA also excludes most funds held by trusts. The only trust funds UPMIFA covers are those for which a charity is the trustee. If the trustee is a bank or an individual, UPMIFA will not apply. Initially, the drafting committee intended to change the scope of UMIFA and include within the coverage of UPMIFA charitable trusts as well as nonprofit corporations. After hearing concerns that trusts might then be subject to conflicting rules if trust law and UPMIFA provided different guidance, the committee decided to maintain the scope of UMIFA and continue to exclude most trusts from UPMIFA.

UPMIFA does not cover charitable remainder trusts as long as the noncharitable interest exists. After the income beneficiary dies or the term of years expires, UPMIFA will apply to the remaining funds, if an institution is the trustee. Often the charitable remainder trust will simply transfer the corpus to the institution on the death of the income beneficiary, so UPMIFA will have little effect on the trust. UPMIFA's prudence norm will apply to any decision making, but the investment decisions will have a short timeframe.

Endowment Fund

An endowment fund for UPMIFA purposes is one that is not wholly expendable on a current basis. The fund may be perpetual or permanent in nature, but the term also includes funds with a fixed term. For example, a fund could be created for a building project, with a plan to spend the fund in ten years. The term only applies to donor-restricted funds and not to board-designated funds.

Gift Instrument

The written documents that establish the terms of a gift are called a gift instrument. An institution and donor may enter into a formal gift agreement, which will set the terms of the gift. In addition, a letter from the donor to the institution outlining the donor's intentions with respect to an enclosed check will constitute a gift instrument under UPMIFA. Solicitation materials prepared by an institution and responded to by a donor will also be considered gift instruments. A gift instrument will be important in determining whether and how a donor restricted a gift. Institutions should consider carefully any printed solicitation materials they use because those materials may create restrictions on gifts received in response.

STANDARD FOR MANAGING AND INVESTING INSTITUTIONAL FUNDS

UPMIFA updates the prudence standard for managing and investing institutional funds. The standard applies to all funds held by a charity. The charity will consider the factors in different ways depending on the purposes and time horizon of the fund. A charity will invest a fund for operating expenses differently from an endowment fund.

In creating the standard, the drafting committee used language from the Revised Model Nonprofit Corporation Act (2008) and from the Uniform Prudent Investor Act (UPIA). By mixing these two sources of language, the drafting committee intended to convey its belief that the standard for investing funds held by a charitable institution is the same regardless of the organizational form of the charity. The standard is consistent with the business judgment standard under corporate law, as applied to charities and charitable managers.

From the Revised Model Nonprofit Corporation Act comes the general standard:

> Each person responsible for managing and investing an institutional fund shall manage and invest the fund in good faith and with the care an ordinarily prudent person in a like position would exercise under similar circumstances.

The standard provides that a manager should incur only reasonable costs in making investments. A decision to hire an investment advisor may be prudent, but the costs should be appropriate in the context of that institution. A manager should make reasonable efforts to verify facts relating to the management and investment of the fund.

This duty is a traditional trust law duty to investigate the accuracy of information used in making decisions.

After stating this general standard, UPMIFA then directs those managing an investment fund to consider a list of factors. The factors come almost directly from UPIA, with minor language changes necessary for a statute focused on charities.

A manager must consider all of the following factors that are relevant:

- Intent of the donor expressed in a gift instrument
- General economic conditions
- Possible effect of inflation or deflation
- Expected tax consequences
- Role of each investment in overall portfolio
- Expected total return
- Other resources of the institution
- Needs of institution to make distributions and preserve capital
- Asset's special relationship to institution's purposes

In considering these factors and making decisions, the manager must consider assets as part of a portfolio with an overall investment strategy having risk and return objectives suited to the fund and the institution. The manager should not consider an investment in isolation.

The institution should diversify investments because modern portfolio theory, on which UPIA is based, deems diversification central to prudent asset management. However, UPMIFA permits an institution to determine that because of special circumstances nondiversification will better serve its purposes.

After receiving gifts of property to be held as investments, the institution must review the property to determine the suitability of retaining the property and may need to make investment changes to rebalance the portfolio.

A person managing an institutional fund must use the person's own judgment and experience, including any special skills or expertise the person has.

A prudent investor can consider material environmental, social, and governance (ESG) factors as part of a robust financial analysis. Studies have shown that funds using ESG integration and other forms of impact investing has financial results that are either the same or better than actively managed funds that use only traditional financial metrics. The choice of manager and continuing oversight, as well as the other factors listed earlier, continue to be important.

A written investment policy is a best practice because the policy will guide prudent decision making with respect to investments and can include the factors that under UPMIFA must be considered in making decisions to expend funds from an endowment.

Another best practice will be to record the consideration given to the factors as part of the decision-making process. If the institution makes a decision not to diversify, the institution should document its annual review of that decision.

UPMIFA does not take a position on mission-related investing, and the comments do not discuss mission-related investing. Two provisions in UPMIFA support the idea that an institution can consider its mission as a factor in making investment decisions. At the beginning of the standard of conduct, UPMIFA states that an institution "shall consider the charitable purposes of the institution and the purposes of the institutional fund" in making investment decisions. This is a statement of the institution's fundamental duty to keep the purposes of the institution in mind, and it suggests that the purposes can influence decision making. In addition, this section directs the decision makers to consider, if relevant, "an asset's special relationship or special value, if any to the charitable purposes of the institution."

EXPENDITURES FROM ENDOWMENT FUNDS

Under UMIFA an institution could spend appreciation above historic dollar value, based on a general prudence standard. UMIFA defined historic dollar value as the amount a donor or donors had contributed to an endowment fund and did not adjust the amount over time. For an old fund with a reasonable investment record, historic dollar value was so low it was meaningless. For a new fund, a drop in the stock market shortly after a donor made a gift could mean the fund was under water and unable to spend appreciation. Under UMIFA an institution could continue to spend "income" defined as interest and dividends even if a fund was under water. The consequence was that investment decisions might be based more on the need to generate income than on a portfolio standard that might yield better overall returns.

Under UPMIFA an institution can spend from its endowment the amount the institution determines to be "prudent for the uses, benefits, purposes, and duration for which the endowment fund is established." UMPIFA directs the decision maker to consider the following factors:

- Duration and preservation of the fund
- Purposes of the institution and the fund
- General economic conditions
- Possible effect of inflation or deflation
- Expected total return
- Other resources of the institution
- Investment policy of the institution

Best practice will be to document the exercise of discretion under UPMIFA.

UMIFA used a rule of construction to interpret a donor's use of the word "endowment" in making a gift. If a donor made a gift "for endowment" or directed a charity to hold the property and "pay only the income," the direction to the charity was not clear. "Income" might mean only interest and dividends and if so, the charity would be unable to spend capital gains. UMIFA provided that these terms, without more specific direction from a donor, meant that a donor wanted to permit the charity to spend a prudent amount of appreciation. UPMIFA updates this rule of construction.

Under UPMIFA, terms like "endowment" and "income" are interpreted to mean that the donor intended to create an endowment fund of permanent duration and not to limit otherwise the authority to spend from the fund. The effect of this rule is that UPMIFA's spending rule applies unless a donor is more specific.

UPMIFA includes a rebuttable presumption of imprudence that applies if spending in one year exceeds 7 percent of the fair market value of the endowment fund. For purposes of the presumption, the value of an endowment fund is computed based on market values averaged over a period of not less than three years, and for an endowment fund in existence fewer than three years, for the existence of the fund. This rebuttable presumption does not create a safe harbor for spending below the applicable percentage. Fewer than half the states have adopted a rebuttable presumption of imprudence, probably due to concerns that it would be read as a safe harbor.

The prudence standard of UPIA depends on the ability to delegate, so the power to delegate is included in UPMIFA.

RELEASE OR MODIFICATION OF RESTRICTIONS

If a donor consents in writing, an institution may release or modify a restriction on management, investment, or purpose of a fund. The fund cannot be used for a purpose other than the charitable purpose of the institution. The donor does not control this process, which could create a concern in connection with the deductibility of the donor's gift. Rather, the donor can agree to a change proposed by the institution, and the donor and institution can work together to develop an appropriate modification.

This provision will be helpful if the donor can be found and consulted, but in many cases the need for modification arises after the donor's death or for a fund with numerous donors. If consent cannot be obtained, the institution must seek court approval for the modification, unless the fund meets the "small, old fund" criteria.

If a restriction on management or investment becomes impracticable or wasteful or impairs the management or investment of the fund, or if due to unanticipated circumstances modification will further the purposes of fund, an institution may be able to modify the restriction. The proposed modification must be in accordance with the donor's probable intention. The institution must notify the attorney general, who can choose to participate in the court proceeding. A court must approve the modification.

If a purpose or a restriction on use becomes unlawful, impracticable, impossible, or wasteful, an institution can ask a court to modify the restriction in a manner consistent with the purposes in the gift instrument governing the fund. The institution must notify the attorney general, and the attorney general can participate in the court proceeding.

UPMIFA adds a process through which an institution can release or modify a restriction without the cost of going to court. If a restriction meets the requirements for cy pres (the restriction has become unlawful, impracticable, impossible to achieve, or wasteful) and if the fund is small (under $25,000) and old (more than twenty years have passed since the fund was established), then the institution may give notice to the attorney general and make the modification without court approval. If the attorney general does not respond within sixty days following the notice from the institution, the institution can proceed with the modification. The statutes in some states have increased the amount considered "small."

CONCLUSION

UPMIFA is entirely default law. An institution and a donor can agree to whatever terms they choose, in keeping with the charitable purposes of the institution. If the institution agrees, the donor can impose restrictions on how funds are invested, how they are expended, and the purposes for which they are expended. An institution and donor can also agree on a modification process to use if modification of the restrictions becomes necessary or desirable. By providing for flexible ways to modify provisions in the future, the donor and institution can save court costs and allow more resources to be used for charitable purposes.

ADDITIONAL READING

Budak, Susan E., and Susan N. Gary. "Legal and Accounting Challenges of Underwater Endowment Funds." *Prob. & Prop.* (January/February 2010): 24.

Gary, Susan N. "Charities, Endowments, and Donor Intent: The Uniform Management of Institutional Funds Act." *Georgia L. Rev.* (2007): 41.

Creating a Capital Campaign for the Los Alamos Historical Society

Heather McClenahan, Executive Director, Los Alamos Historical Society

Board members and staff of every nonprofit dream of checks with lots of zeroes just showing up in the mail because of all the great work that organization does.

The reality: Fundraising is hard work.

Fundraising requires serious organizational skills, teamwork, getting out of your comfort zone, and asking people for—*gulp*—money. It means hearing the word "no." It means staff and volunteers getting overwhelmed or becoming embroiled in misunderstandings. However, with perseverance, it can also mean success. The following are practical principles and lessons learned during the Los Alamos Historical Society's multimillion-dollar fundraising campaign.

BACKGROUND

The Los Alamos Historical Society was founded in 1967 as the laboratory that developed the world's first atomic bombs approached its twenty-fifth anniversary. Community members wanted to ensure the history was preserved, and they acquired a pre–World War II log and stone cabin to serve as the museum building. Through the years, the collection grew, the number of publications soared, and the founding volunteers passed the reins to new generations. Still, by the early 2000s, the organization remained a small operation with only three part-time staff members and a budget of less than $100,000.

All of that changed in 2004 when President George W. Bush signed legislation authorizing the National Park Service to study the feasibility of a Manhattan Project National Historical Park. After the historical society and other champions spent a decade working with Congress, President Obama signed that park into existence in December 2014. It is a noncontiguous park, with sites in Oak Ridge, Tennessee, and Hanford, Washington, as well as Los Alamos. A National Park Service presence in the middle of our downtown meant potentially tens of thousands of new visitors could be walking through the museum's doors.

With museum exhibits from the early 1990s housed in the cabin and the collections stored in a beautiful but wholly inadequate prewar log lodge, the leaders of the organization determined it needed to make changes for the incoming visitors. In 2011, the society completed its first strategic plan, based on the knowledge and hope that the park would be passed by Congress—someday. The ambitious plan to move collections into a new facility, to expand and redo museum exhibits, to increase educational programs, and to fully fund the publishing operation amounted to needs of more than $6 million, about $1.5 million for capital projects and the rest for endowment growth. That was a daunting number for an organization with a budget of less than $150,000, a brand new endowment of $200,000, and no staff member devoted to development.

It was also a daunting number in a small community with little philanthropic history. Los Alamos did not exist as a town until the 1940s, and almost none of the population came from "old money." While the community is regularly listed as one of the nation's richest because of its concentration scientists and engineers with high-paying jobs at the lab, that wealth did not often flow to local nonprofits. The Los Alamos Historical Society set out to change that situation.

After conducting a feasibility study—seventy interviews with community leaders and stakeholders that determined we could achieve the goal—the board of directors opted to conduct a multimillion-dollar fundraising campaign. The following advice and lessons were learned from that endeavor.

DEVELOP YOUR OBJECTIVES AND CREATE A STRONG CASE FOR SUPPORT

First and foremost, to make a compelling case to your donors, you need clearly defined and realistic objectives about why you need to raise money. Your donors are making an investment in your organization. Show them how that investment will pay off in the future.

Take time to develop the objectives. Work with your stakeholders to achieve buy-in and to make sure you are on the right path. You can do this by holding formal meetings or informal gatherings such as an afternoon tea. Use your newsletter or other mailings as well as social media to share information and ask for feedback.

You need to be able to answer the following:

- How will the money be used?
- Why do you need so much money?
- What tangible results will the donor see?
- How will the organization sustain its growth and progress?

With these questions in mind, you will develop a document to share with prospective donors, your "case for support." The document needs to reflect who you are (your brand, you might say) as well as what you are trying to accomplish. It is a useful tool for those who are asking for money as well as for those who are being asked. It should be left with prospective donors so they can contemplate and reflect on the importance of their gift.

The Los Alamos Historical Society had six investment opportunities, with a mix of capital and endowment goals for each. The funds would allow for new exhibits, the acquisition of a historic property in which to expand the museum exhibits, more educational programs, more staffing, and better collections care. These were all tangible topics that interested our donors, and their funding produced visible results. Even now, in the first few years after the campaign, the results still have our donors excited about the difference they were able to make for our organization and for our community.

GET HELP, GET WELL TRAINED, AND GET CONFIDENT

The Los Alamos Historical Society highly recommends hiring fundraising counsel. This may be hard as it takes funds up front. How do you find the money to raise money? However, the advice and service you get from the experts who do this every day are invaluable and worth the investment.

When looking for a consultant, have high expectations. The consultant should be with you every step of the way, walking you through the complete process, training volunteers and staff, answering questions, and guiding your organization to better fundraising practices overall. Keep in mind that the consultants are not the ones who will be asking for the gifts. Rather, they should train your team well, offer advice, and help crunch numbers for you in your gift analyses and donor asks, but they will not be knocking on your donors' doors.

COMPLETE A TRUSTWORTHY GIFT ANALYSIS

The gift analysis is another reason to hire a good consultant. How many gifts of what size do you need to reach your objective? There is actually a pyramid-like formula, with one lead gift equaling about 15 to 20 percent of the goal.

Who are your prospects? If you have members, that list is where you begin. Past board members are an important resource. Do you have other stakeholders? Other community-minded people? As you are developing this list, you may also want to employee a data service such as Wealth Engine (https://www.wealthengine.com/) to help you determine the wealth of those on your list of prospects. You cannot rely on town gossip for this information. Just because someone owns a large apartment complex or shopping center does not necessarily mean he or she has disposable wealth for your projects. The data services can provide a breakdown that helps when it comes to asking for the right amount.

BEGIN QUIETLY

Standard practice in big fundraising is not to announce your intention until at least half of your goal is met. This is difficult, especially in a small community where everyone knows everyone else. How do you balance this "best practice" with the other important "best practice" of transparency in your nonprofit organization? The key is understanding the difference between "quiet" and "secret."

If people ask, be open and honest about your fundraising efforts. Let them know what you are doing and why, but do not publicize it to the media or make any big announcements.

When you are ready to make the campaign public, make a big splash with it. Invite community leaders and the media to a big announcement event. At that point, you also have an opportunity to recruit new volunteers who are interested in your cause but may not have known about it previously. You will also have some people who will become interested in donating—but don't expect the checks to come raining in. The hard work of contacting donors and making an ask must continue.

BE WILLING TO TAKE RISKS

You cannot be told "yes" if you don't ask.

Will some of your donors be offended by an ask? They might. Will some of them say no? You bet. Will some disappoint you by the amount they give? Unfortunately, yes. Rejection is certainly a risk any time you ask someone for something. Do not let any of this be a hindrance.

Finally, do not take no personally. There are many reasons people might not give to a campaign, from hidden financial obligations (an ill family member, grandchildren's college tuition) to other philanthropic commitments. And some, it turns out, just may not like your goals. That's okay too. If you are confident in your objectives, continue moving forward with those who are giving. Always remain polite with those who do not give. You never know how their circumstances might change in the future.

WHO SHOULD BE INVOLVED IN A CAPITAL CAMPAIGN?

A major fundraising campaign cannot be undertaken without full support of the board of directors. It may mean you lose a director or two who can't commit. That's okay. You need to have 100 percent buy-in from the board.

Staff also need to commit. Even if they cannot give in large amounts, it is important for them to take pride in the organization and be able to tell anyone who asks about the campaign that they support it. Myriad fundraising resources exist for nonprofit staff. Whether you have development staff or not, staff members can look through blogs like those at Network for Good (https://www.networkforgood.com/non-profit-fundraising -resources/) or Classy (https://www.classy.org/blog/) to familiarize themselves with terms, ideas, and best practices.

You will need an active cadre of volunteers to make a campaign work. These are people who have made top-level commitments to the organization and are willing to work hard. Remember to be thankful and to reward the efforts of all who work to make the campaign a success. Some suggestions include handwritten thank you notes from the campaign leadership, a special "volunteers only" event in your museum, or a group dinner or lunch together at a favorite restaurant. Each opportunity should be used to thank and encourage the volunteers to make it to the end.

HOW WE DID

The Los Alamos Historical Society's campaign was based on two facets: funding the immediate capital needs and building the endowment for long-term needs. The endowment funds will mostly come through legacy gifts—those from estate donations.

Thanks to the generous donors, the cash capital needs were quickly met (see figure 5.1). The legacy donations are a slower process (that's a good thing!).

Also included in the campaign was the donation of two historic homes, one of which became part of the "museum campus" and the other of which will be added when the family who donated it moves out.

Overall, then, the campaign raised $2.7 million in cash and $630,000 in real estate in four years with a total of just over $5 million pledged. Even though the campaign officially closed, solicitation continues for estate gifts through the new Legacy Society so that endowment goal can be reached in the future.

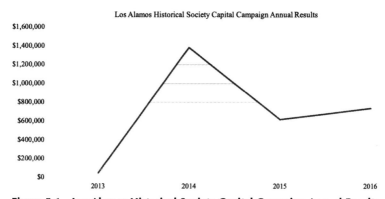

Figure 5.1   Los Alamos Historical Society Capital Campaign Annual Results

PRACTICAL ADVICE

Finally, these last bits of advice may seem small, but they can make all the difference.

Know your state laws! In New Mexico, if a charitable organization raises more than $500,000 in a year, it must complete an audit. We didn't know that, and it delayed our compliance with state regulations for nearly a year. Before you start your campaign, check with your attorney general (or the agency that regulates charities in your state) to determine how you must report income and if there are reporting thresholds. You don't want someone who is interested in donating to look you up online and find that you are out of compliance as a state charity.

Set up a sole-purpose bank account. It may sound oversimplified or superfluous, but set up a new bank account just to accept campaign funds. That way they won't get mixed up with operational funds, and you have a clear record of campaign deposits.

Keep copies of everything. With multiple volunteers talking with multiple people, pledge forms and visit reports being turned in to the office, and money coming in at a quick pace (you hope!), meticulous record keeping is a must. Keep copies of campaign visit reports, incoming and outgoing checks, and any other documents related to the campaign, including your meeting notes. You may not need everything, but you will have it if you do.

When going on an "ask," work in pairs. It will give both of you a bit more confidence. Go in with a specific amount in mind. Listen for what interests the donor. Don't push for an answer on the first visit, but do follow up in a week or two.

As much as possible, get nondesignated gifts. If you have more than one objective, some donors will no doubt want to give to a specific project. That is fine, of course, but as much as possible, guide donors to "greatest need." Keeping track of designated funds can get complicated, whereas donations to the greatest need allow you flexibility, which leads to the next point.

Be flexible! Somewhere along the line, especially during a multiyear campaign, you will find that something does not work out the way you planned. New exhibits may cost more than expected. The building contractor may discover long-hidden asbestos tile. Staffing in one area may become more important than in an area that was originally targeted for fundraising. As long as your overall objectives remain the same, and you keep your donors informed of what is happening with their money, it is important to understand that some of the way the money is used will change during the campaign.

There's no such thing as too much thanks! Thank your volunteers often. Thank your donors profusely and sincerely. Show them through pictures and tours how they have made a difference. Stay in touch with them on a regular basis, and say thank you each and every time.

Finally, have fun! Well, actually, the work of fundraising is not fun. It's sometimes hard, sometimes intimidating, and sometimes frustrating. What is fun, though, is opening an envelope and seeing a $10,000+ check. In fact, it's a thrill you never quite get over.

Section III

CONTRIBUTED INCOME: FUNDRAISING

Contributed income refers to income derived from contributions, sponsorships, and/or grants. In this book, we will subdivide contributed income into two main categories: 1) fundraising and 2) grants. This section focuses on fundraising. Section IV will discuss grants. Fundraising encompasses membership, individual giving, and giving by entities (for example, corporations).

Understanding macro trends in donor giving will help you refine your membership and fundraising strategies and tactics. In terms of individual donors, low interest rates, decreased annual average income, and reduced labor force participation have negatively impacted giving (Rhine 2014). Simultaneously, over the past five years, the percent of recurring donors has steadily increased; the annual retention rates for recurring donors were almost 70 percent higher than for single gift donors (Rhine and Smith 2016). Those retention and recurrence trends should benefit your membership programs. Data mining and surveys can help you understand how to motivate your members and donors to next level tiers, as does using the profiles of your most loyal existing donors to identify potential future loyal donors from new members (White 2018).

As discussed in chapter 1, the US Census Bureau calculated the revenue by type (product line) in 2012. Table III.1 and III.2 show the contribution of membership and private contributions income to the total revenue of institutions that earn such income types.

Table III.1   Membership Income as Percent of Total Revenue by Institution Discipline 2012

All institutions	7.2%
Museums	6.6%
Historical sites	5.8%
Zoos and botanical gardens	7.2%
Nature parks and other similar institutions	9.2%

Table III.2 Private Contributions, Gifts, and Grants Income as Percent of Total Revenue by Institution Discipline 2012

All institutions	30.1%
Museums	31.9%
Historical sites	35.3%
Zoos and botanical gardens	18.9%
Nature parks and other similar institutions	50.1%

Table III.2 includes both fundraising and nonfundraising income, so if you want to compare your internal data to these percentages, you will need to combine your fundraising and private grant income.

The National Center for Charitable Statistics (NCCS) reports the actual revenue generated from different types of contributed income, and rates of change can be computed therefrom. However, the NCCS combines membership, fundraising, grant, and gift income into one category, per the structure of the 990, thus limiting the usefulness of that data. NCCS does provide specific data for income from fundraising events.

Looking at the same income categories by institution discipline, we see the following.

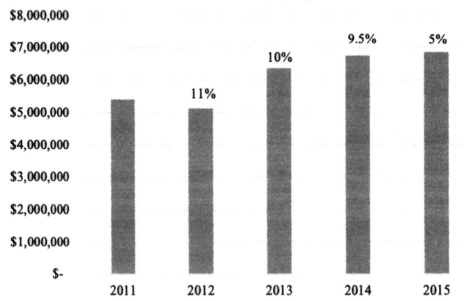

Figure III.1 Gifts, Grants, Membership Fees Income with Rate of Change for All Institutions 2011–2015 ($1,000) in US$

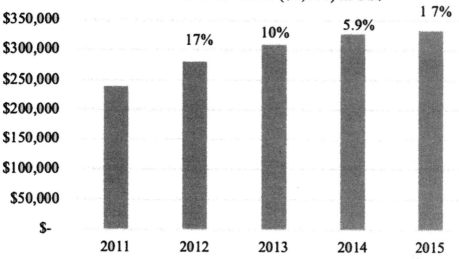

Figure III.2 Income from Fundraising Events with Rate of Change for All Institutions 2011–2015 ($1,000) in US$

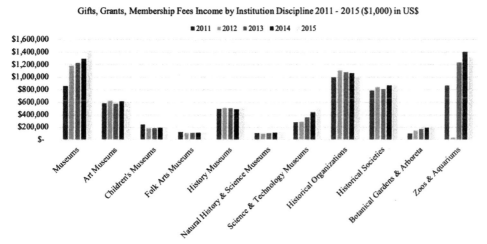

Figure III.3 Gifts, Grants, and Membership Fees Income by Institution Discipline 2011–2015 ($1,000) in US$

Table III.3   Rates of Change of Gifts, Grants, and Membership Fees Income by Institution Discipline 2011–2015

	2011–2012	*2012–2013*	*2013–2014*	*2014–2015*
Museums	38.2%	3.6%	5.2%	9.9%
Art museums	7.3%	−7.6%	6.1%	−2.7%
Children's museums	−24.8%	1.5%	0.6%	3.5%
Folk arts museums	−6.9%	−0.4%	−2.0%	1.9%
History museums	2.9%	−0.6%	−4.0%	6.9%
Natural history and science museums	−4.4%	4.6%	8.2%	9.1%
Science and technology museums	5.8%	21.1%	24.5%	16.1%
Historical organizations	11.4%	−2.7%	−1.8%	−6.3%
Historical societies	7.7%	−3.2%	6.1%	1.2%
Botanical gardens and arboreta	44.3%	15.6%	10.4%	7.0%
Zoos and aquariums	−95.9%	3,331.7%	13.4%	−5.9%

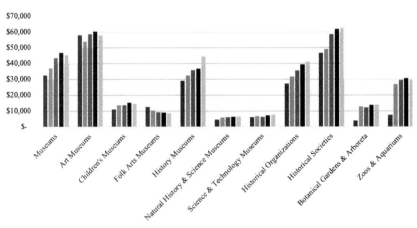

Income from Fundraising Events by Institution Discipline 2011 - 2015 ($1,000) in US$

■2011 ■2012 ■2013 ■2014 ▪2015

Figure III.4   Income from Fundraising Events by Institution Discipline 2011–2015 ($1,000) in US$

Table III.4   Rates of Change of Income from Fundraising Events by Institution Discipline 2011–2015

	2011–2012	*2012–2013*	*2013–2014*	*2014–2015*
Museums	13.8%	17.6%	7.7%	–3.1%
Art museums	–7.1%	8.8%	2.7%	–4.0%
Children's museums	23.1%	0.6%	11.3%	–4.3%
Folk arts museums	–17.1%	–11.9%	–1.7%	–6.2%
History museums	11.4%	9.9%	2.8%	21.0%
Natural history and science museums	34.0%	3.3%	4.3%	1.7%
Science and technology museums	7.9%	–4.4%	13.9%	3.6%
Historical organizations	16.0%	12.0%	10.6%	4.8%
Historical societies	5.4%	18.9%	5.8%	1.5%
Botanical gardens and arboreta	236.8%	–5.9%	13.2%	1.2%
Zoos and aquariums	256.8%	9.9%	3.1%	–1.8%

There is an anomaly with the 2012 gifts, grants, and membership fees income for zoos and aquariums data. Because the variability in the other data is relatively consistent with the fluctuations seen in other charts, the 2012 gifts, grants, and membership fees income for zoos and aquariums dataset could have been miscoded or calculated incorrectly.

CHAPTERS PREVIEW

Membership can be the first step toward a deeper and longer-term giving relationship. Suzette A. Sherman begins this section with a discussion of museum culture. Suzette advocates using membership as a bridge to migrate attendees from transactional visitors to loyal members to philanthropic donors. She details how museums can shape their membership programs to facilitate this matriculation, culminating in philanthropic gifts that improve an institution's long-term financial sustainability. Cari Maslow, associate vice president, engagement at Carnegie Museums of Pittsburgh, delves further into the creation, maintenance, and evaluation of membership programs. Cari provides guidance on pricing, benefit costs, campaign strategies and tactics, targeting, collateral design, visitation, and relationship building. Like Suzette, Cari emphasizes the importance of guiding visitors through their membership journeys and appreciating their support. Suzette and Cari also both discuss the importance of reevaluating membership programs and making appropriate changes. In the next chapter, Nicole Krom, Nicholas D'Addezio, and Melissa Dietrich describe how Longwood Gardens completely changed its membership program by consolidating membership levels and revising benefits. The team incorporated focus group feedback, internal sales data, surveys, and internal financial goals to craft a new membership program. The contributors also discuss how they used consultants in the process and how they anticipated a loss of membership during the transition. After the change, the new Longwood Gardens membership program generates consistent monthly revenue and has seen an increase in member visitation.

Understanding the needs and motivations of donors is critical to effective fundraising. After reviewing fundraising data and effectiveness measurement tools, Beverly Sakauye, chief development officer at the National Civil Rights Museum at the Lorraine Motel, explains the concepts of cultivation and maintenance, providing tools and examples for both concepts. She also reminds us that donors are people who want to feel involved, engaged, and appreciated by your institution. Connecting donors with visitors who have benefited from your institution strengthens that bond. Your board can also facilitate a deeper engagement between donors and your institution. In an "Expert Opinion" segment, Tonya Matthews, equity and nonprofit executive strategy consultant of the Michigan Science Center, presents her three principal techniques to help boards become more effective fundraisers. Like our previous contributors, Tonya advocates creating individualized plans and goals for each board member, establishing buy-in, maximizing their comfort levels, and building their confidence for the ask. Special events like galas are opportunities for board members and institutional staff to ask and to recognize their donors. In an "Expert Opinion" segment, Gina Rogak, director of special events at the Whitney Museum of Fine Arts, shares how she develops special events, creates budgets, partners with other departments, and sets goals to create successful fundraising events.

Then Tim Ardillo, a consultant with Johnson, Grossnickle, and Associates and the former director of institutional advancement for the Indianapolis Zoo, discusses how developing a diversified philanthropy program maximizes potential fundraising revenue. After reviewing donors' philanthropic motivations, Tim explains the importance of the case statement, the written vision for the future of your institution, and its impact on major gifts. He argues that individuals are the greatest area of potential philanthropic revenue growth. Major gifts represent the opportunity to fund endowments, programs, operating funds, and capital campaigns. Julie McDearmon, the director of institutional advancement at the Indianapolis Zoo, continues the discussion of major gifts by returning to the recurring theme in this section: connecting the individual to the institution. Julie emphasizes the importance of establishing the relationship between the individual and the institution. Charismatic or popular staff members can certainly spark interest, but the relationship should remain regardless of the institution's staff. Julie shows you how to use the portfolio approach to cultivate and manage current and prospective donors.

That same approach can be applied to other types of fundraising, like crowdfunding. The next two chapters offer "Expert Opinions" on crowdfunding projects. Jennifer Hayden, director of PR and marketing for the National Museum of Nuclear Science and History, traces the evolution of her institution's crowdfunding initiatives beginning with restoring a B-29 Superfortress plane to restoring multiple planes. Jennifer discusses the reasons why they switched from Kickstarter to Indiegogo and how using crowdfunding platforms expanded audience and community awareness of the museum and its fundraising campaigns. Kimberly A. Kenney, assistant director and curator of the McKinley Presidential Library and Museum, describes how the museum used crowdfunding with a simple PayPal button on the homepage of their website to fund the acquisition of the Ida McKinley tiara. The campaign was announced with one press release that spawned interest from National Public Radio, the *New York Times*, the Associated Press, and local television stations. Kimberly also discusses the decision to not offer rewards or levels and the incorporation of offline events to support the campaign, enabling everyone from school children to major donors to fully participate in what became an exciting event.

This section closes with three chapters that reinforce and summarize the major themes from the previous chapters. Building on the themes of partnership and relationships, Margaret Walker, assistant curator at the Vanderbilt University Fine Arts Gallery, explores how two different institutions, the Vanderbilt University Fine Arts Gallery and the National Society of the Colonial Dames of America, leverage partnerships to facilitate their respective fundraising. As part of Vanderbilt University, the Fine Arts Gallery can leverage internal partnerships for financial and awareness benefits, but access to those benefits depends on the ability of the Fine Arts Gallery's small staff to continuously build relationships throughout the university. The National Society of the Colonial Dames of America owns and operates three museums and other philanthropic ventures, like a network of ninety other museums, historic sites, and memorials managed by local chapters. The risk of fundraising cannibalization and overlap is concerning. Over the past five years, all of these institutions have attempted to form a more organized network to share resources and best practices. Success will depend on buy-in from all the partners. Measuring success is the purview of Allison Porter, president of Avalon Consulting Group. Allison describes how benchmarking, metrics, and reporting are critical to generating the analytics needed for successful fundraising. Using a case study of a new museum, Allison builds a membership and fundraising program for an institution that had not even finished construction when her efforts began. By establishing metrics and donor behavior tracking at the beginning of the process, the new museum was able to effective and efficiently spend scarce resources on its most promising and committed supporters—a lesson for all institutions. She also provides examples of metrics that your institution could use to evaluate your fundraising campaigns.

Kristin Bertrand, director of development at the San José Museum of Art, and James G. Leventhal, deputy director and chief development officer at the Museum of the African Diaspora (MoAD) in San Francisco, close this section by sharing resources that you can use to improve your fundraising skills and campaigns. As they note, resources, databases, and tools change over time, but the skills learned from these resources are universal. As our other contributors have underscored, membership and fundraising are about building relationships and connecting people with the same passions. Bertrand and Leventhal then integrate all these thoughts, concepts, and approaches into two words: subtle and humane.

RESOURCE LIST

Rhine, Carol. *The State of Nonprofit Fundraising*. St. Louis: American Museum Membership Conference, 2014.

Rhine, Carol, and Michael J. Smith. *Benchmarking to Drive Fundraising Success*. Chicago: American Museum Membership Conference, 2016.

The Urban Institute, NCCS Core Files, 2011–2015. https://nccs-data.urban.org/data .php?ds=core. Accessed January–November 2018.

US Census Bureau. 2002, 2007, and 2012 Economic Censuses. https://www.census.gov/ programs-surveys/economic-census/data/tables.html. Accessed January–November 2018.

White, Willard, Usha Subramanian, Christine Zrinsky, and Marcos Voss. *Loyalty Programs: Long Game but Rich Rewards*. Phoenix: American Alliance of Museums Annual Conference, 2018.

6

Membership on Center Stage between the Transactional and Philanthropic

Suzette A. Sherman, President, Sherman Consulting Group

SETTING THE STAGE

Membership can play a leading role in how both internal staff and the visiting public understand your museum. While marketing staff may focus on maximizing ticket sales and development on raising major gifts, membership represents a place of common ground where visitors seeking a richer relationship can begin to embrace the mission. When the connections between constituents—from visitor to member to donor—are managed seamlessly across the organization, with all staff prioritizing long-term relationships over short-term gains, then the stage encourages the transactional to evolve into the philanthropic.

Shifting a museum culture to one focused on membership and philanthropy requires dedicated leadership and demonstrating the financial impact and lifetime value of a first-time visitor who returns, becomes a member, and continues to develop an increasingly philanthropic relationship with the museum. The net revenue from the longtime relationship will far exceed the one-time visit. Furthermore, the cost of attracting a new visitor will be much greater than attracting a repeat visit from someone who has already enjoyed a museum experience. Plus, a positive referral from a member or frequent visitor to a friend will be more persuasive and believable than paid advertising or other marketing messages from the organization. Building lasting constituent relationships through membership represents a net win on both the revenue and expense sides of the equation.

The leadership challenge entails developing a shared understanding across all functional areas regarding the importance of, and approach to, growing relationships beyond a transaction, for example, the purchase of an admission ticket to a relationship such as that achieved through membership. Within a membership program, the opportunities are many for encouraging higher levels of participation, engagement, and support. Figure 6.1 illustrates the connections between the transactional and philanthropic, positioning membership between the two poles.

Furthermore, membership represents an important step in building loyal relationships with constituents and engaging a community of individuals who have stepped forward to become involved in a museum's activities and mission in a deeper way

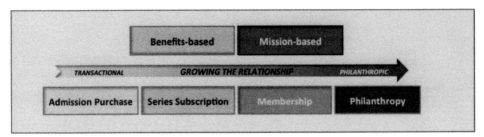

Figure 6.1   The Transactional to Philanthropic Continuum

than that of a one-time visitor. Members have raised their hand to say they're "in" beyond a single visit or transaction. The museum's job is to deliver on the promise of value, connection, and an exceptional, yearlong experience.

MANAGING THE CONSTITUENT JOURNEY TO DEVELOP LOYALTY

A museum-wide commitment is required to deliver exceptional experiences for visitors, members, and donors across all touch points—on site, online, over the phone, and through traditional and new media. Responsive service teams, regular and informative communication, and ongoing programming that encourages involvement and frequent visits will foster loyalty and growth in relationships. An important step in managing the quality of the experiences involves mapping the constituent journey before, during, and after the experience, whether it's a visit, a membership year, or a philanthropic relationship. By identifying the touch points along the journey and the staff who most impact or own responsibility for them, you can manage the process of delivering quality experiences that increase loyalty and are key to success.

When mapping the experience, it is important to understand that the work of retaining a member begins on the first day of the membership year as initial impressions can make or break the quality of the overall experience. After attracting and welcoming newcomers into the membership community, the focus then shifts from the work of acquisition marketing to relationship building, engagement, and retention. A loyal membership base provides an essential pipeline for philanthropic support and demonstrates organizational strength to the board, funders, and community.

By developing strategies to connect members to the mission, you'll turn members into advocates, referral agents, and loyal supporters. Layer communication efforts with messaging about how additional gifts of support and membership upgrades will further the mission and provide new ways to become more deeply engaged in the museum's work. Moving members from introductory levels to mid-level circles and high-level donor groups will increase the overall return from both earned and contributed sources.

SHAPING MEMBERSHIP TO ENCOURAGE ENGAGEMENT AND CULTIVATE RELATIONSHIPS

The structure of a membership program can contribute to its ability to bridge the transactional and philanthropic by encouraging upgrades to higher levels of engagement. Using research and analysis to understand what benefits and experiences current members and membership prospects value and use provides an essential starting point. Of course, the introductory or lower levels of membership must include the essentials that encourage onsite and online visitors to step into a member relationship based on their plans to visit—how often (visit frequency), with whom (party size and composition), what services are desired (free or discounted parking, strollers, and coat check), and how involved the visit might be (general admission only or tickets to exhibitions, films, and other activities).

Objectives for these lower levels, often considered the general membership program with benefits for one or two individuals or a family, typically involve growing the household count. The number of member households, along with attendance, provide a source of pride for museum leaders, and often top off the list of metrics in museum dashboards and reports of key performance indicators. Some museums prioritize admissions revenue over membership or the member household count over membership revenue, but all earned and contributed financial metrics and revenue streams should be managed together for optimal long-term financial strength, with constituent loyalty and relationships living at the heart. When the short-term race drives the priorities, then organizations often neglect their relationships with visitors, members, donors, and employees, which negatively impacts loyalty and long-term financial strength.

Membership builds a bridge between the transactional and philanthropic constituencies, and the most effective programs create a ladder of engagement. The ideal membership program will offer the right number of membership categories, packaged with the right bundle of benefits, and priced to attract new members, while also encouraging current members to renew and upgrade to higher levels of participation. Museums often err on the side of offering too many membership levels, benefits, and choices, making the purchase or upgrade decision overwhelming. Work to simplify the decision-making process involved with the purchase by avoiding overly complex structures that might confuse and frustrate prospects. Instead, streamline the membership program and present it in a clear and persuasive way that helps visitors or current members choose the option that best meets their interests and visiting plans.

Structuring a membership program for growth in the member household count requires entry-level categories packed with valued benefits and priced right when compared to the cost of admission and tickets. Museums with free general admission need to make a compelling case for support and offer other benefits with high perceived value, such as special access and private hours, exhibition previews, and insider perspectives.

In the introductory levels, offering a bundle of strategic benefits at optimal prices for one or two individuals and/or families that will encourage repeat visits is important for positioning membership as an attractive alternative to a one-time admission purchase. These levels typically provide unlimited free admission, members-only programs, exhibition tickets and previews, discounts, and member communications as a starting point.

In the mid-levels, often priced between $250 and $1,000 depending on specific museum and market characteristics, the combination of benefits should provide rich experiences designed to encourage upgrades from the introductory levels. For these mid-levels, museum staff should work to understand member and donor interests as a basis for developing loyal relationships and cultivating philanthropic aspirations. Benefits in these levels should create a window into the inner workings of the organization through behind-the-scenes opportunities, insider communications, special access to museum curators or content experts, and presentations by the museum director. This is the space where the transactional begins to fade away and an opportunity to cultivate loyal relationships and philanthropic interests can flourish.

Positioning and branding the mid-levels as a distinctive group that offers engaging experiences and social opportunities, while also supporting the work of the organization, is also important. This can be accomplished by using names for each of these levels to communicate a supportive relationship, such as Supporter, Patron, or Benefactor, and then naming the entire mid-level group as a circle or patrons group. Members often prefer a descriptive naming approach for the grouping rather than clever or complicated alternatives, but it depends on the organization and market. For example, Museum Patrons, Museum Circle, Discovery Circle, or Garden Circle often outperform catchy alternatives like The Cezanne Circle, Galileo's Guild, or Magnolia Society in research studies.

Above the mid-levels, the major giving groups top the pyramid of member and donor participation and support. Involvement here is mostly philanthropic, though it remains important to provide intimate experiences, such as private tours with curators, receptions in the homes of board members and other philanthropists, or dinners with the museum's director, content experts, and thought leaders. These major giving levels are often branded as leadership circles or societies.

Figure 6.2 illustrates how a ladder of engagement can be shaped to encourage upgrades, resulting in net revenue gains and strong constituent loyalty across all membership groups from introductory to major giving societies. The engagement will involve levels of communication from email and digital to more personal notes, phone calls, and face-to-face meetings, as well as levels of programming. Some programs, such as special hours or previews, will serve many, while other events will be designed as more intimate gatherings where discussion is fostered and personal relationships are developed.

In terms of communications, today, even smaller organizations have easy access to high-tech tools for customer relationship management, website development, e-commerce, e-marketing, and social media marketing. With these tools, museums are able to personalize communications to all members, speaking to them by name and acknowledging their level of support, plus offering relevant program information based on their interests and past participation, as well as highlights on the benefits they could enjoy at higher levels. Combining this personalization using high-tech tools with high-touch experiences, appealing to their specific interests and philanthropic

Figure 6.2   Ladder of Engagement

goals, can effectively encourage upgrades from lower to higher levels for greater involvement, participation, and loyalty.

CREATING A CULTURE OF PHILANTHROPY

The process of rethinking the membership structure can contribute to an organization-wide culture of philanthropy because of membership's role as a bridge between the transactional and the philanthropic. With a research-based understanding of what constituents value and an in-depth analysis of performance metrics and trends, museums can structure the membership benefits, levels, and price points for maximum financial impact. Creating a ladder of engaging experiences that encourages members to step up to higher levels of participation and support will contribute to loyalty and overall growth in net revenue from both earned and contributed sources. Membership represents a doorway into a relationship where loyalty and commitment can be cultivated.

Museum leaders who take a holistic view—one that balances earned revenue streams with contributed income from membership and philanthropic gifts—will be equipped to optimize long-term financial strength. By delivering experiences that encourage first-time visitors to return and become members for a yearlong relationship with opportunities to experience museum offerings in new ways, they can develop a base of loyal constituents. Then they can inspire members with the mission-based work of the museum and encourage additional support, further grow loyalty, and strengthen relationships. With membership on center stage, this pathway will transform the transactional into loyal relationships that can be stewarded into philanthropic supporters.

7

The Value in Membership

Cari Maslow, Associate Vice President, Engagement, at Carnegie Museums of Pittsburgh

Membership is where earned and contributed revenue meet for your museum. Unlike performing art subscriptions that are often seen as a comparable product because both purchases demonstrate loyalty or at least a commitment to be a more frequent participant, the nature of the US tax code means that the benefit typically most highly valued by people purchasing a membership—unlimited free admission—does not impact tax deductibility, so most membership purchases can be treated as contributions with a goods and services portion. This creates a dilemma for many organizations and I would argue a trap—do I treat my members like donors or do I assume that their primary motivation is value and treat them as value-seeking consumers? The basics of a strong membership program are the same either way—the difference really lies in how you spend your resources, how you look at your program, and at its root whether your emphasis is on the long-term or short-term value of members. Museums do not have alumni and at least currently most do not capture visitor contact information. This means that our member bases are our most reliable source of future donors.

This chapter will outline key elements to consider when building or evaluating a member program across that viewpoint continuum and will attempt to bring considerations from both perspectives. Like many aspects of a membership program, the type of museum you work in may heavily influence your perspective on this, so I'll point out when things are typical to various types of programs. For instance, if you work for a museum that truly has free admission all of the time without a blockbuster exhibition program with ticket costs, then your membership program falls clearly in the contributed revenue end of the spectrum.

KEY ELEMENTS: PRICING AND BENEFITS

The price of a membership should always be based on how much admission is to your organization. You need to know where the tipping point is, which is essentially how many visits would have to be made for the membership to be paid for. The standard practice is for this to be about three visits. So for example, if your basic family-level membership covers two adults and four children, you would calculate

Table 7.1 Tipping Point—Membership

Admission Value	Member Price	Tipping Point
(2*$15) + (4*$7) = $58	$150	2.6 visits

how much a full price visit would cost for that group of people and divide your membership price by that amount to calculate this value. The tipping point is rarely the same for all levels of membership. It's typical to focus on what it is for your most popular member level.

You should always look at the pricing of the two products in tandem. That relationship is key to membership sales, especially at the admissions desk. Sales tools should clearly draw the connection for visitors with the goal of making a decision to become a member seem an obvious choice to anyone who thinks they will visit multiple times. It's also a good practice to let visitors decide to join after their visit by applying their admission ticket costs to the price of a membership.

There are a variety of different types of research you can do to ensure that both your admission and your membership price are on target. The least effective but cheapest is to benchmark your pricing by looking at other museums in your area and then keep your pricing on par with theirs. If this is all you can do, focus on keeping your tipping point in line rather than your actual membership price. The biggest problem with this method is that it makes the assumption that someone in your market is doing more research than just benchmarking with your museum. If not, your entire cohort might be undervaluing admission and membership. Other methods are various types of surveys and focus groups that try to get at what people are willing to pay. Conjoint analysis, which is a form of surveying that presents respondents with a variety of options to choose from and bases follow-up questions on the choices they make, is one of the better techniques to use, especially when you are making significant changes to your membership product.

The benefits of membership should be examined in conjunction with price. You want to consider multiple things when looking at benefits:

- Cost to the organization—look at both the cost of the item and the cost to deliver the benefit
- Impact on tax deductibility for the member
- Incentivize upgrade behavior
- Foster engagement with the organization

You need to consider the cost of benefits when you look at the return on investment (ROI) of your membership program, but make sure to take a long view. For example, a magnet is a cheap benefit and can be mailed in a #10 envelope, but a free ticket to a low-cost event at the museum will immediately encourage visitation, which in turn is a driver of actually renewing the membership. The ticket may cost more in the short term, but only a portion of your members will redeem it, lowering your actual cost. They're also providing you with useful information about themselves that you can use to engage them in the future. Even better, if free tickets to the event are a benefit with a higher level of membership, you are also demonstrating a reason to upgrade.

Don't forget to look at benefits from the perspective of your member. As stated earlier, unlimited free admission does not affect the tax deductibility of a membership purchase. While the impact of charitable donations for the majority of people changed with the 2018 tax code revision, the rules around valuing goods and services did not, so you should observe the tax regulations required around soliciting for a contribution when selling memberships and look carefully at your benefits from this perspective. For instance, ten free parking vouchers would impact tax deductibility for a member but a 15 percent discount on parking would not. You need to understand the rules and view benefit options with them in mind because this calculation will impact the member's perception of the value of membership and the impact of his or her membership purchase on your organization.

The vast majority of members do not use all of the benefits of membership and will often not visit enough times for the membership to "pay for itself," so make sure you're conversant in key measures—lifetime value, member per capita, and percent of donors who began as members—when you make key decisions. That doesn't mean that the answer is to overload your membership program with benefits, but it does mean that you want to be thoughtful about how members are perceived by museum staff and ensure that decisions are made with both short- and long-term benefit in mind.

KEY TOOLS: ACQUISITION, RENEWAL, AND UPGRADE CAMPAIGNS

There are three key tools for driving membership revenue: acquisition, renewal, and upgrade campaigns. They are all important, but the most important is renewal. It makes very little sense to spend money acquiring members if you don't have a comprehensive renewal strategy. You want your plan for all three types of campaigns to include multiple channels—mail, telemarketing, email, online, on site, etc. To generate the most revenue, the efforts in all channels should work together.

The channel that will be most successful for you will depend on both what type of museum you are and your market. For instance, zoos often do most of their acquisition on site in the summer months and may not do any acquisition mail. Museums that don't charge admission don't invest as much effort in onsite sales as museums that do charge admission. The tool that's almost universal in the United States is direct mail, but in Europe and Canada, where postage is far more expensive, mail plays a lesser role and electronic fund transfer (EFT) and other forms of recurring giving are far more important. You want to think carefully about your investment mix considering your museum type, the demographics of your current and desired members, and what has been successful in the past. Don't assume that young people don't read mail or that what you would respond to is what your members will respond to. You can find in-depth information about response rates to various marketing channels in research done by the Data and Marketing Association that can help you build a case to support your choices when you are presenting the membership budget to your finance office or senior leadership.

Acquisition

Acquisition campaigns are often the largest expense in a membership program's budget and the first place that budget cuts are made. These campaigns are an important part of ensuring that you're building your member base. It's important to look at both revenue and member counts when making decisions about acquisition. If you look at only revenue, you can miss drops in counts that will have an impact in the long term. Direct mail is an important component of acquisition, but it's expensive, so you need to be sure you're spending your resources wisely by making sure to use the science behind direct mail and not your personal preferences. It is often wise to have an outside firm handle a large acquisition mailing. They can bring an expertise on direct mail to the table that most in-house staffs don't possess, and when you factor in the time it takes to work with a designer, rent and trade mailing lists, and work with a printer, there is not as much additional cost as you might assume. A firm can also bring information and insight into what and how to test in order to continually improve your results.

Renewals

Every member of your museum should be asked to renew on a fixed schedule that you don't waver from. The surest way to leave revenue on the table both in the short term and the long term is not to do this. For example, long-term members have been shown to be some of the best planned giving prospects for museums. In the United States, direct mail is the backbone of most museums' renewal strategies. It can be supported by email, telemarketing, and online work, but be wary of doing away with mail to save money. The general rule of thumb on how many mail hits to send is to mail until you start to lose money.

Figure 7.1 shows an example of a renewal schedule.

You'll note that this example shows when the member will receive an upgrade mailing and a request to make a donation to the annual fund. You want to make sure to take all solicitations into account when you build your schedule. This example is based on members who expire in August and is a monthly renewal schedule. Smaller

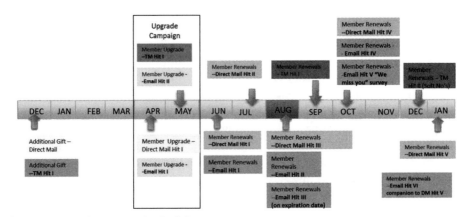

Figure 7.1   Member Renewal Schedule

museums may not have the capacity to renew members every month. The important thing is to find a schedule that works for you and stick to it. If you can, you also want to test in renewal mail and email to find the most effective packages for your membership base. If you're lucky, your testing will reveal a variety of packages that work equally effectively so you have options to choose from.

Upgrades

There are two standard types of upgrade campaigns: campaigns that 1) ask a member to renew early and upgrade to a new level mid-cycle with the benefit of starting the new level immediately, and that 2) ask the member to pay the difference in the levels and then when it's time for renewal ask them to remain at the upgraded level. Both methods have their benefits, with the first usually seeing more members remain at the higher level and a higher average gift on the mailing itself but typically a smaller response rate, and the second seeing more respondents but a lower average gift and fewer members remaining at the new level. Either could be effective for your organization.

KEY ELEMENTS TO A CAMPAIGN: TARGET AUDIENCE, DESIGN, AND OFFER

There are three key elements to consider in all campaigns: the target audience, design, and offer. All three elements can and should be tested to ensure that you're using your expense budget wisely.

The target audience is who you are mailing to or targeting online. In acquisition, your decisions on who to target should be based on who your current members are. Be careful about what channels you use to try to expand your audience demographic and how you try to do it. Direct mail is not the channel to break ground with in this respect, so while you can certainly target different elements of your base, it will be costly and likely ineffective to go beyond that. So for instance, if you are a science center, your member base is probably largely families with young children. You may have a strategic goal of bringing in more single adults, but just sending your typical direct mail package to lists with more nonfamily names is not likely to be successful both because your core product will likely appeal to fewer people and because your sales are likely to be your less expensive memberships, which will also bring your average gift down. In renewal and upgrade campaigns, your target audience is to some extent defined by your current member base, but in some instances further refining can be done by modeling of typical responders, geographic targeting, or by using other demographic information. For instance, a museum that's in a city with a great deal of tourism that had a large influx of members due to a blockbuster exhibition might decide not to mail any renewal notices to first-year members who live outside a certain geographic radius.

Design is essentially what the package, ad, or signage looks like. It should correspond both with your institutional branding and your target audience. It is probably the place where you're most likely to make a mistake in direct mail because it's challenging to remember that science needs to rule here, not your personal preference. Even color choices can impact results, so be thoughtful and make sure that you test carefully. The language and copy length need to be based on research about what's effective in each particular channel. For example: Email is typically better structured with short messages and limited links that can pull your recipient away from the response form and completing the purchase. Direct mail on the other hand tends to be long and repetitive, and have multiple pieces because most recipients won't actually read the whole piece. Its typically designed with skimming in mind.

The offer is how you entice people to do what you want them to do when you want them to do it. Offers should be constructed with a deadline and should be designed to incent people to buy membership at a certain level, so whether you're using a premium or a promotion, set it up in such a way as to move people to choose your higher-priced membership levels. First-year members behave very differently from multiyear members, so you should consider implementing different offers with them in renewal campaigns. Retention rates of first-year members is a key metric to impact, so giving them an extra month of membership or a discount tends to be money well spent in the long term. In renewals, you also want to be careful in how you sequence your offers so that the best one is used in your first mail or email hit. You want your members to renew early so you save money in mailing costs. It would be a mistake to teach them to wait for your final offer to renew to get the best deal.

IMPACTING THE NUMBERS

The most cost-effective method of increasing your member base and your member revenue is to focus on increasing retention. First-year member retention of 30 to 40 percent is seen as solid performance, but it means that each year we need to acquire more and more members to grow. To see what an impact increasing retention can have, take your member count, calculate how many member households make up 1 percent, and then multiply that number by your average membership gift. The number you get is the value of increasing your retention by a single percentage point.

Table 7.2 shows an example for a small museum and a mid-sized museum.

By focusing on retention, you'll impact both the short-term and the long-term ROI of your program because many of these techniques do not significantly impact costs, but some may have impact to immediate revenue. Here are a couple of things that you can look at doing to increase your retention rates.

Table 7.2 Member Retention Impact

Member Base	1%	Average Membership	Value of a 1 Percentage Point Increase in Retention
5,000	50	$75	$3,750
25,000	250	$125	$31,250

Drive Visitation

The one thing that everyone in the field seems to agree on is that repeat visitation is a driver for retention both because there's an inherent value to the member and because it gives us more opportunities to provide great experiences and build relationships. The common belief is that three visits is the magic number in ensuring renewal. I'm not sure that this is true though because what really matters from a value perspective is a member's perception of how often he or she has visited. But because most of us don't have the skills or the resources to employ regression analysis to identify what factors are our own drivers of retention, common sense will lead you to focus your efforts on getting members to visit. Data can help you do that by identifying members who aren't visiting so you can target invitations and visit-based promotions like extra discounts in the store to them. You can also focus your benefits on things like discounts on admission for guests and special member preview hours that inherently drive members to visit again.

Recurring Giving

Recurring giving has been shown to be one of the surest ways an organization can grow its contributed revenue. It has been used outside the United States for years and was pioneered here primarily by public radio and television. Membership organizations have struggled to find ways to incorporate it in the past, primarily because of limits in technology, but it is one of the most effective ways you can impact your member retention rate and build a steady stream of revenue for your museum. Today, you can create a digital member card, credit card processors can auto-update card expiration dates, and culturally Americans are catching up to their Canadian and European peers and are now comfortable with EFTs and recurring charges. You do need to think through your process, how you're going to handle a monthly membership sale at the admissions desk, and how you're going to position it within your existing membership products. It's tempting to explain it as "joining with twelve easy payments" as opposed to as a recurring gift to your museum. That approach will undermine the value of implementing a program like this, so you want to avoid this type of language. You also need to think through how you're going to continue to engage your recurring members and how you plan to implement additional giving and upgrade campaigns with this audience both in your existing campaigns and behind the scenes in your customer relationship management software.

An unexpected benefit that several museums that have implemented recurring giving programs for membership have noticed is that monthly givers tend to be less affluent and younger, so it seems to be a viable tool to consider if one of your museum's priorities is to diversify its audience in these ways.

A MORE COMPREHENSIVE APPROACH TO
MEMBERSHIP: VERTICAL INTEGRATION

Decades of survey data and other research for your organization will likely show that members below a certain membership level are your value seekers and that at a certain point in your organization's membership continuum this changes. The problem with this thinking is that it completely ignores the demographic distribution of your base population. For example, the empty nesters are likely to have had a membership that allowed them to bring their children and now that the children have left home may downgrade to a membership that allows admission for just two adults. That's very logical purchase behavior—especially if your membership program and related material focus exclusively on value- and admission-based benefits—but those empty nesters are also entering the time in their lives where they will have more disposable income and are therefore entering what can be their most charitable decades. Long-standing membership practice would drop them into a list of people being asked to return to their previous level of membership—an approach unlikely to work in this situation and that by default will support the organizational belief that members are value seekers.

There is value in looking at your membership solicitations, your donor communications, your annual fund program, and your major gift program in a continuum guided more by demographics, financial capacity, and behavior than membership level. In order to do this effectively, you need to become an advocate for ensuring that your various database systems at least talk to each other so you can use visit behavior, email opens, store purchases, additional giving, etc. as data points that inform how you communicate with and solicit your members. This is a daunting task for a small membership program and perhaps even more daunting for a large museum that has disparate, unconnected data and an infrastructure that isn't conducive to these areas of the business working together. Most of us don't have an easy time increasing our expense budgets and our staff count is also not something that we can easily grow. By using data more effectively to target mailings or to prove that an event is not as successful as leadership believes it to be, you can free up resources to focus on building relationships with members. Efforts like calling all new members to welcome them and adding communications about impact can make a decided difference to retention rates and if appropriately targeted can be focused on the members that have the greatest likelihood of becoming larger supporters of your museum.

It's also important to train your staff to build relationships with members. Applaud them when they spend extra time speaking with a member or going the extra mile to ensure that someone is happy. Those little things can make all the difference to how your organization is perceived and whether it is somewhere a member will want to be and have fond memories of when he or she is asked to make a contribution. I know that I'm doing my job correctly when I receive personal emails from members sharing information or thank you cards from children or I see members at every single member event and they recognize me at the grocery store. I want to have relationships with my members, I want them to want to be here, and I want them to tell me when they aren't happy about something. Even responding to a complaint is a chance to build a relationship, so empower your staff to listen and fix things—a $5 coupon or a free month of membership is a small price to pay when you're trying to build a relationship that will last a lifetime. Then take everything you're doing with members and apply it to your staff because to make this really work you also need to retain your staff.

CONCLUSION

It will always be most effective to sell a membership like you're speaking to that value-driven consumer, but to retain them in a world where a vast majority will, despite all your efforts, not visit enough times to actually receive that value, you need to convince them that they decided to join at least in part to support your museum. To do that, you want to talk to them as if they are donors right away, so include impact messaging in everything you do—let them know how many school children visit for free and that their joining enabled the museum to impact those children's lives. Treat them as if they are valued members of your community, and not value-driven shoppers, if you want to ensure that they don't make the decision to renew every year around the value they received from you. Most nonprofits would not undervalue a donor who consistently makes a $100 annual gift, so don't let your organization do it because that donor is a member. Instead do everything you can to ensure that once someone joins your museum you communicate with him or her as if he or she made that choice in order to support the museum and the value it brings not only to him- or herself or his or her family and friends but also to the community. You can do that and encourage him or her to visit with special opportunities to both support his or her decision to join from a value perspective and expand his or her view of why he or she made that decision. Research shows that people give to feel good about themselves and their decisions, so validate members' decision to join at every opportunity and in turn they will support your institution with a lifetime of participation and support.

RECOMMENDED RESOURCES

The American Museum Membership Conference happens every eighteen months and is an excellent forum for membership professionals to learn and build their professional networks. http://americanmuseummembership.org/.

Colleen Dilenschneider has a very useful website and blog *Know Your Own Bone*. https://www.colleendilen.com/.

Culture Track is a research study and initiative conducted by LaPlaca Cohen that provides information on how Americans look at culture. https://culturetrack.com/.

The Data and Marketing Association has information and research on direct mail and other forms of direct marketing. https://thedma.org/.

Simplicity, Flexibility, Loyalty, and Profitability

Revamping the Longwood Gardens Membership Program

Nicole Krom, Membership and Outreach
Manager; Nicholas D'Addezio, Director of
Marketing; and Melissa Dietrich, Associate
Director of Membership, Longwood Gardens

Residing in the suburbs of Philadelphia, Longwood Gardens spans 1,083 idyllic acres in Chester County, Pennsylvania. Philanthropist Pierre S. du Pont purchased the land in 1906 to save a collection of trees slated to be cut down for lumber. Over the years, du Pont designed and created a collection of indoor and outdoor gardens and steered the path for Longwood to become one of the great gardens of the world. Today, Longwood Gardens welcomes more than 1.5 million guests a year, has more than four hundred employees, and continues to inspire people through excellence in garden design, horticulture, education, and the arts.

THE HISTORY

A relatively new program, membership at Longwood began in 2007. Prior to 2007, "membership" was structured as a frequent visitor pass. Over the past ten years, the growth in the program has been quite extraordinary. In 2007, Longwood transitioned everyone from the frequent visitor pass to membership, accounting for sixteen thousand households. After expanding benefit offerings and focusing on the guest experience and innovative displays, Longwood jumped to more than fifty-one thousand household members by early 2014. It was at this time that Longwood began reviewing growth projections for future years and questioning if the membership program, as it stood, could support additional growth while continuing to deliver an extraordinary guest experience for these members. Providing a first-class experience while managing capacity at programs, events, and generally busy days was becoming a challenge. In addition, because of recent Longwood admission price increases that were not aligned to membership price increases, many guests sought a membership for its value

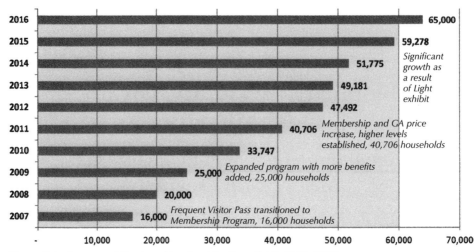

Figure 8.1   Longwood Gardens Membership Growth FY 2007–2016

versus a membership based on supporting Longwood. As Longwood began these membership program discussions, membership continued to increase and hit its peak in April 2016 at more than sixty-five thousand households (see figure 8.1).

THE PROCESS

Knowing its current limitations, Longwood embarked on a multiyear project to refresh its membership program. Key goals for the new program were to continue to deliver an extraordinary experience that members had come to expect, while also ensuring that the program was a financially viable one for Longwood that supports the mission and vision of the organization. Over the course of two years, staff assessed the program in place and created a road map for future changes. Beginning with internal analysis and member survey data, the membership team launched a request for proposal to bring two consultants on board to assist in the development. The first consultant conducted a data mining study to understand current member behaviors and visitation patterns. The second consultant conducted focus groups and surveys and developed membership models to test among current and lapsed members. This component of the work took approximately one year.

Using the qualitative data, Longwood uncovered some interesting findings on member behaviors. For example, while a very small percentage of the total member households (less than 5 percent) attended events like concerts and education classes, members still accounted for 55 percent of the audiences at these events. The Café saw more than 60 percent of total sales from members, while the GardenShop saw close to 37 percent of total sales. The data showed that members bought an additional eighteen thousand tickets to bring guests along with them, resulting in close to $350,000 in revenue. Last, the data confirmed the increased value of long-term members over time, with those that had been a member for more than five years contributing an additional $700 in spending for every $100 they originally spent on membership. In addition to buying behavior, the data uncovered a negative trend related to new members. While overall member households were increasing, the number and percentage of first-time members was decreasing. Using these findings and other analyses, Longwood was able to determine which benefits were most important to members and which benefits significantly impacted other areas of the organization.

Qualitative data from the focus groups and surveys also revealed useful information. As expected, value proved the driver for purchasing memberships. Most respondents did not think about the support they were providing the Gardens and did not make the decision to purchase a membership based on need of the organization. Members loved visiting the Gardens and ranked certain benefits like the Christmas display and the GardenShop discounts as most important to them.

Longwood combined the data taken from focus groups and surveys to develop and test membership models and then surveyed a second dataset of more than twenty-four thousand current and lapsed members on these models. The models, which were available for purchase by those surveyed, tested price sensitivity, new membership levels, new names for the levels, and member benefits. It yielded a response rate of 19 percent. Results showed that there was a small percentage (2 percent to 6 percent of the respondents) that would not purchase a membership in one of the proposed modeled programs. Also, a high percentage of respondents chose to purchase one of the higher membership levels even though there was a significant price increase from previous levels.

With all this information in hand, it was time for Longwood to define its new membership program. Longwood wanted to achieve four main goals in the new program: simplicity, flexibility, loyalty, and profitability. Prior to implementing the new membership program, Longwood had offered thirteen levels of membership from which to choose. To make it more manageable for staff to explain the membership options and for new members to know the best choice for their needs, Longwood aimed to consolidate those thirteen levels. Through focus groups and surveys, Longwood determined that members wanted to visit the Gardens with family and friends more. The structure of the program had limitations in how they could visit, so a goal to increase flexibility in membership admissions arose. At the time of analysis, more than twenty-three thousand households had been members of Longwood for five or more years. Sustaining that loyalty while undertaking such radical change was a very important factor. Finally, the new program had to be profitable. Longwood decided on an average price increase of 40 percent as there was not a high degree of price sensitivity found among those tested.

Longwood spent the second year of the implementation working on internal systems and developing communications, branding, key performance indicators, and staff training with a goal of launching a new membership program in August 2016.

On August 1, 2016, Longwood transitioned all active members to five new membership levels, which included benefits and considerations for larger families and young adults. Members continued to have access to their old benefits until their current membership expired. The new delineation of benefits created a new structure to encourage members to move up the membership ladder. Some benefits were removed and/or restricted to higher levels.

Longwood also enacted an internal and external communications plan. Internally, the membership team presented the new program to the full staff, received full support of the board and CEO, conducted staff trainings, and provided talking points for consistent messaging. Externally, Longwood began communicating to active members two months prior to the transition. Longwood mailed members welcome packets with new membership cards, as well as sent information about the new structure through several outlets, including the monthly e-newsletter and such mailed materials as Longwood's seasonal magazine. Longwood rebranded all this information to support a brand new membership program, and the messaging focused on the excitement of the new program with increased flexibility for members.

THE RESULTS

Longwood expected and planned for a dip in the total number of member households after the new program rollout, but expected to rebound to a range of 62,000 to 64,000 households by the end of the fiscal year via natural growth and acquisition campaigns. The drop-off was realized and the low point of just over 57,000 households occurred eight months after program implementation. This shrinking member base, however, was short lived. Through new acquisition campaigns, increased engagement with members, and increased attendance through the opening of a large revitalization project in the Gardens, member households grew well past the initial goal. Longwood now hovers around 67,000 households with expectations of hitting 70,000 by October 2018.

Financially, in the first fiscal year, Longwood saw a 42 percent increase in revenue, surpassing $9 million. Now, eighteen months into the new program, revenue goals

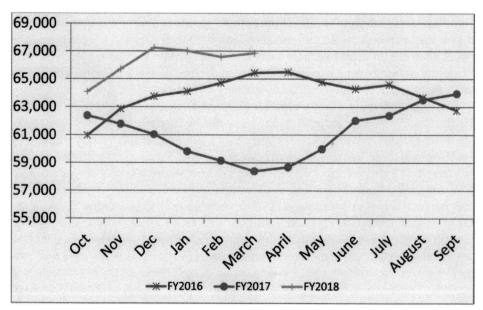

Figure 8.2   Longwood Gardens Member Households FY 2017

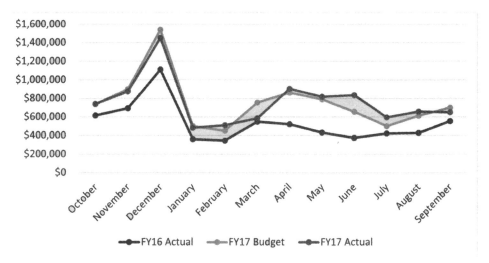

Figure 8.3   Longwood Gardens Financials FY 2017

continue to be exceeded (see figure 8.3) thanks to the increased price coupled with the fact that many members move to higher levels of membership when renewing. Moreover, the average sale increased by 40 percent from $101.89 to $142.60, visitation increased by 20 percent over the prior year with average yearly visits now over twelve per member households, and members now represent a greater percentage of total visitation.

The success of this program transition is attributed to many factors. The whole staff understood that the prior structure was not sustainable, so there was buy-in from the top down. There was no department at Longwood that this transition did not touch. At times, the consultants did recommend against some of the direction that was ultimately decided, mainly concerning the one-time price increase; however, Longwood wanted to make all changes at once. It was imperative to have the data to understand how members were using their membership and what benefits they were most interested in. While valuing the consultants' recommendations, Longwood acting on its deep knowledge of current member behaviors was key to program success. Preparation was also important, including anticipating member feedback, drafting talking points, focusing messaging on the positive changes in the program, and working to ensure systems were tested.

CONCLUSION

While membership is one piece of the income strategy at Longwood, it's a big one, now representing 25 percent of overall earned revenue. It not only results in consistent monthly revenues to the Gardens but also makes up a large portion of attendance, especially during the shoulder seasons when visitation would otherwise be low for a garden. Understanding and tracking performance indicators is an important measure in ensuring that the program continues to be successful and can be used for projecting future growth. Longwood tracks total membership count by household daily, as well as measures both month-to-date and year-to-date revenue against projections daily. Longwood also uses other reports to gauge success, including retention and renewal rates, conversion rates, numbers and percentages of first-time members, upgrades and downgrades, and member attendance.

Understanding data is key to determining how to create, enhance, or restructure a membership program. It helps create buy-in from staff and can be used when responding to member challenges, issues, and complaints. From a revenue side, knowing what is under- or overutilized can help streamline benefits, events, and other member-related facets to discontinue any aspect that would not help increase the bottom line, enhance the member experience, or fit with the vision for the program.

While the idea of the membership restructure seemed a daunting task before implementation, with the right data, a clear roadmap for success, and an eyes-wide-open approach, Longwood realized it was a much-needed journey for both the organization itself and its members.

9

Why Maintenance and Cultivation Are Critical

Beverly Sakauye, Chief Development Officer, National Civil Rights Museum at the Lorraine Motel

The role of the fundraising professional mandates an understanding of the national and local environment that affects your donors and prospects, and thus the fundraising efforts for your institution. Currently, the 2017 Federal Tax Cuts and Jobs Act dominates the national conversation across all sectors, nonprofit in particular. The National Council of Nonprofits forecast a potential $13 billion drop in individual giving, while Marts & Lundy/Lilly Family School of Philanthropy gave three different economic scenarios, each with possible impact on various sources of giving. Contrary to those analyses, InsideCharity.org strongly believes the opposite: that this tax reform will infuse more money into the charitable sector. Though forecasts differ, each organization agrees that maintenance and cultivation are all the more important for every museum and nonprofit organization. Each reminds us that "donors don't support your cause just because they get a tax savings." Una Osili, director of research at the Lilly Family School was quoted in *The Chronicle of Philanthropy* saying that donors give "because they want to change the world" (Joslyn 2018). This section will review relevant national data on effective fundraising and how to measure your institutional effectiveness. Maintenance and cultivation will then be discussed and placed within the context of philanthropy, fundraising models, principles, techniques, and best practices that should inform your development program. Examples of strategies and techniques used by this author will be provided.

NATIONAL DATA ON FUNDRAISING

The Fundraising Effectiveness Project (FEP) was established in 2006 to conduct research and to help nonprofit organizations measure, compare, and maximize their annual growth in giving. The 2018 report summarizes a dataset of 13,601 nonprofit organizations provided by five donor software firms, showing that although giving grew by 2 percent to $11.086 billion, their analysis indicated that the average donor retention rate in 2016 was 45.5 percent, continuing the ten-year trend of consistently weak retention rates (Levis, Miller, and Williams 2018). Gift attrition (when a donor does not renew a donation) or donor turnover is a constant, even with growth in gift dollars through increased or new giving. This emphasizes the need to continually cultivate prospective donors, while also working to retain and upgrade current donors. Your long-term goal should always be to create lifelong donors.

The 2017 FEP reported a new donor retention rate at 23.6 percent. And once they stop giving, few, if any, are brought back. However, if a donor repeats the first gift, the retention rate jumps to 60 percent. Donors who give monthly (usually a set amount) have the highest retention rates: 90 percent. The reactivation rate is 9.9 percent for lapsed donors (getting donors who have not repeated a gift for one to five years). Thus, stewardship (that is, cultivation) to deepen the relationship with those donors, engaging them with your organization, and communicating the impact of your work, is of key importance. The goal for your entire renewal program should be an 80 to 85 percent retention rate (Love n.d.).

The Fundraising Report Card (TFRC) recommends museums compare the number of donations or number of donors from last year to those who gave again this year. Rather than analyzing one donor at a time, they recommend that "what will be more valuable is analyzing your entire database or a large segment of our donors. This way you can see trends, analyze giving behavior and optimize future fundraising performance" (Shefska 2016).

> In collaboration with PSI/Adventist, the FEP (Fundraising Effectiveness Project) has developed the downloadable Excel-based Fundraising Fitness Test that allows nonprofits to measure and evaluate their fundraising programs against a set of over 150 performance indicators by five donor giving levels. . . . Performance indicators include: donor retention rates (new donor retention, repeat donor retention and overall donor retention); donor gains, losses and net; dollar gains, losses and net; growth in giving ($); growth in number of donors; and donor attrition. Gift range categories are $5,000 & up, $1,000 to $4,999, $250 to $999, $100 to 249 an Under $100.

The data you will need are the donor ID, date, and amount for each gift in your database (Growth in Giving Measurement Tools n.d.).

PRINCIPLES OF PHILANTHROPY

The goal of fundraising is not to secure a donation but to develop a donor, one that with your stewardship (maintenance and cultivation) becomes a lifelong donor. It is the means—not the end—of achieving the mission of your museum. A good illustration of the cycle of fundraising (in the book of the same name by Andrea Kihlstedt and Andy Robinson) begins with 1) identifying prospects; 2) educating, cultivating, and involving (the cultivation function); 3) the ask, the point at which prospects become donors; and 4) thank and recognize and involve more deeply (the retention function).

During the cultivation process, the donor/prospective donor is drawn closer to your museum as he or she sees his or her interests and values aligned with the museum's. Maintenance, interchangeably retention, is the process by which the development professional strategically engages the donor so that the donor will renew a gift year after year. Over time a deeper relationship is intentionally developed and strategic solicitation efforts result in larger gifts.

Fundraising, in a broad sense, is the measure of your institution's success and the value donors (whether individuals, corporations, or foundations) place on your organization. Fundraising is guided by principles and ethics that have been developed over time. The Association of Donor Relations Professionals describes donor relations as the "comprehensive effort of any nonprofit that seeks philanthropic support to ensure that donors experience high-quality interactions with the organization that foster long term engagement and investment" (Association of Donor Relations Professionals

A DONOR BILL OF RIGHTS

DEVELOPED BY:

| Association of Fundraising Professionals (AFP) | Association for Healthcare Philanthropy (AHP) | Council for Advancement and Support of Education (CASE) | Giving Institute: Leading Consultants to Non-Profits |

PHILANTHROPY is based on voluntary action for the common good. It is a tradition of giving and sharing that is primary to the quality of life. To assure that philanthropy merits the respect and trust of the general public, and that donors and prospective donors can have full confidence in the not-for-profit organizations and causes they are asked to support, we declare that all donors have these rights:

I
To be informed of the organization's mission, of the way the organization intends to use donated resources, and of its capacity to use donations effectively for their intended purposes.

II
To be informed of the identity of those serving on the organization's governing board, and to expect the board to exercise prudent judgment in its stewardship responsibilities.

III
To have access to the organization's most recent financial statements.

IV
To be assured their gifts will be used for the purposes for which they were given.

V
To receive appropriate acknowledgement and recognition.

VI
To be assured that information about their donations is handled with respect and with confidentiality to the extent provided by law.

VII
To expect that all relationships with individuals representing organizations of interest to the donor will be professional in nature.

VIII
To be informed whether those seeking donations are volunteers, employees of the organization or hired solicitors.

IX
To have the opportunity for their names to be deleted from mailing lists that an organization may intend to share.

X
To feel free to ask questions when making a donation and to receive prompt, truthful and forthright answers.

Figure 9.1 Donor Bill of Rights

n.d.). And thus donor relations should always be values driven, donor focused, intentional, and strategic to help ensure the long-term sustainability of your museum.

A Donor Bill of Rights was created by the AFP along with other philanthropic nonprofit associations and can be used as a guide for donor retention. Basic to this is that donors make voluntary contributions for philanthropy—the love of mankind to create a better world. Donors give to support your cause.

CULTIVATION

Cultivation is a continual process, but who do you cultivate? The universe of people to draw from is large and can be somewhat daunting. The constituency model developed by the Fundraising School, Indiana University Lilly Family School of Philanthropy is helpful.

These concentric circles represent from the center those that are closest and most engaged with your institution, thus where fundraising is most successful. Analogous to people in the third concentric ring from the center, which for my institution are the people who participate in our mostly free public programs. Cultivation builds the base of support and is the method of making prospects aware of the need for an organization's services and for their support. Research can help you segment your prospects by potential capacity to give or affinity or linkages to your museum. Cultivation tools may be used in combination or singly and may include

Constituency Model

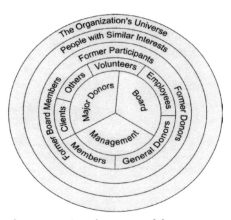

Figure 9.2   Constituency Model

- Newsletters or other print collateral
- Special museum tours
- Luncheons
- Presentations by staff
- Short videos of people participating in programs (perhaps a personal testimonial—real people are often more effective than celebrities)
- Events (we target individuals and personally invite select people to our signature fundraising events)
- Socialization with other donors and organization representatives
- Social media

In our museum, we give complimentary admission passes to board members and staff and also as giveaways for other nonprofit auctions. To be redeemed, the visitor must complete the pass with name, email, date of visit, and guest of. This information is collected and then development inputs it into our fundraising database to use for new prospects. Cultivation is then measured by response rate, number and level of the gifts received, total amount of money raised, effectiveness of each strategy and each vehicle, amount of time spent, total cost and net proceeds, and donor satisfaction with the experience.

After cultivation, the next step in the fundraising cycle is solicitation of prospective donors. At this point, it is helpful to look at the time-honored donor pyramid of fundraising strategies developed by the Fundraising School, Indiana University Lilly Family School of Philanthropy. Here the base of the

Figure 9.3   Donor Pyramid

pyramid represents the universe of prospective donors. The next level is the first-time donor who makes a gift through direct mail/telemarketing/fundraising event/internet/media/door-to-door. That gift indicates he or she has some commitment to your cause. Movement up the pyramid reflects fundraising strategies that grow more and more personal. As the donor's relationship to your institution deepens, the donor's commitment grows and is reflected in the larger size of gifts.

Through this ongoing process, the organization is constantly testing the market's understanding and acceptance of its goals and objectives, its exhibits and public programs, its institutional achievements, and the reputation of the board of directors and staff. Funding is a validation of the organization's operating, special, capital and endowment needs, and the extent of donor relationships.

THE DEVELOPMENT INFRASTRUCTURE AND BEST PRACTICES

What does every development department need to fulfill its role? The foundation of fundraising for any museum is the written case statement and the institutional plans and goals that then inform the integrated development plan with fundraising goals, objectives, and timelines (Seiler 2016c.) Your fundraising budget with expenses and revenue is essential; here working with your finance department is necessary, although that depends on your organization's budget process. And as you are creating cultivation and maintenance strategies and techniques, it is important to remember that not all prospects and donors are alike, so segmenting and prioritizing groups will improve your effectiveness. Integrate into the plan the communication strategies that you will utilize with your various constituencies. Segmentation may include

- Giving levels and cumulative amounts
- Number of years of giving
- Gift frequency

- Giving designation and interest
- Linkage and relationships
- Capacity to give (at a certain level of giving, upgrading opportunities should be strategic and individual to maximize success)

You must continually measure and evaluate the results of your efforts against your plan. If this is done monthly, it may become apparent that adjustments are needed to the plan. Compare results against your past efforts and against national analytics. If you don't yet have a baseline for your fundraising efforts, I suggest that you analyze your data for the past two or three years. You must know where you have been to gauge and plan your efforts going forward.

Other essentials needed for your infrastructure include

- A donor software system to track donors and their gifts, manage relationships through recording contact with donors, appeals sent, demographics, gift dates, and solicitation methods, events attended, visits or tours, family, and employment. Gifts by records and reports for fundraising program productivity—rates of retention, attrition, upgrades, and growth of giving. For donor reports: donor composition, levels of giving, constituency comparisons, technique comparisons, growth rates, responsiveness to events, and levels of involvement.
- Stories of how your institution touched someone—help to compel prospects and inspire donors. Short videos of thirty to sixty seconds are particularly compelling. A collection of these stories is a good resource. I talk to frontline and program staff to seek stories and ask other directors and staff to send any testimonial for the collection.
- Communication tools—print, digital, website, and social media. Depending on your museum, you may need to partner with your marketing department to communicate on a regular basis—social media—to engender a sense of community and connectedness. The Generosity Network suggests in addition to your organization's official page that you encourage individual members of your team as well as outside partners to create personal pages where they share their own messages about your work.
- Acknowledgment system/process—in writing and by phone or in person. The thank you must be timely, accurate, and appropriate. Conversations can lead to understanding why a donor first started giving, what is important to the donor, a referral to a prospect, and potentially a deeper relationship. Develop a tiered acknowledgment system whereby all donors receive their IRS letter signed by your director of development with a personal handwritten note. Certain donors should get a personal handwritten thank you from the president, and still others should receive a brief thank you from a board member (perhaps the development committee chair). At another level, these donors should receive an invitation for special stewardship meetings or recognition in the newsletter. Write a personal note on an acknowledgment. It is recommended that the development officer have a list of donors with the potential to upgrade their gifts to stay connected with either by phone or in-person meeting. It is easy to stay behind your desk, but getting on the street is a more effective use of your time. Regular times must be scheduled on your calendar.

- Recognition tools—giving clubs/societies, donor walls, annual report, meet and greet with the president and board members, and newsletter articles. Prominently displayed on the first floor of our museum is our donor wall to acknowledge donors to our big comprehensive capital/endowment campaign. The minimum level is $5,000 (payable over three to five years). The wall is updated annually, adding new endowment donors and elevating donors to higher-level giving categories as long as the donation is for the endowment fund, as the museum renovation was completed four years ago.
- Collateral—either print or digital—for updates to donors, newsletters, the annual report, and fulfillment pieces. We have a quarterly print newsletter and are working to make a digital version. Depending on the size of your museum, your marketing/communications department is the major partner with which you work to achieve your fundraising goals.
- GuideStar—make sure you take the time register your museum, provide an organizational profile, and keep the information up to date. Some of your communities may have their own version of this that is normally tied to GuideStar. In Memphis it is https://WHEREtoGIVEmidsouth.guidestar.org.

Network for Good and other experts remind us that giving is a human connection and that we need to show people that they can make a difference and that they matter. Call your donors—thank them and ask them why they support your institution. This can give insight into donor motivations that you can then utilize in your planning. Target donors with whom you should meet or host a small gathering.

CONCLUSION

The amount of the donor's contribution is proportional to the involvement and feeling of engagement. This continual process of cultivating and acquiring donors includes involving them in the mission, making them feel a part of the "family," retaining their support, and upgrading their gifts, leading to major gifts and ultimately to a legacy gift. In the end, the focus of your fundraising program must always be on the donor and the relationship you are continually building. You must understand the environment in which you fundraise—national and local. The advice from all experts is to remember that most donors don't give to receive a tax deduction; they give to support the cause. As a development professional, you must continue to talk to and communicate with your donors and prospective donors, share your institutional vision, and invite them to help make it happen; only then will you retain your donors as you further develop and deepen the relationship.

Cultivate, ask, ask again, retain, and upgrade. This is an ongoing cycle that must be strategic and intentional as relationships with donors are developed. Give donors the opportunity to fulfill their philanthropic dreams while they help you achieve yours.

BIBLIOGRAPHY AND RESOURCES

American Alliance of Museums. *Financial Stability. Standards Regarding Financial Stability. Standards Regarding Developing and Managing Business and Individual Donor Support.* http://ww2.aam-us.org/resources/ethics-standards-and-best-practices/financial-stability.

Association of Donor Relations Professionals. *Donor Relations and Stewardship Defined.* http://www.adrp.net/assets/documents/adrpdefinitionsexpanded.pdf.

Association of Fundraising Professionals. *The Donor Bill of Rights.*

Association for Fundraising Professionals. *Resource Center Toolkits and Resources.* http://www.afpnet.org/ResourceCenter/content.cfm?ItemNumber=3136.

Association for Fundraising Professionals Fundraising Effectiveness Project. http://afpfep.org/reports/download/.

Barden, Pamela. "12 Principles of Fundraising." NonProfitPRO, May 1, 2013. http://www.nonprofitpro.com/article/12-principles-fundraising/all/.

Barry, Frank, Lawrence Henze, David Lamb, and Katherine Swank. *Cultivating Lifelong Donors: Stewardship and the Fundraising Pyramid.* Edited by Heather Friedrichs Lyman and Lindsey Houston Salmony. Charleston: Blackbaud, 2010.

Bloomerang. *A Guide to Donor Engagement.* 2018. https://bloomerang.co/engagement.

BoardSource. *Measuring Fundraising Effectiveness: Why Cost of Fundraising Isn't Enough.* https://boardsource.org/news/2017/02/measuring-fundraising-effectiveness-2/.

Chisholm, Sean. *The Donor Attrition Survival Guide.* Classy. https://www.classy.org/blog/.

Craver, Roger M. *Retention Fundraising: The New Art and Science of Keeping Your Donors for Life.* Medfield, MA: Emerson and Church Publishers, 2015.

Donahue, Roberta L., Caitlin Deranek Stewart. "Special Events." In *Achieving Excellence in Fundraising*, fourth edition, edited by Eugene R. Tempel, Timothy L. Seiler, and Dwight Burlingame, 417–21. Hoboken, NJ: John Wiley & Sons, Inc., 2016.

The Fundraising Effectiveness Project, AFP Association of Fundraising Professionals. http://afpfep.org/about/.

Gainpaulsingh, Mena. *Top 10 Donor Stewardship "Rules" to Ensure that Your Fundraising Thrives.* http://www.afpnet.org/ResourceCenter/ArticleDetail.cfm?ItemNumber=42279.

Garecht, Joe. *Beginner's Guide to Donor Cultivation.* The Fundraising Authority. http://www.thefundraisingauthority.com/donor-cultivation/guide-to-donor-cultivation/.

Growth in Giving Measurement Tools. http://afpfep.org/tools/.

Joslyn, Heather. "4% Growth in Giving Is a Possibility This Year—But Impossible to Say Because of Tax Law." *The Chronicle of Philanthropy*, February 13, 2018. http://www.philanthropy.com/article/Giving-in-2018-Could-Grow-4-/242533.

Kihlstedt, Andrea, and Andy Robinson. "Cycle of Fundraising." In *Train Your Board (And Everyone Else) to Raise Money*, 44. Medfield, MA: Emerson and Church Publishers, 2014.

LaRose, Jimmy. *What Tax Reform Means for Charity: More Money, Money, Money.* https://insidecharity.org/2018/01/09/what-tax-ref-rm-means-for-charity/.

Levis, Bill, Manager, Fundraising Effectiveness Project, Ben Miller, DonorTrends, and Cathy Williams, Association of Fundraising Professionals. Contributions by Caity Craver, DonorTrends, and Jim Greenfield, ACFRE. *2018 Fundraising Effectiveness Survey Report, A Project of the Growth in Giving Initiative, 4/12/2018.* 2018. http://afpfep.org/reports/.

Lockshin, Vanessa Chase. *21 Ideas to Refresh Your Donor Stewardship.* http://www.thestorytellingnonprofit.com/blog/21-ideas-to-refresh-your-donor-stewardship/.

Love, Jay. *Donor Retention.* https://bloomerang.co/?s=donor+retention.

Love, Jay. *Follow the Donor Bill of Rights for Donor Retention Success.* https://bloomerang.co/blog/follow-the-donor-bill-of-rights-for-donor-retention-success/.

MacLaughlin, Steve, Chuck Longfield, Angele Vellake, and Erin Duff. *Charitable Giving Report: How Fundraising Performed in 2017.* Edited by Olivia Franzese. Blackbaud Institute. https://institute.blackbaud.com/asset/2017-charitable-giving-report/.

McCrea, Jennifer, Jeffrey C. Walker, and Karl Weber. *The Generosity Network.* New York: Deepak Chopra Books, an imprint of the Crown Publishing Group, a division of Random House LLC, a Penguin Random House Company, 2013.

Miller, Ben. Contributions by Bill Levis, Heather McGinness, Nathan Dietz, Cathy Williams, and Michael Nilsen. *2016 Donor Retention Report, December 31, 2016, a Supplement to the 2016 Fundraising Effectiveness Survey Report.* Urban Institute, Association of Fundraising Professionals. www.afpfep.org.

National Council of Nonprofits. *Tax Cuts and Jobs Act, H.R. 1 Nonprofit Analysis of the Final Tax Law,* Tax Cuts and Jobs Act of 2017, Public Law 115-409, December 22, 2017. Updated February 22, 2018.

Network for Good. *How to Get Donations, 14 Reasons People Give.* https://www.networkforgood.com/nonprofitblog/how-to-get-donations-14-reasons-why-people-donate/.

Network for Good. *6 Keys to Donor Retention.* https://www.networkforgood.com/nonprofitblog/6-keys-donor-retention/.

Qgiv. *Donor Stewardship: Create Lifelong Donors in 10 Steps.* https://www.qgiv.com/blog/donor-stewardship-guide/.

Ralser, Tom. *ROI for Nonprofits: The New Key to Sustainability.* Hoboken, NJ: John Wiley & Sons, Inc., 2007.

Seiler, Timothy L. "Individuals as a Constituency for Fundraising." In *Achieving Excellence in Fundraising*, fourth edition, edited by Eugene R. Tempel, Timothy L. Seiler, and Dwight Burlingame, 49–55. Hoboken, NJ: John Wiley & Sons, Inc., 2016a.

Seiler, Timothy L. "Plan to Succeed." In *Achieving Excellence in Fundraising*, fourth edition, edited by Eugene R. Tempel, Timothy L. Seiler, and Dwight Burlingame, 27–34. Hoboken, NJ: John Wiley & Sons, Inc., 2016b.

Seiler, Timothy L. "The Total Development Plan Built on the Annual Giving Program." In *Achieving Excellence in Fundraising*, fourth edition, edited by Eugene R. Tempel, Timothy L. Seiler, and Dwight Burlingame, 215–22. Hoboken, NJ: John Wiley & Sons, Inc., 2016c.

Seymour, Harold J. *Designs for Fund-Raising.* Second edition. Rockville, MD: Fund Raising Institute, a Division of The Taft Group, 1988.

Shefska, Zach. *Metrics 101: Donor & Donation Retention.* The Fundraising Report Card. November 2, 2016. https://fundraisingreportcard.com/donor-and-donation-retention/.

Tempel, Eugene R., Timothy L. Seiler. "Stewardship and Accountability." *Achieving Excellence in Fundraising*, fourth edition, edited by Eugene R. Tempel, Timothy L. Seiler, and Dwight Burlingame, 417–21. Hoboken, NJ: John Wiley & Sons, Inc., 2016.

Top 75 Fundraising Websites and Blogs to Follow in 2018. https://blog.feedspot.com/50-must-read-fundraising-blogs-you-should-be-reading/.

Williams, Karla A., ACFRE. "Donor Focused Strategies for Annual Giving." In *Aspen's Fund Raising Series for the 21st Century*, edited by James P. Gelatt. Gaithersburg, MD: Aspen Publishers, Inc., 1997.

Expert Opinion: Board Members and Fundraising

Tonya Matthews, Equity and Nonprofit Executive Strategy Consultant

How do you build a board that is effective in fundraising?

I suggest three principal techniques when building a board that is effective in fundraising: clarity, tiers, and personalization.

First and most critical is clarity. Boards must have clarity on the goals and expectations of participation in development support of their organization. This includes clarity on give-and-get amount expectations, specific goals for collective giving of the board, and specific participation expectations—from gala attendance to CEO introductions to asks. This remains the most "awkward" conversation to have with board members, but it is also the most straightforward. This should take the form of written policy and annual goals that are annually updated by development staff, reflected in any board self-review, and introduced in board member orientation—if not, even earlier during the recruitment stage.

Secondly, "tiers" is a way of introducing board members to various stages of fundraising in a deliberately unintimidating way. On the introductory tiers are stewardship moments of current donors, such as thanking current donors for their gifts or giving current donors updates. Giving board members the opportunity to thank donors allows them to experience the enthusiasm donors have about their gift and about the organization. Also, it's good for board members to participate in update calls and meetings with current donors. In this space, board members not only get to experience the donor enthusiasm, but also get practice using talking points about the organization and listening for donor's passion points. Occasionally, they will have the opportunity to see their staff steward react to challenging or tricky questions. These "easy" donor touches demystify donations, add insight into processes underlying giving in "the real world," and, frankly, make development seem a bit less scary.

The upper tiers are, of course, "the ask" and "cultivation of new donors." When possible, it is very effective to include board members in conversations with relationships they are bringing to the organization, as well as relationships they are not as familiar with. When "match-making" unfamiliar relationships, it is critical for staff to consider possible commonalities or other points of connection—for example, same industry, same alma mater, same hometown—to create room for natural, personable conversation. Preparation of board members is key, including organizational talking points and also background on potential donor.

Last but certainly not least, the most critical point in activating board members at higher tiers of participation in fundraising is helping them understand the natural assets they themselves are in fundraising—with leads to the second technique: personalization. Personalization reminds us that our board members are individuals too. Board members bring personalities and connections to the organization just like donors, individuals, and institutions. All the various archetypes—social, business, mission-oriented, community-focused, change and innovation-motivated—are represented on both sides. Celebrating the individual passion and skills of a board member and being deliberate about which asks and cultivations s/he is requested to support adds credence to the statement "Just be you!" and inspires confidence in board members in these situations.

How should a board participate in long-range and annual development planning?

In a perfect world, annual development planning should occur three to four months prior to the close of the current fiscal year and there should always be two or three long-range support options included in the plan. Admittedly, for smaller or newer organizations, this is not often done without a bit of stress and double-duty acknowledging that you are also working in a "real-time" fundraising state to close critical goals for the current year. However, this is the best way to make room for board participation.

Allowing board input and insight into various fundraising strategies and assets—from general operating, to a new show, an innovative exhibit, the next gala—primarily supports buy-in and excitement from board members. This excitement is critical to keeping a board focused and engaged in supporting fundraising. Additionally, it supports board members in being nimble in conversation with prospects. Starting these conversations with the board development committee and then allowing the chair of the committee to present the outline of the plan and bigger, long-term ideas creates peer-to-peer ownership of the plan. While all fundraising should be connected to previous, driving conversation, it is also critical that bigger, long-term ideas/assets in the development plan be connected to the organization's strategic plan and/or signature mission activities.

What are the museum's expectations for board members' personal giving and fundraising activities?

I have worked in organizations with different expectations for personal giving and fundraising activity. The healthiest boards *all* had an expectation for personal giving. I have worked with a smaller institution ($5M operating budget and less) that used the phrase "meaningful gift" to describe to the board personal giving expectation. In contrast, when stewarding a larger organization ($15M operating budget and higher), there was a clearly stated personal giving level required for participation, with strong encouragement to "stretch your support" to support the vision. Recently, it has become widely known that foundations pay attention to personal giving—and this has become a strong motivator to codify personal giving.

In my stewardship of board participation, the most effective strategy for expectation has been to a) have a pledge form early in the year, b) note a save-the-date for gala (attendance and solicitation support expected), and c) have first quarter individualized meetings and tasking of board members, outlining their personal participation for at least the first two quarters. The only prescribed expectation for participation in fundraising activities is often "gala attendance and support." Individualized plans and activities for board members is highly effective and requires significant staff support—the larger the board and the larger the fundraising portfolio, the more staff support is needed.

How do your board members identify and cultivate donors?

Identification and cultivation of board members is a shared responsibility of staff and board, with the heaviest burdens being on staff. Initially, board members are asked to think about their personal and professional circles and connect that to the current donor portfolio. The goal is for board members to bring or cultivate two to three new relationships for the organization every year, in addition to stewarding four or five current donors. (Note that "stewarding" can be everything from hosting meetings to signing thank you cards.)

As board members become more familiar with programs and growth goals, board members are encouraged make note of new companies or new "neighbors" in their professional and personal circles who may resonate with the mission and work of the organization. These names are collected by the development staff for vetting and prioritization. Conversely, development staff are charged with similar responsibilities, plus active research, and bring these names to board members for review, input, and possible additional connections and engagement strategies for those names.

What happens when a board member does not understand his or her fundraising role or embrace it?

Support and, if necessary, nonrenewal of term for board members who do not actively participate in fundraising or personal giving requires a very strong board culture and a highly committed chair. Without proper leadership from inside [the board], participation in fundraising becomes a matter of personal choice and preference, rather than board duty and expectation.

What goals, metrics, and/or indicators do you use to evaluate the performance of your board and your fundraising campaigns?

Metrics and indicators really support clarity in activating a board in fundraising campaigns. There are basic metrics: Yes or No for participation personally and Yes or No for participation in asks to other donors. There are also target metrics. For example, has the board agreed to support a certain percentage of the overall goal for the campaign? For annual giving this tends to be an overall target dollar amount—perhaps even tied to a percentage of the operating budget for the board to support. Whereas for bigger campaigns, there may be a combined 100 percent target as well as having the board collectively have total support at a particular giving tier of the campaign.

Indicators for board engagement is similar—but strongly benefits from trend data. Indicators are most helpful if they are tracked and compared year over year. For example, is overall individual giving participation stable? Increasing? Declining? Or is the overall giving amount of the board stable? Increasing? Declining? And how does that compare to board size and composition?

Another interesting metric/indicator is comparing board composition to the composition of the donor base. Who is on the board tends to be very indicative of where overall support is coming from and can often be very helpful in setting goals for new board member skills, connections, and community.

11

Expert Opinion: Special Events and Staff Participation in Fundraising

Gina Rogak, Director of Special Events, Whitney Museum of American Art

How do you identify and cultivate donors?

My specialty being events, I am constantly on the lookout for appropriate honorees, co-chairs, and honorary chairs for our fundraising events. Honorees often come from our board, but we have also honored artists on occasion, and corporate and foundation leaders as well. We research any potential honorees for their support base, boards they serve on, colleagues in their industry, other organizations they support, looking for individuals who may be asked to support our events in their honor. We will also ask honorees directly for a list of constituents who can be solicited either via a letter or via the event invitation, to purchase tickets or a table, or make a contribution.

Essentially the formula is the same whether you're seeking a major gift or selling event tickets—identify, cultivate, make the ask, close the deal.

How do you create a budget for fundraising events? Do you seek in-kind donations or partnerships?

At the Whitney we have net fundraising goals, so we start with how much money we need to raise and work in the expenses of actually putting on an event (catering, rentals, invitations printing, etc.). With years of experience it's fairly easy to estimate what things will or may cost and what the threshold is in terms of ticket prices. For example, you can't typically charge as much for a ticket to a luncheon as you can for a dinner. To maximize our fundraising abilities, we often add something—a limited edition print you can purchase, premium seating for an additional cost. And sponsorship is a very significant source of income for fundraising events. We do seek in-kind donations as they provide budget relief, primarily liquor donations. On occasion sponsors have also done some in-kind, such as an auto sponsor providing cars for VIP guests.

What goals, metrics, and/or indicators do you use to evaluate the success of a fundraising event?

The obvious measure of success for fundraising events is whether we meet our financial goals. But we also look at patterns of participation—have previous table and tickets buyers participated again this year? Who is a new participant? Has strategic seating at the event been fruitful (that is, did a curator of an upcoming exhibition successfully impress the potential donor seated next to her)? Was the sponsor satisfied and likely to come back next year? What was the feedback from trustees, from the honoree and the co-chairs? Did we use the event to appropriately and successfully demonstrate our values? We do a full post-mortem after every fundraising event with participation from many departments in order to identify what worked and what didn't.

How do you use that information to develop future events?

Even though we strive to improve year after year, I am always surprised when after every major gala I am told "that was the best one ever." An event is a living, breathing thing involving thousands of details big and small as well as dozens, sometimes hundreds, of people (including the guests), and there is potential for things to go wrong every second. By analyzing what went right and why it worked, we can try to repeat the following year, or with the next event.

It's been difficult to create new fundraising events because I believe you have to target a new audience, and new audiences are not yet engaged enough with the museum to spend a lot of money. You can't ask your trustees and major donors to buy expensive tickets to more than one major event a year. You have to tailor your event to your desired audience without sacrificing your values and mission. It's harder than it sounds, especially when you are an institution with ambitious goals and multiple projects to fund.

It's easier to target younger donors, but events for young supporters don't typically make much money. In developing an annual fundraising event, I think it's very useful to plan out to the next five years, line up your honorees, featured artists, sponsor prospects, and cultivate them like any other prospects by inviting them to the event year after year and engaging them long before you ask them to help you fundraise.

In summary, we don't use the information gained from post-mortem to develop future events so much as to improve existing events, or at the very least to ensure that this year's event is as good or better than last year's.

How does the museum staff participate in long-range and annual development planning?

The Whitney development department consists of five areas: major gifts, special events, corporate partnerships, foundations and government, and membership.

In our biweekly senior development staff meetings, we tackle ongoing issues and ideas for development initiatives, and share information from our respective areas that may have useful implications for others.

As a development department head, I participated in a strategic planning committee that is working on the next five years. I was asked to join the "architecture" committee that is focusing on our physical space, both existing and potential future opportunities. With intimate knowledge of our facility gathered from three full years of doing events in our new building, I am aware of both the assets and shortcomings of our current spaces and well positioned to make recommendations for any future additions or renovations being contemplated.

How are the museum staff educated or trained in fundraising?

The major gifts staff worked with a fundraising consultant on cultivating individual donors for our capital campaign. The tools they acquired were communicated to the rest of the senior level development staff and are applicable in many ways.

I encourage my staff to seek professional development opportunities all year long, from going to fundraising conferences, to speaking with colleagues, to asking me questions about fundraising. We have also worked as a team to brainstorm fundraising ideas as they pertain to events, including coming up with new ideas for fundraising events. I talk through fundraising issues with them in our weekly staff meetings and in the individual bi-weekly meetings I have with each staff member.

What are the most effective techniques or ways that museum directors can support fundraising?

Helping to identify appropriate honorees and co-chairs; signing letters to potential honorees or co-chairs and sometimes to trustees and major donors. Directors are key to making asks or closing deals after major gifts staff have cultivated and positioned them. Directors can make themselves available during the cultivation process when needed. Our director meets every week with the major gift staff to review a list of donors who he has seen to download information about the meeting, and to identify those he needs to see or reach out to with an ask.

Directors can also be key to making decisions about where to direct an ask—or a donor—when there are multiple priorities, as they typically have the larger strategic objectives in mind.

Making the Case

Motivating Your Museum's Major Gift Prospects

Tim Ardillo, Consultant,
Johnson, Grossnickle, and Associates

Museums and other cultural institutions do not necessarily have built-in constituencies like educational institutions do—alumni, parents, faculty, etc., who often provide high levels of philanthropic revenue to diversify the institution's funding model. Yet museums do have the same need for a diversified revenue model that includes earned revenue, sponsorships, income from endowments, and, of course, philanthropy. The challenge is how to increase revenue from philanthropy by identifying, engaging, and motivating major gift prospects.

In order to maximize revenue from philanthropy, museums and other cultural institutions need to develop a multichannel, diversified philanthropy program that engages and earns support from its donors, members, and other interested community members. To do this, museums must present a clear vision that begins with the top leadership, understand the motivations of their donors, make their case to prospective donors in a convincing way, and focus a predominant portion of their fundraising resources on major gift development.

PHILANTHROPY IN CONTEXT

Let's first examine the need for museums to focus on major gift development by understanding the sources and recipients of philanthropic dollars in the United States.

As reported in *Giving USA 2017, The Annual Report on Philanthropy* published by the Giving USA Foundation, $390.05 billion was given to charitable organizations in 2016. While organizations do need to have balanced development programs that seek support from corporations and foundations, it is important to remember the greatest source of potential support is from individuals. As noted in figure 12.1, individuals

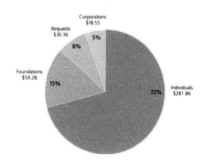

2016 contributions: $390.05 billion by source (in billions of dollars – all figures are rounded)

Figure 12.1   2016 Contributions by Source

drive charitable giving in the United States. Fully 72 percent of philanthropic dollars were contributed by individuals. And when you take into account family foundations (7.5 percent), which are also directed by individuals, and bequests (8 percent), individuals influence approximately 87.5 percent of all philanthropic contributions.

What types of organizations receive those funds? As noted in figure 12.2, nearly 60 percent of all philanthropic contributions went to religious, educational, and human service organizations in 2016. Over the last several years the allocations of those charitable contributions have not shifted much. It is interesting to note, however, that during the Great Recession contributions to human services overtook contributions to education as more donors decided to support organizations focused on direct day-to-day needs of the public. Postrecession giving has returned to a more normal allocation of charitable giving however. The remaining 40 percent of all charitable dollars supported all of the other sectors including arts, culture, and the humanities. Specifically, giving to arts, culture, and humanities, which includes giving to museums, comprised 5 percent of philanthropic giving in 2016. Giving to this sector has seen an uptick in giving for several consecutive years, something that many attribute to innovative approaches to fundraising and connecting with constituents.

2016 contributions: $390 billion by type of recipient organization (in billions of dollars)

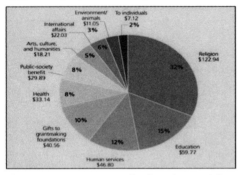

Figure 12.2   2016 Contributions by Recipient Type

UNDERSTANDING DONOR MOTIVATIONS

While it is important to understand the context of the philanthropic marketplace, it is also helpful to understand what drives donors to make their charitable gifts.

Institutional vision is an important factor in motivating donors to make transformational gifts. In an effort to understand the characteristics of institutions that receive million-dollar and above gifts, Johnson, Grossnickle, and Associates and the Indiana University Lilly Family School of Philanthropy conducted a research study titled "Million Dollar Ready: Assessing Institutional Factors that Lead to Transformational Gifts." Among the key findings of this project, which studied 1,449 higher education institutions that had received at least one gift of more than one million dollars, was that longer presidential tenure and the ability to articulate a vision was associated with higher numbers of million-dollar-plus donations.

According to Craig Weatherup, a donor to Arizona State University who was quoted in the study, "My wife and I have made these philanthropic investments because of the president's compelling vision and articulation of a clear need to make the vision a reality." While this study focused on higher education, key lessons can be learned and applied across all sectors, including the arts. Clearly, trust in an institution's chief executive and the vision for the future is a key driver in a donor's willingness to make a transformational gift.

Additional research also supports the importance of mission in motivating high net worth donors to give, among other motivators. The *US Trust Study of High Net Worth Philanthropy* found in 2015 that belief in the mission, belief that their gift can make a difference, and personal satisfaction were the top three reasons high net worth donors cited as motivation for making a gift.

The key message here is to engage leadership and articulate the impact of your mission on those served. To build strong donor relationships and grow major gifts, communicate your vision in a way that connects with your donor's philanthropic goals. In addition to the motivations listed earlier, the simplest rule to remember is that donors also give because they are asked! As fundraisers, we offer donors the opportunity to support an endeavor about which we know they care deeply and that advances their own philanthropic interests. It is that perspective that should be taken into account when making the case for increased philanthropic support through major gifts.

ROLE OF A CASE STATEMENT

When sharing a vision for the future of the museum with a prospective donor, it is important to articulate that vision for the future of your museum in a way that clearly describes your philanthropic priorities, informs discussions with donors, and provides a key starting point in the discussion of impact and relevance. A case statement serves as a written message to convey that vision. Not only does it ensure that everyone responsible for sharing the vision is on the same page, it also gives the prospective donor something to react to and discuss as you enter into major gift conversations.

While case statements come in many shapes, forms, and sizes, the parameters are consistent. This document should appeal to the heart and the head. Not only should it get to the emotion of what your museum is trying to accomplish, it should also include enough facts and figures to satisfy the donor or prospect who wants to know how it is going to work and how the museum is going to sustain it for the long term. The case statement should also be concise and easy to read.

The case statement should also include photographs and illustrations that depict the ultimate outcome once a gift has been made. Nothing connects with people more than seeing photos of other people. For instance, don't just show the new museum gallery; rather, show a family enjoying the future space. To further humanize the fundable opportunity, include quotes from experts, curators, members, and donors. Quotes and testimonials help tell the story and help illustrate the impact of the donor's or prospect's major gift on the museum and its mission. Ultimately, this document should excite donors with a vision of what the future of the museum, the community, and even the world can be with the help of their transformative gift.

THE IMPORTANCE OF MAJOR GIFTS

As stated earlier, individual giving comprises a significant portion of the philanthropic pie in the United States. And for most institutions, a small percentage of dedicated and committed donors provide the majority of annual philanthropic revenue, especially in the context of a campaign. The vast majority of successful campaigns are based on a relatively small number of lead and major gifts that are supported by a broad array of other gifts at various levels. On average, 90 percent of campaign funds are contributed by just 10 percent of an organization's donors. This highlights the important role major gifts can play in securing philanthropic revenue for your museum.

How does your museum define a major gift? Is it a $50,000 gift? Is it a $100,000 gift? Or is it even a $10,000 gift? Regardless of the gift size, the process of cultivation, solicitation, and stewardship is the same.

To start, museums must identify the prospects most likely to make major and transformational gifts. But it is not just a question of capacity. The best prospects are those who have the greatest financial capacity coupled with the greatest interest in the museum. The local billionaire who has absolutely no interest in your mission is not likely to become a donor unless you can develop this interest. If you have asked this person for a gift in the past and know that she or he has no interest in the museum, then you might be wasting your time. Instead focus on the people closest to the museum who have the greatest wealth or access to wealth. In addition to focusing on the top 10 percent to 20 percent of your donors and prospects, think of other factors that may indicate major gift potential in the future: future giving potential, the *recency* and frequency of their giving to your institution, and their overall involvement with you.

Of course, this needs to be balanced with introducing new potential donors to the institution. Fundraisers do not have control over a prospect's capacity, but they do have a role to play in their connection to the institution. So who are these individuals and how are they uncovered? There are a number of ways to identify new prospects. Start with the museum's database and look at people whose giving has lapsed and people who have not made a gift. They are in the database for a reason—start talking to them and focus on those who have the ability to be major donors. Additionally, ask the board members and organizational volunteers to provide names of people who they believe can make a significant gift and with whom they would be willing to make an introduction. Also, regularly scan the newspaper, business journal, and other publications for people who might naturally be potential donors for the institution. In general, it will take longer to qualify these individuals and establish a long-term relationship with the institution—as much as a year—however, commit the time and resources in the development program to ensure that this untapped market gets some attention.

Additionally, consider the ways in which the museum recognizes its major donors. Art institutions offer a plethora of opportunities to recognize donors, whether that be by naming physical spaces, entries on donor recognition displays, or in printed and online publications. Keep in mind that not all donors want the recognition, and some even make gifts on the condition of anonymity, while others are motivated by public acknowledgment. Talk to them and work to understand the motivations for their philanthropic giving.

CONCLUSION

While the overall structure of successful revenue models for museums and other cultural institutions may look similar, the greatest area of potential growth lies in philanthropy from individuals. An engaged and cultivated base of major gift donors are your best prospects for operating gifts, capital and programmatic gifts, as well as endowment gifts. Growing the donor base as well as increasing major gifts need to be top priorities. Investing wisely in the museum's development program for the long term is key to this growth. There is no secret formula to good fundraising. Good fundraising is based on building relationships with your donors, aligning your mission and vision with their philanthropic priorities, and asking for major gifts!

BIBLIOGRAPHY

Developing Major Gifts. https://philanthropy.iupui.edu/professional-development/courses-seminars/the-fund-raising-school/developing-major-gifts.html.

Giving USA: The Annual Report on Philanthropy for the Year 2016. Chicago: Giving USA Foundation, 2017.

"Million Dollar Ready: Assessing Institutional Factors that Lead to Transformational Gifts." 2013. Johnson, Grossnickle, and Associates and the Lilly Family School of Philanthropy at Indiana University–Purdue University Indianapolis.

The 2016 U.S. Trust ® Study of High Net Worth Philanthropy. New York: U.S. Trust Philanthropic Solutions and Family Office Group, 2016.

13

Major Gifts

Relationships Matter

Julie McDearmon, Director of Institutional Advancement at the Indianapolis Zoo

INTRODUCTION

Major gifts are just one piece of a well-rounded fundraising program within a nonprofit organization. It's common to hear new fundraisers, executive directors, or a president or CEO ask which part of a fundraising program is the most important method to focus on within their own organization. That's not an easy answer because every organization is different. But it's even more important to note that without a strong annual fund, an organization won't have low- to mid-level donors to feed its major gifts program. Without a strong major gifts program, there are less planned giving prospects. Without special events, there are no new audiences to connect with the mission. No single fundraising method is more important than another, and most of them take an equal amount of time and effort, but they all require unique and different strategies. A sustainable major gifts program strikes a delicate balance between searching for new donor prospects, qualifying and cultivating those prospects, and stewarding current donors. Major gifts include things such as capital campaign gifts, annual gifts, and other special projects. Major gifts work is methodical and takes a lot of planning on the front end to make it successful.

IT'S ALL ABOUT RELATIONSHIPS

Major gifts fundraising professionals do not operate in a black-and-white situational world; their world is gray. Every donor is treated uniquely and each situation is looked at differently, depending on how the donor expects to be treated. Relationships are at the very core of major gifts fundraising. Some of those relationships take more work, others require little if any effort at all in exchange for the end goal: the donation.

An organization should never have just one point of contact with its donors, and more specifically, its major gifts donors. The organization should take the time to plan out who will have access to each donor and how to facilitate those relationships. It's imperative that the core of the connection exist between the donor and the organization rather than between the individuals. That way, when staff move on or retire (or abruptly leave), others in the organization can pick up the relationships.

MANAGING PORTFOLIOS

Within most nonprofit organizations, major gifts officers manage a dedicated portfolio of current donors and viable prospects. Similar to a financial-based portfolio of clients, major gifts portfolios help fundraisers stay focused on those top prospects they should either be continuing or building relationships with and connecting to the mission of the organization. Most major gifts officers will say that 100 to 120 prospects in their portfolio is just enough thank you very much, and they are correct. Major gifts officers should focus on making three to four relevant calls and visits per week. Their job is to move those in their portfolio through a cycle: qualify (or disqualify) prospects, cultivate relationships with those that are deemed prospects, make the ask, get the donation, and steward donors until the process starts all over again. Major gifts officers must be very strategic about this process and cater their plan to the individuals. What major gifts is not is a one-size-fits-all approach. People have different ways they wish to connect with a nonprofit organization, and it's the major gifts officer's job to find out how to do that.

Much like a major gifts officer's portfolio, those in top leadership positions should also have a dedicated portfolio with a mix of current donors and viable prospects. These should be donors and prospects that have a high capacity to give or are current principal donors to the organization. While it is crucial that the executive director, president, or CEO be a primary point of contact for the donors or prospects in their portfolio, it is not uncommon for the major gifts officer or director of development to drive that donor cycle process or to also have direct contact with those donors. It's always a good idea for the major gifts officer or director of development to plan out those special touches for the donor and for the executive director, president, or CEO to be the one to follow through with the action.

DONOR MEMBERSHIP SOCIETY

Most membership-based organizations do not have a natural base of donors who support annual operations. An organization's annual fund is a key tool to get low- to mid-level donors interested in the organization and its mission, and it should be the goal of fundraising staff to move these donors into major donors, planned giving donors, and capital campaign donors. General low- to mid-level annual fund donations to organizations such as museums vary, but many range from $25 to $500 annually.

One way to move these low- to mid-level annual fund donors through the giving pipeline into annual major donors is via a donor membership society. These donor membership societies often include an annual membership to the organization and other special major donor benefits that could include a complimentary annual appreciation dinner, unlimited guest admission, behind-the-scenes access, and donor-only previews to new exhibits. Many organizations start their donor membership society at a level such as $1,000+ per year. The donors who contribute to this donor membership society are assigned to a major gifts officer portfolio and this staff fundraiser provides high-level stewardship for the donor throughout the year. It should be the intention that membership to these societies is strictly annual, and renewal should be sought out annually as well, with the intention to upgrade the donor.

Also keep in mind that a donor membership society is just one form of a major gift to an organization. Major gifts come in many different forms, including funding for special programs or capital projects, and do not always fall under an annual operating cycle. It's up to an organization to set the bar for what constitutes a major gift for their organization, whether it's a donor membership society or for special and capital projects. Some organizations will say a major gift starts at $500 and others will say $10,000. Size of operating budget, fundraising staff, and fundraising goals are just a few ways to determine a major gifts threshold.

FINDING THE BALANCE

In major gifts, it's important to find a good balance between keeping current donors and looking for new donors. For membership-based organizations, there is not an automatic audience, unlike, for example, universities or colleges. Membership-based organizations such as museums must build their donor base from the bottom up and continue to find new donors constantly. But while it's important to mine for new donors, an organization does not want to neglect its current donors. Many organizations find this challenging because common fundraising metrics are based on the number of new donors, renewal and retention rates, etc. However, major gifts work should not be based on transactions; it's based on the relationship the donor has with the organization. One frustration often pointed out by major gifts professionals is that they are expected to produce results immediately or very soon after hire. Major gifts fundraising is a highly relationship-based, strategic form of fundraising, and sometimes it takes months or years to see the results of a major gifts officer's efforts. If an organization is only basing success on the number of visits or phone calls made in a day, week, month, or year, its major gifts fundraising results will suffer and the organization risks high turnover rates among its major gifts staff due to unrealistic expectations.

If your organization is fortunate enough to have a staff person dedicated to prospect research, that frees up time for fundraising professionals to focus on the qualifying and cultivating of prospects and stewarding of donors. Unless your organization is quite large, that is not often the case, and major gifts officers end up doing a majority of the research to seek out new prospects. Searching for new prospects and stewarding current donors is often regarded as the easy part of the major gifts equation. The "cold calls" to get appointments with potential donors and the ask are then often regarded as the hard part of the major gifts equation. Therefore it's important to remember that one of the main reasons donors or donor prospects don't give is because they aren't asked! Even the most well-intentioned and skilled fundraiser can spend too much time searching but never get around to the ask. It's also easy to provide excellent stewardship to a current donor. Many organizations struggle to find the perfect balance, but to be successful at a major gifts program, the organization must find the balance that works best for them.

THE ASK

The ask is often perceived as the scariest part of major gifts fundraising work. It's the one thing fundraisers, executive directors, presidents, or CEOs can prepare for relentlessly but delay due to fear of rejection. It's important to remember that a donation ask for an organization is not the same thing as an ask for a personal loan from a bank. If the organization has a solid case for support and if the person asking is adequately prepared, that puts the organization one step closer to its next big donation.

When preparing to make an ask, it helps to have a solid history of other projects the prospect has supported, both in the community and in the organization. Find out what his or her philanthropic goals are and if those are a good fit for your organization. Depending on the size of the ask, taking another person such as a board or executive-level staff member along eases the nervousness. This also allows for continuity between what the prospect said in the meeting and what was heard. Before the meeting, plan out the ask appropriately. Find out who will tee up the topic and who is responsible for the ask. Script the ask out and practice if needed. Make sure that once the ask is out there, the prospect has time to respond to the ask. Leave time for questions. It's not always appropriate for the prospect to give an answer right away; perhaps he or she needs to involve his or her spouse or partner in the decision. Additionally, when setting up the meeting to make the ask, always include the spouse or partner in the invitation for the meeting. It's easy to insult a prospect by ignoring the fact that many philanthropic decisions are made as a family. Finally, be prepared to follow up within the agreed upon timeframe.

CONTACT REPORTS

Say the organization had a great meeting with a donor or prospect, but if the synopsis of what was said and the outcome of the meeting is not documented somewhere in the organization's donor database, the meeting never took place! Contact reports should include: purpose of visit; staff in attendance; donor or prospect and guests in attendance; materials and info shared with donor or prospect; any new information learned such as employment, family, children, hobbies, interests, clubs, and affiliations; next action steps; others who need to be involved; and thoughts/strategies for the future. The information on the report should be concise and avoid gossip, hearsay, or anything that might embarrass the donor or prospect if he or she were to see a copy of the report. If the contact reports were done correctly, the next person who is assigned to the donor should have the notes needed to continue the relationship.

AVOID CRISIS FUNDRAISING

It's imperative that every organization not rely strictly on major gifts but continue to seek multiple donors from diverse funding sources. Depending solely on one or two funding sources is never optimal, and that's where a diverse fundraising program plan comes into play. Consider a scenario such as this: XYZ museum currently receives 50 percent of its funding from its local and state tax revenue. The fundraising model is such that its focus is on low-end annual fund gifts and the remainder of the annual fundraising goals are supplemented via the tax revenue. A new mayor is elected and passes a budget that decreases the allocation of tax revenue to nonprofit organizations throughout the city. That leaves XYZ museum scrambling to determine how to balance the organization's budget, which puts a strain on staff and subsequently sends the fundraising team into crisis fundraising mode! Crisis fundraising mode is reactive, not proactive, and often includes various consequences, just to name a few: begging current donors to increase their donation after they've already made their commitment, possibly causing donors to second-guess their donation or lose confidence in the organization; resorting to sales pitch–type fundraising models that aren't a good fit for the organization; haphazardly planning a special fundraising event that uses many resources (including staff time and expenses) but has low ROI; and mission drift because sometimes organizations see some money for something as better than no money for nothing (that is, taking grant funding for a program they can't sustain).

It's essential for organizations to develop and build a solid and diverse annual and long-term fundraising plan that makes sense for the organization. These plans should fit what works best for an organization and its resources and should outline who is responsible for which portion of the plan. While many organizations are successful at social media fundraising or can sustain a high-expense special event, those fundraising elements don't work for every organization. It's up to the organization to determine its needs, what works with its audience, and what resources it have that will allow the organization to realistically meet its goals and objectives.

CONCLUSION

Major gifts work requires a strong, strategic taskmaster at the helm and planning, persistence, and perseverance above all else. It's about building relationships and connecting people to the mission of the organization. It is indeed a little bit of art and a little bit of science. Last, it's important to remember that major gifts fundraising is just one piece of what should be a very diverse fundraising plan!

RESOURCES

CASE Sample Contact Report. https://www.case.org/Publications_and_Products/Fundrais ing_Fundamentals_Intro/Fundraising_Fundamentals_section_10/Fundraising_Fundamen tals_section_102.html.

Kent Dove Sample Script. http://majorgivingnow.org/downloads/pdf/dove.pdf.

Supporting Advancement Sample Contact Report. http://www.supportingadvancement.com/ forms/sample_forms/trinity_contact_report.htm

14

Expert Opinion: Crowdfunding Projects at the National Museum of Nuclear Science and History

Jennifer Hayden, Director of PR and Marketing, National Museum of Nuclear Science and History

What prompted you to begin using crowdfunding?

A very talented museum volunteer brought up the possibility of crowdfunding as we were looking at fundraising initiatives to help us restore our B-29 Superfortress in 2015. We needed to raise a substantial amount of money in a fairly short amount of time, and after looking into crowdfunding as a possibility, we thought it would fit very well with our efforts in raising money to restore the exterior of this large aircraft. We were also hopeful it would help increase community awareness of our museum.

How do you decide when to use crowdfunding versus other funding tactics?

We have utilized crowdfunding on four different fundraising initiatives, and all of them have been for our Operation Preservation Campaign, a multiyear campaign to restore the many aircraft in our nine-acre outdoor exhibit area, Heritage Park. We use crowdfunding in addition to other funding tactics, as restoring our aircraft comes with a hefty price tag. We aim to raise a portion of the overall cost to restore each airplane through crowdfunding, and we work to raise the remaining funds through other initiatives such as special events.

Which platforms (that is, Kickstarter, Indiegogo) do you use and why?

For our very first crowdfunding campaign, we decided to go with Kickstarter. Our B-29 Superfortress, one of only seventeen B-29 bombers left in existence, is one of our most popular artifacts, and we hoped it would receive a large following because of its history. Because Kickstarter is "all or nothing" in regards to raising the funds—if you do not meet your entire goal that is listed on your promotional page, you will not receive a penny, even if it is only dollars away from your goal—and it only gave us thirty days to raise the $44,000, it created an extreme sense of urgency to our supporters and donors. It was a successful campaign, reaching $47,751, but it did come with a fair amount of stress for staff and volunteers in spreading the word and trying to reach the goal.

For the next restoration project, our B-52B Stratofortress, and all of our future crowdfunding campaigns, we decided to go with Indiegogo. With this platform, even if your goal is not met, you will still receive all the donations promised by supporters. This did prove itself to be a less stressful campaign, and we knew our efforts would not be lost if we did not reach our goal. This did provide a different reaction from supporters though. Since it was no longer "all or nothing" campaign with an intense sense of urgency, many donors decided to bring their donations directly into the museum so their donations wouldn't be hit with the Indiegogo fees. They wanted the museum to receive 100 percent of their donation. This, and all of our future campaigns, have been a huge success, but we stopped reaching our goal as it was seen on the crowdfunding web pages. On our pages, it would show we only hit a portion of our goal, however, we did reach our goals in their entirety due to generous donations that were actually walked through our doors at the museum.

We had looked at other platforms as well, but Indiegogo and Kickstarter seemed the best fit for our nonprofit institutions and the huge restorations on which we were focusing. They were very business friendly and incredibly easy to use.

How do you manage or accept offline donations for a crowdfunding campaign?

The donations that were given offline remained offline. They were given directly to the museum, to our finance department, to go directly to our Operation Preservation Campaign. We tried to verbalize to all of our crowdfunding supporters that our campaigns were still a success, because of these offline donations added with their support through Indiegogo.

How do you sustain campaign momentum?

These campaigns were an all-hands effort. We asked all of our staff, board of directors, volunteers, members, and supporters to help us spread the word. We utilized collateral that our in-house graphic designer created, such as bookmarks to be handed to all museum visitors, postcards sent out to our mailing lists, flyers to be distributed around town, and signs throughout our museum. We tried to remain constantly in the public's eye by sending out new releases through Newswire, hitting publications all over the world, boosting Facebook posts, and utilizing other social media platforms. We were able to catch our local media's attention, and we lined up many radio and television interviews to talk about these campaigns. The key was to keep the campaign constantly out in front of the public and our constituency. We did pay some marketing dollars to help spread the word, but much of it was done through media, social media, and word-of-mouth.

How do you determine the rewards and levels?

We determined our rewards and levels internally, with all of the staff it would directly affect. We had our museum store purchaser involved, our office manager who coordinates the mailing and disbursement of the rewards at the end, our finance manager, our restoration coordinator who works on all the airplanes, our director of development, and our marketing director. For our first campaign with Kickstarter, we gave many more rewards at lower levels, hoping it would entice people to give support.

We found the rewards were not that big of an enticement, as many only wanted to give their money, not wanting us to spend any on them in return. Because of this, our future rewards were given at higher financial levels. We chose the rewards based on popular items we sell in our museum store, as well as ease of mailing these items. As we choose rewards for the higher giving levels, we incorporate things such as visits to the museum, special tours, and even permanent recognition outside by the aircraft.

Did crowdfunding expand your institution's audience or community awareness?

Crowdfunding absolutely expanded our institution's audience and community awareness. The initiatives themselves—restoring historic and iconic aircraft at a Smithsonian affiliated and congressionally chartered museum—were impressive and caught the attention of many people around the world, but the fact they could easily show their support through a safe and known entity such as Kickstarter or Indiegogo was a huge plus. People who give to these platforms were also informed about our initiatives through the crowdfunding platforms, and we received support from these people as well—people who may have not otherwise have heard about us or our initiatives.

Expert Opinion: Crowdfunding the Ida McKinley Tiara Acquisition for the McKinley Presidential Library and Museum

Kimberly A. Kenney, Assistant Director and Curator, McKinley Presidential Library and Museum

After learning that Ida McKinley's diamond tiara had been sold on the television show *Pawn Stars*, Kimberly Kenney contacted Rick Harrison, co-owner of the Gold & Silver Pawn Shop in Las Vegas, and asked if the museum could acquire the tiara. Harrison had purchased the tiara with the intention of using it to raise money for the National Epilepsy Foundation, for which he, who suffers from epilepsy, is the national spokesperson. Because he felt a connection to Mrs. McKinley, who also suffered from epilepsy, Harrison agreed to sell the tiara to the museum for the price he paid for it, $43,000, if the museum could raise the money in three months.

What prompted you to use crowdfunding to raise money to purchase the tiara?

Although we are a presidential library, we are not part of the National Archives system, which means we are a private nonprofit, like most museums. We knew we did not have the funds to purchase the tiara on our own, so we contacted the media to publicize our efforts [by sending] a press release out to our regular media list. . . . It became "crowd sourced" organically, because the story was distributed nationwide through the Associated Press. The momentum built from there.

Why did you decide to use crowdfunding versus another funding tactic?

When considering a crowdfunding campaign, the end goal has to be exciting to a wide, general audience. It has to be something that people will want to rally around. The story of Ida's diamond tiara being sold to a pawn shop in Las Vegas resonated with people. They wanted to "bring it home." In fact, one of the first checks we received was from someone living in Las Vegas! If the object of your fundraising doesn't have popular appeal, then no "crowds" will get behind it.

Which platforms (that is, Kickstarter, Indiegogo) did you use and why?

We did not use any crowdfunding platforms. We set up a PayPal button on the homepage of our website, and we used social media to point people to it. Our board was leery of the fees and wanted us to try to raise the funds without using one of those services. If the campaign hadn't exploded the way it did, we might have tried one of them. But we were successful on our own.

How did you manage or accept offline donations for the campaign?
   Our front office manager logged each donation that came in the mail and compiled a list of names and addresses in a spreadsheet. We intended to return all of the donations if we failed to meet the fundraising goal within the three-month time frame that Rick Harrison . . . gave us. We used this donor information to invite each person to a special preview of the tiara after it arrived at the museum. It was very exclusive, donors only, and we had a line out the door. The tiara went on display the next day for the general public.

How did you sustain campaign momentum?
   I maintained a chart in the lobby of the museum and an identical chart online. I made forty-three diamonds, and filled one in for every $1,000 we received. I posted the chart on our Facebook page every time we filled in another diamond. The most exciting part of every day was when the mail came! We received at least one check in the mail just about every day during the campaign.

How do you determine the rewards and levels?
   We didn't have rewards or levels. Every donor, no matter how much they gave, was invited to the preview.

Did crowdfunding expand your institution's audience or community awareness?
   We could never have purchased the publicity we received for this project! We were in the *New York Times*, several NPR stations, and TV stations throughout northeast Ohio. One of my favorite moments was when a child on a field trip, probably in second or third grade, came into the building and immediately said to me, "Did you get Ida's crown yet?" Everyone was talking about it! Several schools did fundraising on their own and brought their donations with them on the day of their field trip. It really took on a life of its own, and we sat back and watched the money come in. Our cause inspired people to give, which is the key to a successful crowdfunding campaign. We had one donor who gave $5,000, and maybe ten who gave $1,000. The rest were small donations—$20, $50, $100—that all added up. We even had a "drive-thru" event where people could drop off their loose change! The Ohio Pawnbrokers Association solicited donations from their members and sent them to us in one check. It was a lot of fun, and we were so grateful to each person who made this happen for us. Ida's diamond tiara is still an attraction for us. It is on permanent display in the McKinley Gallery.

Since this campaign was so successful, have you considered similar campaigns for other initiatives/projects?
   We would definitely do this again if we had the opportunity to purchase something that we thought would resonate with a large number of people.

16

Making Partnerships a Priority in Fundraising

Margaret Walker, Assistant Curator at the Vanderbilt University Fine Arts Gallery

So much of life is transactional, but people are drawn to museums—as visitors, donors, or employees—because they offer something "more," something less tangible. It is the mission, the collection, the personal stories, and the history of a place that spark the interest and consideration of people in the modern day. A partnerships-driven approach to fundraising leverages this inherent intangible quality and provides a greater depth of involvement and nonmonetary returns for partners as well. This chapter will focus on two case studies of different approaches to using partnerships as a key factor in fundraising, showing how this is more about setting a priority than fitting a particular model. One institution is a small academic museum situated within Vanderbilt University and the second is a network of historic houses nationwide connected with the National Society of the Colonial Dames of America (NSCDA).

When beginning to think about partnerships in fundraising, it is important to consider what would make them strategic. For the purposes of this chapter, a strategic partnership will be defined as one that involves stakeholders outside of the museum, is targeted by aligned interest, and is appropriately timed. Additionally, every institution must consider its mission when planning for fundraising, especially if considering new directions.

The first case, of the Vanderbilt University Fine Arts Gallery (henceforth, the Gallery), looks at a small academic museum with a roughly encyclopedic collection of about seven thousand objects and a full-time staff of two. The author is one of those two employees and not a development professional but necessarily wears that hat on many occasions. While a free museum for the general public, the Gallery's central mission is to support the academic enterprise of the university as a whole and engage its student body. The scope of the Gallery's activities includes a wide range of exhibitions and programming, class visits with art pulled from storage for viewings, and occasional displays of art elsewhere on campus. Partnerships and fundraising are often crucial for exhibitions and related programming.

The NSCDA is a lineage society that promotes appreciation for the people, places, and events that led to the formation and development of our country. Its members are female descendants from an individual who rendered efficient service to our country during the colonial period. The NSCDA was an early leader in the field of historic preservation, and the forty-four state societies often have at least one museum property significant in local or national history that they own, maintain, or support. Additionally, there are three properties supported by the national society. Dumbarton House in Washington, DC, is owned solely by the Dames, and two properties are owned by other entities: George Mason's Gunston Hall in Mason Neck, Virgina, home of the author of the Virginia Declaration of Rights, which was an important influence on both the Declaration of Independence and the Bill of Rights, and Sulgrave Manor in Oxfordshire, England, the ancestral home of George Washington. These three properties as well as the local museum properties nationwide receive financial support for regular operating and project needs through ownership by or partnership with the Dames.

VANDERBILT UNIVERSITY FINE ARTS GALLERY

The partnerships-driven approach to fundraising used by the Vanderbilt University Fine Arts Gallery may be particularly applicable to other academic museums and galleries, as they will likely have similar constraints and opportunities. Because the Gallery is part of a larger nonprofit institution, its goals must fit within the fundraising goals of the university as a whole. While it does receive some gifts—both monetary and of art—from alumni and outside donors, these are often unsolicited or achieved by working closely in tandem with development and alumni relations. Given constraints on solicitation of individuals, the focus of this study, and truly of the Gallery, is on forming partnerships within the university across departments. This has the advantage, too, of being clearly missional as the Gallery seeks to be ever more interdisciplinary in the reach of its collections and exhibitions.

One of the strongest recurring partnerships has been with the Freshman Commons. Each year, the first-year students read a book that is then tied to a curriculum that runs outside of regular classes for the first half semester of school in "Visions" groups. Since 2010 the Gallery has linked its fall exhibition with the first-year read. The Gallery approached the dean of the Commons with the idea of this partnership in 2010 because that year it moved into a building near all of the freshman dorms. At times the link has been a direct connection, as with *Race, Sports and Vanderbilt, 1966–1970*, which was tied to the book *Strong Inside: Perry Wallace and the Collision of Race and Sports in the South*. Other years, the exhibition has been more thematic, allowing students to make connections with the book and the curriculum without that link being directly obvious, as with *Who Are We? Identity and the Contemporary Photographic Portrait*. Commons is always a lead financial sponsor of the Gallery's fall exhibition. Beyond that monetary support, benefits for the Gallery include higher student visitor numbers and awareness. Commons, in turn, creates a natural avenue to expose students to a resource on campus in their first year and a new and exciting venue for the curricular "Visions" groups to meet. Further, they are listed as a sponsor on all exhibition materials, which are distributed throughout and beyond campus.

Another recurring partnership is with the "Exhibiting Historical Art" class, taught annually in the department of history of art. This class results in a small, student-curated exhibition, often using material from the collection. The budget is typically split between the Gallery and the department of history of art. The Gallery, while its own department, shares a building with history of art and also the program in classical and Mediterranean studies. This proximity logistically facilitates partnerships with these disciplines to which there is also frequently a natural intellectual link.

Expanding on this idea of a recurring partnership, academic museums could think about exhibitions that pair well with lecture series or endowed programs at their colleges and universities. Municipal museums could think about exhibitions and programs that link with annual events for which the city is known.

More often, partnerships are formed for specific exhibitions or programs associated with them. Asking other departments and centers on campus to co-sponsor a project provides funding, visibility, an additional visitor constituency, and therefore higher visitor numbers, as those partners will often use the exhibition a number of times during its run. Furthermore, the partners benefit by having access to original art and a unique venue in which to engage topics of interest. (With regard to artwork in the collection, access is never truly a barrier, but having an exhibition generates the necessary excitement and visibility for greater engagement.) Typically, the partnership creates little extra work for either side, but, when appropriate, the Gallery has adopted a co-curation model. Some exhibitions have also been planned with specific classes in mind.

Memento Mori: Looking at Death in Art and Illustration provided an excellent opportunity to partner with Vanderbilt's Center for Biomedical Ethics and Society as well as its medical school. This project included both exhibition-general funding and program-specific funding. With regard to the latter, the Gallery was able to work into a regularly occurring and fully funded lecture series in the medical school, creating a program in which a physician, a medical historian, and an art historian spoke on the same image from Andreas Vesalius's 1543 book on anatomy, an early edition of which was in the exhibition.

Race, Sports, and Vanderbilt, 1966–1970 was linked with the annual Commons partnership but also received sponsorship from the department of athletics and the office of diversity, equity, and inclusion. The exhibition was centered on the story of Perry Wallace, a Vanderbilt basketball player who was the first African American to play in the Southeastern Conference. Several teams and groups of coaches came to visit the exhibition, an audience that is normally difficult to reach outside of class visits because of their very busy schedules.

For *The Dada Effect: An Anti-Aesthetic and Its Influence*, the gallery adopted a co-curation model, working with the assistant director of the W. T. Bandy Center for Baudelaire and Modern French Studies, which is housed inside the central library. The Gallery styled this as a postdoctoral internship for him, as he explored curatorial career options. The library, therefore, as well as the department of French and Italian and the department of theater helped to sponsor this exhibition. It was planned to open around the same time as an important conference at Vanderbilt for scholars of Paul Verlaine, so the Gallery organized an exhibition preview event supported by the department of French and Italian.

These partnerships are formed in a variety of ways, often through formal and informal networking within the Vanderbilt community. The Gallery has a faculty

committee of about eight members who meet four times annually. They often facilitate this process, making the initial connection. This, for instance, was the case with
Memento Mori, for which one of the committee members, faculty in both French
and biomedical ethics, was a co-curator. Other partnerships have evolved when the
Gallery director was approached by a faculty member who had an idea but needed
professional museum expertise and a venue to continue with it. Some partnerships
have come about through "cold" emails too, inquiring first about interest and potential
involvement and later about financial support. Additionally, the Gallery sent a survey
to all faculty in spring 2018 about future growth of the collection and collaborations
with classes, creating a list of follow-ups for potential partnerships to be explored in
the future.

These are just a few examples of how the Vanderbilt University Fine Arts Gallery
has worked in recent years to leverage the many benefits of existing inside of a university, including potential for cross-campus collaborations and working to align exhibitions and programming to existing opportunities in the university community, be they
classes, conferences, or lecture series. This approach minimizes the need to fundraise
outside of the university and generates or builds on existing energies on campus. The
detraction is that this model exclusively covers budget items related to exhibitions and
programs and does not provide support for general operating expenses or ongoing care
of collections. Success is measured, to some degree, by the amount of an exhibition
budget offset by partner contributions. This allows the Gallery to accumulate income
from endowments for future growth of the collection. To a large degree, though, success is measured by number of attendees at the exhibition opening or related events,
for the whole run of a show, and, importantly, the number of student visitors.

THE NATIONAL SOCIETY OF THE COLONIAL DAMES OF AMERICA

The NSCDA was founded in 1891, around the time that a number of societies interested in preserving the history of the United States sprang up. Preservation has always
been at the heart of the NSCDA mission, beginning with the New York Society
assuming stewardship of the Van Cortlandt House in 1896. While the Dames are
involved in a number of efforts, including patriotic service and support of veterans
and their families, museums and preservation remain critical to their mission and
vision for the future. There are many layers to the networks of partnership among the
museum properties and between the properties and the members of the NSCDA.

The National Society is headquartered at Dumbarton House in Washington, DC,
which is owned and operated wholly by the NSCDA. Two additional museums are
supported by the National Society. George Mason's Gunston Hall, in Mason Neck,
Virginia, is owned by the Commonwealth of Virginia, but governed by Dames who
make up the entirety of its board of directors, the Board of Regents of Gunston Hall,
Inc. The house has a friends group of Dames, who contribute unrestricted funds, and
also receives financial support from a Dames-funded foundation and the Commonwealth of Virginia. Sulgrave Manor, the ancestral home of George Washington, was
purchased by public subscription in 1914 to commemorate one hundred years of peace

between Great Britain and the United States. At that time, the Dames established an endowment fund for its benefit and today two Dames, the senior and junior representatives to the Sulgrave Manor Trust, sit on its board at any given time. The endowment continues to provide financial support, as do funds from the US-based 501(c)(3) Friends of the Sulgrave Manor Trust. Together, the friends groups and endowments provide both unrestricted and project-specific funds.

Dames across the country are familiar with these three properties and often make financial contributions to them through their state's dues, annual solicitation campaigns, and/or local fundraisers. Many also make efforts to visit them. Recently, the three properties have coordinated a schedule for annual fund solicitations in order to reach the members of the National Society more effectively and to avoid "donor fatigue."

On the other side of the coin is the network of over ninety museums, collections, historic sites, and memorials that are considered part of the Great American Treasures: NSCDA Museum Alliance. Forty-five of these are directly owned and/or operated nationally or by a corporate society. The remaining forty-seven have affiliations of varied ranges, from regular fundraising and volunteering for municipal parks and historic sites, to owning a collection but not a site, or furnishing a room of a larger museum. Some corporate societies do not have museum properties, but most have at least one that is directly supported in a number of ways, one of which is almost always through fundraising. Dames are aware of museum properties in corporate societies beyond their own and may support them financially or in other ways.

Furthermore, part of the most recent strategic planning efforts by the National Society that began about five years ago included forming an organized network for these affiliated institutions so that they could begin to better share resources and best practices. The network had of course always existed, but had not yet been fully leveraged. Current and future initiatives through the network include professional development, joint programming and marketing, and possibly shared support staff (say, of a conservator). There have now been three meetings for directors and staff, the most recent one timed and located adjacent to the 2017 annual conference for the American Association for State and Local History in Austin, Texas. This alignment with relevant professional conferences is likely to continue in the future. Dumbarton House Executive Director Karen Daly said of the effort to formalize this alliance that "our museum properties are all individually doing great work in their communities, but our cumulative impact and ability to tell such a broad range of the story of this country is far greater when we work together."

Daly says of the partners within the NSCDA Museum Alliance that success is measured through primarily quantitative metrics—attendance figures, grant awards received, and funds spent on conservation and preservation. They do have plans to both expand collection of quantitative data and implement collection of qualitative metrics, a process that has already begun at Dumbarton House through visitor evaluations funded by the National Endowment for the Humanities and the Institute of Museum and Library Services Interpretive Planning grants. The organized partnership of these ninety-some properties presents an opportunity to more efficiently share practices and financial resources for implementing such data collection strategies.

The National Society is in the process of raising funds for an endowment to support the museums of the corporate societies. Central to this vision is that a portion of the income from the endowment would be distributed through competitive grants to properties in the NSCDA Museum Alliance. The funds for this endowment will come primarily from the membership base of the NSCDA. A benefit of the connection to this member base is a regular, national constituency from which Dumbarton House, Gunston Hall, and Sulgrave Manor can fundraise. Furthermore, that national member base is aware of the preservation legacy of the organization nationally and may therefore be supportive of funding national Museum Alliance efforts that will benefit sites outside of their own communities. Their less-tangible return is a feeling of belonging at NSCDA properties nationwide—no small thing. The membership is a limited pool though. In recognition of this, many of the Dames' museum properties have invited outside partners into this area of their work, for instance by inviting community members onto the board of a site owned by a corporate society. The partnership between the Dames and these properties is foundational to their financial stability and history, but the corporate societies and museum properties are all working in ways distinct to their situations to build partnerships outside of the Dames as well.

CONCLUSIONS

Smaller professional networks often serve a unique purpose for museum professionals, especially in small institutions, as they can tailor programming and support more easily and offer more frequent and manageable opportunities to build professional relationships. Often these are local, as in the academic community at Vanderbilt or corporate societies for various Dames properties. However, the institutions studied here are both part of moderate-sized national networks, the first being the Association of Academic Museums and Galleries and the second being that of the NSCDA, its membership, and its Museum Alliance. As the world becomes increasingly more connected, those wider-spreading networks become easier to maintain and all the more important for broadening perspectives.

Vanderbilt's partnerships in recent years have been strategic in their efforts to reach populations on campus that would not normally use museum collections but whose work and goals align with the subject of an exhibition. Furthermore, the Gallery makes efforts to time these partnerships so that the sponsoring departments and centers will be able to maximize their use, for instance during the run of a class or at the time of a related conference. The NSCDA network is strategic along the same lines but in different ways. Because of the ninety-some properties' relationship beyond their corporate societies with a national entity, there is interest and financial support for them nationwide. This is successful, in part, because each of the corporate societies has the same mission, at the core of which is prioritization of historic preservation and telling the stories of the places and events that have led to the development of this country. Timing will be specific to each property and the community in which it is situated, but coordinating a schedule for solicitations on a national level, while too new of an initiative to have data, seems to be a step in the right direction.

This chapter has not discussed all forms of partnerships that can be leveraged for the fundraising needs of museums. Others include strategic board building, corporate sponsorships, and in-kind donations, which may be good avenues for other institutions to explore. Furthermore, as more for-profit companies focus on corporate social responsibility and impact investing from a business-minded angle, new metrics for measuring the success of partnerships and fundraising will almost certainly be vetted. Partnerships can be formed to support all areas of a museum's work—operations, exhibitions, collections growth and management, and programming. What that partnership looks like and what it is used to support will vary based on mission and, if successful, will create some sort of "buy-in" among the partners that goes beyond the dollar amount of a contribution.

BIBLIOGRAPHY

Karen Daly (Dumbarton House Executive Director). Phone interview by Margaret Walker, February 26, 2018.

17

Donations and Fundraising

Management, Evaluation, and Metrics

Allison Porter, President of Avalon Consulting Group; and Faith Brown Kerr, Writer and Editor

Museums are doing more than ever before to deliver compelling, hands-on exhibitions to their visitors, with cutting-edge digital engagement, apps, and virtual tours. Museum marketers have similarly upped their game, with state-of-the-art, data-driven, multichannel marketing campaigns that build member value, engage new generations, and reward members for their loyalty.

My colleagues at Avalon Consulting Group and I have developed a powerful combination of membership experience and mission-driven fundraising best practices to help our museum clients raise funds. The key components of this practice include benchmarking the numbers—forensically examining available data to support strategy; maximizing the drivers that affect a museum's metrics; and paying strict attention to accountability and reporting—so we have clear and extensive analytics to inform how we move forward.

MAXIMIZING INDIVIDUAL GIVING

With regard to individual giving programs for museums, we can never settle for a set-it-and-forget-it approach. Instead, our experience has shown that arts and nonarts donors are different types of donors who must therefore be cultivated in unique ways, with tailored engagement strategies.

Arts donors:

- put 90 percent emphasis on membership benefits and 10 percent on philanthropy;
- view supporting the arts as important but not the most critical issue in their lives;
- base the decision to join on "what's in it for me?" and "how will this further bind me to the organization?";
- give locally—they want direct and immediate benefit from their gifts; and
- want a quality product and direct access to it.

Conversely, nonarts donors:

119

- put less emphasis on benefits, more on mission;
- view the issues they support as critical in their lives (for example, charity, humanitarian aid, health, the environment);
- give to be part of a higher cause;
- give nationally/internationally—they want to help someone or improve society as a whole but do not expect personal benefit; and
- want results and to impact positive social change.

Beyond what we know to be generally true about arts donors, we know that data-driven marketing is the best way to maximize their giving. We can make educated guesses about what motivates donors to give or listen to their anecdotal feedback or our gut, but we have learned that nothing works better than concrete data to inform why donors give and what will encourage them to give again.

We also consider the impact of where a museum is in its lifecycle to determine how we market to existing and prospective museum members: pre-opening (as excitement builds and members want to be in on the ground floor), grand opening (with media attention and the thrill of the first look), post-opening (when interest among members can wane), and anniversary years (as the museum settles into maturity and needs to find new ways to engage both visitors and supporters).

A NEW MUSEUM'S STORY

Avalon began an ongoing partnership with a new museum in Washington, DC, and we were tasked with helping the museum to build a file of loyal charter members throughout its construction and grand opening phases.

During this time, before there was a museum to visit, we focused on several fronts to generate engagement and support, always employing tried and true multichannel strategies (direct mail, online, telemarketing) to build a file of charter members who would stay with the museum after the excitement and publicity of the opening diminished. We put so much emphasis on multichannel donors because we know they are the best donors—with higher average gifts, multiple gifts per year, and long-lasting commitment.

We established the basics that every individual giving program requires: donor acquisition, special appeals, renewals, cultivation, and acquisition. The following, in broad brushstrokes, gives a sense of the programs and unique campaigns we launched for this museum, which evolved as the museum grew from an idea, to a foundation, to a new building that donors could visit.

We created a renewal series as a standalone program: a multi-effort, expire-based monthly series that ran separately from the appeals. In this way, we delivered significant net revenue, while also profitably reinstating lapsed members. Going forward, with the museum now open, we are always seeking to refine and improve the renewal series by extensive testing and cost cutting as we identify the optimal mix of mail and mirrored email efforts to maximize response. This is the time to continually push the creative envelope by testing package elements to see how a tweak or a wholesale change can raise the performance bar.

We also initiated a Membership Month to recruit online members by sending targeted emails with ever-increasing urgency toward the monthly recruitment and revenue goals. These efforts to engage new supporters resulted in the most successful month of online fundraising in the museum's history. After a hugely successful Membership Month, we designed an online list-building campaign through carefully targeted online advertising, as well as a petition campaign to engage and sign up new online supporters.

Targeting the generous giving season at year end, we created a year-end appeal with a highly personalized touch to encourage members to contribute at the end of the calendar year, raise additional, necessary funding, and provide an insider's look at the in-progress structure of the new museum. This was the highest grossing appeal of the fiscal year, giving donors a stake in the planning and construction phase, while seeing their support in action.

Among any organization's most valuable donors, sustainers commit to give regular, monthly gifts and, through cultivation, tend to be extremely loyal. So we created a monthly sustainer program for the museum—branding it with a unique name and ongoing stewardship. The standalone direct mail invitation, which resulted in 105 new sustainers, took just 3.52 months to make back our invitation costs. Coming off the museum's grand opening and successful year end, an e-invitation encouraged anyone who had joined the museum in the previous six months to deepen their commitment and join the sustainer program. This digital approach grew the program by 17 percent for a tremendous jump in steady, monthly revenue.

Well into its second year of operation, we focus on honing the strategies that proved so successful in the construction phase—stewarding existing charter members with meaningful cultivation tools like newsletters, emails, and other communications to keep them informed of what is happening at the museum.

This cultivation results in further bonding to the museum, and our deep dives into the data help us to target which charter members are ready to upgrade their giving, become monthly sustainers, or simply give again.

DRIVERS OF KEY METRICS

Always consider what drives key metrics in marketing because the numbers don't lie. Most people have a gut feeling about how testing will turn out, but time and time again, we are proved wrong, which is why we test and retest. And why we scrutinize the data to look for clues as to what will attract a donor's attention, entertainment, or charitable dollars.

For example, timing can be key. Soliciting a donor while he or she is having a great time at the museum, or shortly after, is very effective for some museums. But think about what visitors will be doing at the museum and the potential touch points during that time. Will they stay all day? Have lunch? See an in-house film? Will they have children in tow and therefore be distracted from hearing a fundraising message? What special exhibitions will draw them to the museum? Can those special exhibition junkies be encouraged to join, or are they fair-weather friends? Are regular ticket buyers good candidates for membership conversion? Will the benefits package speak to them and encourage loyalty? Finally, what is the museum's market reach, and how can it hold the market's attention?

The answers to these questions will help to define each museum's unique market—and its compelling case for support and the perceived value of its benefits will help reach beyond it. A benefits audit can uncover opportunities to entice benefits-focused arts donors, with testing to determine what best motivates them. Benefits should cover a range of giving levels and can include admission discounts, parking vouchers, gift shop and restaurant coupons, as well as free catalogues, books, and behind-the-scenes tours.

A full benefits audit for one client uncovered ways to better tailor the offerings to the members. For example, because of the museum's location outside of the United States, many members cannot visit the actual museum, but they support its mission and would enjoy a comprehensive virtual tour or insider phone call with curators. When we instituted a tiered benefits structure, including a base level of membership, followed by subsequently higher giving levels, we saw an immediate improvement in our donor acquisition average gift. Improving the back-end fulfillment structure and acknowledgment programs added simple, but meaningful, touches to ensure members feel valued. This included sending out temporary membership cards, followed by permanent cards in renewal mailings, quarterly newsletters, and other touchpoints.

ACCOUNTABILITY AND REPORTING

In managing key metrics—which will inform all marketing strategies—the first step is to define which metrics present the full picture of challenges and opportunities. A regular review of key performance indicators allows museums to keep tabs on developing trends and changes as marketing programs evolve. It is a good idea for nonprofit organizations to keep tabs on industry benchmarking reports to provide context to their program's results. These include the Blackbaud Charitable Giving Report, the M+R Benchmarks Report, the donorCentrics Report, and the Giving USA Report on Philanthropy. Additionally, Avalon's blog at www.avalonconsulting.net/blog includes a number of posts about metrics including tracking your second gift rate, factoring in future retention when crafting acquisition strategies, and measuring acquisition's long-term impact. See the "Suggested Reading" list at the end of this article to source these reference materials.

Digging into campaign- and program-level data—including response rate, average gift, net per member, and cost to raise a dollar—can provide concrete evidence that messaging and case for support are working or not. These metrics inform all testing plans and rollouts, help to compare results across fundraising channels, and provide a baseline on which we build engagement and upgrading strategies.

Member-level data come from dashboard reports and master file analyses—the truly deep dives into the numbers that can tell so much about donors and help pinpoint those most likely to give. The metrics include member retention, gifts per member, and fiscal year/year-over-year results, among others. Also critical are file composition, file trajectory, and the impact of the acquisition program, member value, cross-channel analysis, and the potential of your major donor pipeline. These metrics can help to determine the health of the file, the correct acquisition investment to stem attrition and/or grow the file, upgrade potential, and segmentation strategies.

Our leadership reporting includes quarterly and annual reports to ensure that we are on target and making adjustments as necessary, so there are no surprises at the end of the fiscal year. This accountability also includes helping our clients to report and translate results to their boards, tracking progress to long-term strategic goals and investments, and where they are on key performance indicators. In addition, we continuously evaluate our goals, resetting and forecasting as we go along. Our reporting includes daily and monthly reports—for both big-picture and drill-down views that ensure we proactively identify and respond to real-time challenges and opportunities.

Carefully define and track all data over time to ensure file health remains strong and that museums continue to invest appropriately. Benchmarking among your peers and year over year are critical because metrics can vary widely by organization depending on where it is in the lifecycle of the program. The priority should always be on building and maintaining a strong and stable base of support from valuable, multichannel, long-term members who are committed to the museum's goals and mission, and who believe that they benefit from being a part of the organization.

MOVING FORWARD

Museums use myriad tactics to engage, sign up, cultivate, and thank donors. The key is continual engagement—driven by the data—across multiple communications channels to further bond members to the museum. This is the chance to tell the stories of all that the donors' support has accomplished and describe the opportunities for continued partnership that lie ahead.

Along the way, closely monitor each museum's donor file data to ensure that all programs stay on track and are cost-effective and that members and prospects are being properly cultivated and engaged. Staying on top of the data helps to identify trends in giving—positive or negative—so we can make adjustments as necessary, while targeting those donors who are ready to give again, upgrade their giving, or become monthly sustainers. This also ensures long-term, sustainable revenue and healthy, productive museum membership programs, as well as providing key accountability to leadership.

SUGGESTED READINGS

Avalon Consulting Group. "Avalon Cultural Coalition Benchmarking Presentation." Available upon request from info@avalonconsulting.net.
Blackbaud Institute for Philanthropic Impact. "2017 Charitable Giving Report." https://institute .blackbaud.com/asset/2017-charitable-giving-report/.
donorCentrics. https://www.blackbaud.com/target-analytics/donorcentrics.

Hillinger, T. J. "Measuring Acquisition's Long-Term Impact." Avalon Consulting Group's *FYI* (blog). https://www.avalonconsulting.net/blog/measuring-acquisitions-long-term-impact/.

Hillinger, T. J. "Your Second Gift Rate Is Talking. Are You Listening?" Avalon Consulting Group's *FYI* (blog). https://www.avalonconsulting.net/blog/your-second-gift-rate-is-talking -are-you-listening/.

Indiana University Lilly Family School of Philanthropy. "Giving USA 2017: The Annual Report on Philanthropy for the Year 2016." https://givingusa.org/tag/giving-usa-2017/.

Kerr, Kerri. "Where Is the Acquisition Variable in the Retention Equation?" Avalon Consulting Group's *FYI* (blog). https://www.avalonconsulting.net/blog/wheres-the-acquisition-variable -in-the-retention-equation/.

M+R. "Benchmarks 2018." https://mrbenchmarks.com/.

18

Lead and Learn

Resources for Fundraising Success

Kristin Bertrand, Director of Development at the San José Museum of Art; and James G. Leventhal, Deputy Director and Chief Development Officer at the Museum of the African Diaspora (MoAD) in San Francisco

If you are reading this chapter, it is likely that the responsibility for fundraising is a new part of your job or you are looking to deepen your understanding so that you can raise more money for your museum, either as a professional or as a volunteer. In this brief chapter, we want to direct you to useful resources that are longer and have more space to capture specific and salient details like database management, an effective call report system, and preparing for major gift campaigns of various scales. We will go over the purposefulness needed to rally contributed resources effectively to support museums and culture in the twenty-first century and will share a few inspiring precepts that we have found helpful.

Every stage of fundraising can be learned and useful texts are important. Contextualizing your fundraising as a shared learning experience makes your work both more fulfilling and successful. Through fundraising you typically get involved in activities by which you learn all kinds of things—traveling with donor groups to new locations; developing funding resources for a new exhibition about an artist with whose work you were previously unfamiliar; and even and especially getting to know more people, learning from their wisdom and life experiences. Over time, you improve at the fundamentals of communication, cultivation, and solicitation. It helps to begin with an appreciation for best practices and a foundational conceptualization of why your work matters to you, to the donors, and to the world in which you are having an impact.

PROCESS AND PURPOSE

Two good books we recommend to begin with are *The Complete Guide to Fundraising Management* by Stanley Weinstein and Kay Spinkle Grace's *Beyond Fundraising: New Strategies for Nonprofit Innovation and Investment*. The first is a consolidated review of tactical needs and the structure of execution of a solid fundraising plan, and the second is one of the more inspiring books on how and why fundraising matters. Finding the balance between process and purpose is essential to a successful program.

Part of the challenge of writing or teaching about fundraising is being able to put language to work that you might take for granted and to articulate processes. In terms of brass tacks, Weinstein's *Guide to Fundraising Management* is invaluable. It is not unlike other foundational books on the mechanics of asking for money. It is a solid place to begin, and, as with any research you do, you should check the footnotes and bibliography for more good books, articles, and online resources. Here is an example of an essential lesson and how Weinstein walks through it, namely regarding solicitation timing:

> The precise timing of a request for funds is as much an art as a science. A few broad guidelines can be helpful. In general, solicit board members and those closest to the organization prior to approaching people not as close to the organization. Marketing experts tend to view this process as a series of concentric circles indicating primary, secondary, and tertiary markets. Approach affluent members of the planning team soon after the conclusion of the planning process, or soon after the needs become manifest. (Weinstein 2002)

In this the author reinforces the need to start with your board, to focus on those with the proven propensity to be generous to your museum, and to utilize a sense of urgency in your solicitations. While these delineated activities may seem self-apparent, to articulate them helps to clarify intent at each stage, and these basic tenets may not be obvious to everyone. Another classic book that covers fundamental procedures is *Hank Rosso's Achieving Excellence in Fund Raising* edited by Eugene R. Tempel, Timothy L. Seiler, and Dwight F. Burlingame. Either one of these terrific overviews is important to add to your shelf and resource and share regularly.

Several of the steps Weinstein details earlier and further in the book, while essential to understand and articulate, can at times be what Kay Sprinkle Grace might describe as the "tin cup" approach, in which your hand is always out to board members and other volunteers. Donors can tire of constantly being asked. Rather than talking about fundraising, Grace writes and speaks more about "development." The process is not so much about raising money but engaging in deep relationships and together helping to transform organizations and their positive influence in the world. In Kay Sprinkle Grace's *Beyond Fundraising*, she defines development as follows:

> Development consists of those often subtle, frequently intangible, and not immediately measurable acts which draw donors and volunteers closer to the organization into an understanding of shared values. (Grace 1997)

It is this kind of subtle and humane approach that can make a great difference when working toward higher-level giving. At the same time, the basic building blocks that Weinberg lays out remain in play, including getting your current and prospective donors actively involved in the planning to deepen their ownership of the museum's needs and intended impact. Helping others lead and learn is the hallmark of any successful fundraising campaign.

PRECONCEPTIONS AND POTENTIALITY

Studies are integral to validating your work now. Two important studies that come to mind that also complement each other are "The Giving Code" and the interrelated studies published by the Center on Wealth and Philanthropy consecutively in 1999 and 2003 on the so-called wealth transfer that is still in play today.

Major donors come to your organizations with a lot of preconceptions. In "The Giving Code," Alexa Cortés Culwell and Heather McLeod Grant, co-founders of Open Impact, capture the ethos of the new generation of philanthropists:

> Many of Silicon Valley's philanthropists—individuals, corporations, and foundations—feel compelled to be strategic in their giving rather than just compassionate. They talk about needing time to make thoughtful decisions, and many worry about making mistakes. More than 52 percent of wealthy individuals report that their philanthropy "keeps them up at night," and cited such worries as whether they were making an impact, having their money wasted, or donating enough to a cause given the sometimes overwhelming need. . . .These experiences are in some ways an unintended consequence of the "strategic philanthropy" movement of the past two decades. Feeling an intense sense of responsibility to be good stewards of their philanthropic dollars can paradoxically slow down the process and make givers more risk-averse. They often want to do philanthropy the "right way," only to discover that there is no right way. (Culwell and Grant 2017)

The same tension exists for fundraisers and it is important to find the balance. As "The Giving Code" goes on to emphasize, impact is really one of the most important operative terms. As noted in "The Giving Code,"

> the challenge of having to measure results may also leave a whole segment of nonprofits behind, as they struggle to serve the critical needs of some of our most vulnerable populations with no capacity to meet the demands of donors with such different worldviews and expectations. Nevertheless, nonprofits would do well to try and measure what they can, even if it's only leading indicators. There's no sign that this focus on impact and results is going away anytime soon.

Engagement, too, is so important, as the writers point out:

> These philanthropists are compelled to seek new approaches to solving age-old social and environmental challenges. They are also much less likely to be compelled by more traditional approaches to fundraising such as galas or direct mail. As one focus group participant told us: "Don't invite me to a gala to tell me about a great organization. Invite me to a meeting to discuss how together we will solve the problem."

Right now we are living in extraordinary times for philanthropy. If your case is great, the resources exist; and it is so important that you harness your giving communities' finest potential. In 1999 a report was published by the Center on Wealth and Philanthropy (CWP) at Boston College titled "Millionaires and the Millennium: New Estimates of the Forthcoming Wealth Transfer and the Prospects for a Golden Age of Philanthropy" by Paul G. Schervish and John J. Havens. The CWP is a multidisciplinary research center specializing in the study of spirituality, wealth, philanthropy, and other aspects of cultural life in an age of affluence. It is an inspiring read. Following the cataclysmic events of September 11, 2001, Schervish and Havens and the CWP updated the report and published "Why the $41 Trillion Wealth Transfer Estimate Is Still Valid: A Review of Challenges and Questions" in 2003. These reports detail how, through increased investment planning, estate gifts, and the conservatively estimated realization of a century's worth of wealth, charities in the United States should expect to see $41 trillion in gifts made by the year 2052.

Extraordinary museum fundraising efforts like SFMOMA's successful $610 million comprehensive campaign to secure the costs of its new building and triple its endowment are testament to the potential at all levels of museum fundraising in the current climate—with the $41 trillion wealth transfer in full swing and when the right work is being done. Creating the balance of lessons from studies such as "The Giving Code," you can transcend barriers and achieve great things by

- emphasizing and articulating the impact of your mission;
- properly structuring your program to focus on donor engagement;
- openly confronting challenges and preconceptions; and
- bringing everyone together to focus on the potentiality.

As noted in "The Giving Code,"

> One young donor now giving away millions told a story of being so anxious about giving "strategically" that it was not until an older mentor gave her permission to experiment more freely that she was able to begin giving on a larger scale.

HURDLES AND HIGH NOTES

This work is not easy and there are hurdles to overcome, but museums matter and your work is essential. Two other important, recent studies that also complement each other are "Critical Issues Facing the Arts in California" published by the Irvine Foundation and the most recent work done by the American Alliance of Museums (AAM) with support from the Andrew W. Mellon Foundation looking at museums as economic engines.

With the proliferation of museums comes the challenge of sustaining both the ongoing operations and special programs driven by the ever-increasing community need for education. Challenges abound, especially on the West Coast with newer—so possibly less established—museums than on the East Coast and greater fluctuations in wealth. Published in 2006, the James Irvine Foundation's "Critical Issues Facing the Arts in California" paints a grim portrait of the future of the arts and culture nonprofit industry in California, for example. According to the Irvine Report's findings, "The number and size of nonprofit arts organizations now exceeds available public and private sources of support," adding that this is not part of a typical or cyclical downturn but "a permanent, structural change" (Irvine 2007). The most important impact that the Irvine paper sees is the decline in public funding at all levels, and the study notes that earned income is not making up the difference. Further, as demands for accountability in the nonprofit sector have increased, organizations have become more businesslike and expend more on administration. Even though the report was published over a decade ago, its findings are still relevant and need to be explored; in fact, since the report was published, the James Irvine Foundation itself has changed its guidelines to focus on poverty and no longer funds the arts.

Given the very real challenges, it is essential to build the case for museums. Consistently museums have proven to attract more visitors than all sporting events combined. They are special places of wonder and gathering and safe spaces for shared learning. In the AAM report "Museums as Economic Engines: A National Report" (2017), Laura Lott, CEO of the AAM, notes,

> Throughout this detailed study, the numbers tell an indisputable story about museums as true economic engines for their communities, supporting jobs and wages that are vital to the health of their hometown . . . beyond this cultural impact, the museum sector is also essential to the national economy—generating GDP, stimulating jobs, and contributing taxes. (American Alliance of Museums 2018)

The AAM report provides examples of how other museums describe their economic impact, such as:

> Cincinnati's Museum Center took a similar approach, quantifying their economic impact and ongoing construction impact to the tune of $114 million (annually) to the regional economy. The museum also sought to call further attention to their societal contributions by providing quantitative evidence of their community engagement and education programs such as ECSITE, which provides training to dozens of pre-K teachers, who in turn impacted more than 1,200 young learners in 2012.

As a basic truth, embrace your numbers, whatever they are. The only way you can help them grow is to see them and to share them. With a deeper understanding of what they suggest, you can learn to work more effectively to serve your audience better. Nicholas Penny, former director of the National Gallery, London (2008–2015), published a piece in *Apollo* with a clear prescription:

> Attractions that grow their visitor numbers sustainably share some common behaviour. This includes a willingness or ability to invest in refurbishment and refreshing their core offering; a decision to foster creative partnerships with unusual suspects; a determination to tell the stories of their collection, people and places in more engaging ways, attracting new audiences as a result; and a resolve to be bolder in their public programming, including trying new income-generating events. (Penny 2018)

As a fundraising professional you will do well to increase the resources that make this work possible, while providing the guidance and advice to help your museum make sound decisions.

We hope these have been helpful and lead you to other resources and teachers to help you grow and build your network, change the world for the better, and learn together. It is important to put a process in place and to articulate a plan. Provide names of prospects, be clear about their current giving, and create protocols for peer-to-peer review. Wealth indication tools like Blackbaud's Target Analytics are important in identifying underutilized resources within your database, and nothing is more invaluable than face-to-face engagement with as many donors as possible. And remember: The world needs you because your industry needs you and museums are having a profound impact.

It is imperative that the museum community focus on training tomorrow's leaders to grapple with the funding challenge and opportunities head-on. The Irvine paper puts forward a call for new leaders, observing,

> Neither is the sector attracting sufficient numbers of capable young people to replace the generation of cultural leaders that will retire in the next 10–15 years. The Bridgespan Group's recent report on leadership transition suggests that as many as 1.2 million new senior managers will be needed in the nonprofit sector by 2016. This figure for the non-profit arts sector in California is likely to be in the tens of thousands. (The James Irvine Foundation 2006)

As Lilya Wagner, a leading fundraising consultant, recommends, "the more fundraising is integrated into the entire organization, the more successful it will be" (Wagner 2001). These new leaders must be familiar with a holistic approach to development work. Be strong and reassured: the work is not easy. Remember: The need for funding and demonstrated impact underlie all of your museum's work, making the effective management of a meaningful fundraising operation fundamental for the current and future health and viability of your museum.

BIBLIOGRAPHY

American Alliance of Museums. "Museums as Economic Engines: A National Report." 2017. https://www.aam-us.org/2018/01/19/museums-as-economic-engines/. Accessed April 2018.

Culwell, A. C., and H. McLeod Grant. "The Giving Code." 2017. https://www.openimpact.io/giving-code. Accessed April 2018.

Grace, K. S. *Beyond Fundraising: New Strategies for Nonprofit Innovation and Investment.* New York: John Wiley & Sons, Inc., 1997.

Havens, J. J., and P. G. Schervish. "Millionaires and the Millennium: New Estimates of the Forthcoming Wealth Transfer and the Prospects for a Golden Age of Philanthropy." http://www.bc.edu/content/dam/files/research_sites/cwp/pdf/m_m.pdf. Accessed April 2018.

Havens, J. J., and P. G. Schervish. "Why the $41 Trillion Wealth Transfer Estimate Is Still Valid: A Review of Challenges and Questions." *The Journal of Gift Planning* (January 2003). http://www.bc.edu/content/dam/files/research_sites/cwp/pdf/41trillionreview1.pdf. Accessed April 2018.

The James Irvine Foundation (with AEA Consultants). "Critical Issues Facing the Arts in California: A Working Paper from the James Irvine Foundation." September 2006.

Penny, N. "Are Museums Too Preoccupied with Visitor Numbers?" *Apollo Magazine*, April 23, 2018. https://www.apollo-magazine.com/are-museums-too-preoccupied-by-visitor-numbers/. Accessed May 2018.

Tempel, E. R., T. L. Seiler, and D. F. Burlingame. *Hank Rosso's Achieving Excellence in Fund Raising*, second edition. San Francisco, CA: Jossey-Bass, 2003.

Wagner, Lilya. *Careers in Fundraising*. San Francisco, CA: Jossey-Bass, 2001.

Weinstein, Stanley. *The Complete Guide to Fundraising Management*. San Francisco, CA: Wiley, 2002.

Section IV

CONTRIBUTED INCOME: GRANTS

Contributed income refers to income derived from contributions, sponsorships, and/or grants. This section discusses grants. Grants include government grants and grants from private organizations. Readers are probably most familiar with government grants. Federal departments like the Institute of Museum and Library Services (IMLS), the National Endowment for the Arts (NEA), the National Endowment for the Humanities (NEH), and the National Science Foundation (NSF) offer webinars, publish guides, and appear at conferences to educate institutions on their grant processes. At the state and local government level, arts and humanities councils may also exist. Representatives from those government departments may appear at your regional or state museum association conferences.

Private organizations like foundations, industry associations, and corporations also provide grants. Because foundations are the most well-known private organizations, be sure to consider those other entities that may offer grants in smaller amounts or for very specific purposes. For example, the Hotel Congress in Tucson supplies grants under $10,000 to local nonprofit organizations, in addition to its in-kind contributions (http://hotelcongress.com/giving/, accessed November 2018), and the Association of Science-Technology Centers' Fund-the-Bus mini-grant program subsidizes transportation costs for schoolchildren (https://www.astc.org/fund-a-bus/, accessed October 2018).

The "Resource Lists" provided by our contributors and collected at the end of the book contain information about directories and other resources to help you identify grant-making organizations.

As discussed in chapter 1, the US Census Bureau calculated the revenue by type (product line) in 2012. Table IV.1 and IV.2 show the contribution of private contributions and government income to the total revenue of institutions that earn such income types.

As discussed in section III, these tables include both grant and nongrant income, so the data are broadly informative. The private contributions, gifts, and grants income table includes both fundraising and nonfundraising income, so if you want to compare your internal data to these percentages, you will need to combine your fundraising and private grant income. You would similarly combine all of your institution's

Table IV.1   Private Contributions, Gifts, and Grants Income as Percent of Total Revenue by Institution Discipline 2012

All institutions	30.1%
Museums	31.9%
Historical sites	35.3%
Zoos and botanical gardens	18.9%
Nature parks and other similar institutions	50.1%

Table IV.2   Government Contributions, Gifts, and Grants Income as Percent of Total Revenue by Institution Discipline 2012

All institutions	13.5%
Museums	12.6%
Historical sites	15.1%
Zoos and botanical gardens	14%
Nature parks and other similar institutions	26.2%

government contributions, gifts, and grants income to accurately benchmark against the percentages above.

The National Center for Charitable Statistics (NCCS) gifts, grants, and membership fees income data were presented in section III. As you may recall, the NCCS combines membership, fundraising, grant, and gift income into one category, per the structure of the 990—restricting the ability to analyze grant data from that source.

CHAPTERS PREVIEW

Our contributors discuss all aspects of the grant process, from writing to managing, and the different types of grants. Holly Piper Lang, grants specialist, begins this section with a discussion of the federal grant application process. Both new and experienced grant writers will benefit from Holly's detailed discussions of the preparation needed to find grants, secure in-house staff support, and navigate government bureaucracy and technology. She also explains how panelists evaluate grant applications and the importance of reading the panel reviews. Then Andrew J. Verhoff walks readers through the intricacies of state-level grants. States may have multiple grant programs with their own individual requirements and funding sources. Andrew describes how you can combine grants from state, national, and other entities to achieve your strategic and tactical goals. Andrew also shares his perspective about grant applications from his point of view as a grant coordinator for the Ohio History Connection.

Theory becomes reality as Zinia Willits describes her three-year, ultimately successful effort to secure a $250,000 Sustaining Cultural Heritage Collections Implementation Grant from the National Endowment for the Humanities for the Gibbes Museum of Art. Though Zinia had written several small grants, this much larger grant was a more complicated endeavor. After describing the first and second failed attempts, she applies the lessons learned from those failures and was finally awarded the grant on the third attempt—a tribute to her persistence and attention to detail. Marie Berlin brings us full circle with her guide to managing the implementation and reporting requirements of an IMLS grant. The Young at Art Museum (YAA) received both an IMLS grant and foundation grant to open and support the initial programming at a new YAA ArtHouse, a community center for residents and local artists. Marie discusses how she balanced construction issues, community engagement, and program development with grant management requirements and logistical setbacks—ultimately establishing a popular community center.

This section ends with a focus on private foundation grants. Lily Williams, director of development at the Fabric Workshop and Museum, provides an in-depth methodology for identifying, writing, and monitoring foundation grants. She identifies and describes how the foundation grant application process differs from the government grant application process. Her research tips will help you unearth additional funding opportunities and subtleties to strengthen your application. Then Gary N. Smith, president of the Summerlee Foundation, offers his "Expert Opinion" on building relationships between foundations and grant recipients. Alyssa Kopf and Kelly Purdy from the Denver Foundation explain how the foundation manages the Greenwood Fund, a donor-advised fund (DAF), which provides collection care and preservation grants to museums in Colorado and Wyoming. The application process for the Greenwood Fund differs from the typical grant application process by using a request for proposal procedure; its reporting requirements are streamlined compared to a typical grant. As Martin Levine explains in the final chapter in this section, DAFs have been used for almost one hundred years and seem to be growing in popularity. A DAF allows a donor to control the distribution and timing of his or her donations according to his or her own philanthropic goals—similar to a foundation without the structure and overhead. Museums themselves can actually be DAF sponsors. Martin reviews the legal and tax implications of DAFs and provides a guide for deciding if your institution could become a DAF sponsor. Your institution's attorney, investment advisor, and accountant should be consulted too. All of this section's contributors remind us that expertise in specialized disciplines is required to succeed with grants.

RESOURCE LIST

Institute of Museum and Library Services. www.imls.gov.

National Endowment for the Arts. www.nea.gov.

National Endowment for the Humanities. www.neh.gov.

National Science Foundation. www.nsf.gov.

National Trust for Historic Preservation. www.preservationnation.org.

The Urban Institute. NCCS Core Files, 2011–2015. https://nccs-data.urban.org/data .php?ds=core. Accessed January–November 2018.

US Census Bureau. 2002, 2007, and 2012 Economic Censuses. https://www.census.gov/ programs-surveys/economic-census/data/tables.html. Accessed January–November 2018.

Applying, Navigating, and Managing Government Grants

Holly Piper Lang, Grants Specialist,
Holly Piper Lang Grant Writing Services

Congratulations! Whether you are beginning the application process or currently manage a federal grant, you have made impressive strides in furthering the financial health of your museum. Federal grants from agencies such as the National Endowment for the Arts (NEA), the Institute of Museum and Library Services (IMLS), the National Endowment for the Humanities (NEH), and other agencies not only provide substantial, crucial support for programming but also heighten the prestige of your organization and will help build your professional reputation.

However, the application process can be quite overwhelming regardless of how many times you have applied. I have found the keys to success are proper preparation and practicing flexibility.

IDENTIFICATION PROCESS

Identifying viable prospects is more or less a chicken before the egg or egg before the chicken game. Prospects can, and will, come about two ways:

1. A staff person will come to you with a project/program idea and ask if a funder may be interested in it; or
2. A grant opportunity will come across your desk, and you will present it to program staff for consideration, even if you do not have a project in mind yet.

Either way, it is best to keep a running list of prospects to easily reference as identifying national, state, and regional opportunities can be difficult. Through all my research, I have yet to find a well-thought-out, all-encompassing website or directory. Rather, you should look to those staff members with tribal knowledge and institutional records, especially if you are new to this type of grant work. Go through hard and electronic file folders, talk to leadership about past grants the institution may have submitted before, and use Google to identify opportunities using keywords such as "federal art grants." If you dedicate enough time sleuthing through local and federal websites one by one, you will find that almost all agencies offer grant or contract opportunities, even cities and county branches. I also suggest subscribing to agency e-newsletters as they often announce funding opportunities.

If you are new to grant work, it is a good idea to build your confidence and experience before applying for a large, federal grant, such as an IMLS grant. "Wet your whistle" with a more localized opportunity. For example, I live in California, and because I worked on a number of city grants and California Art Council grants (the state's arts funding arm) earlier in my career, I felt better prepared to apply for and managing IMLS and NEA awards.

PREP ACCORDINGLY

The biggest favor your institution can do for itself is its due diligence. Research the notice of funding (NOF) or request for proposal (RFP)—federal agency websites can be tricky to navigate. If this is your first, second, or even twentieth time visiting a site, be sure to dedicate at least an hour or two to not only reading through the RFP or NOF but also researching grants that were recently funded under the same category. Once again, subscribe to their e-newsletters, attend webinars of interest, and take heed of the program officers' names and contact information. You will need to make contact with the agency to introduce yourself and the organization.

If you are new to the process and curious about seeing what a "winning application" entails, you can contact the agency and request the narrative of your choice under the Freedom of Information Act. This is especially helpful for those who are new to proposal writing. If you are not new to grant writing, it is still a good idea to request recently funded grants and to also pull past "winning" grants that may have been produced by your institution before your arrival. Before you delve too deeply into the process, secure buy-in from your project team. Your hours of preparation will become obsolete if your team is fractured or not supportive of the process.

SECURING BUY-IN

The majority of federal funders establish consistent deadlines. For example, IMLS offers the Museums for America opportunity up until December 1 at 11:59 p.m. each year. Use these consistencies to your advantage and inform your leadership team and potential principal investigator (PI, otherwise known as the project lead) three to six months before the deadline.

Schedule your first meeting at least three months before the deadline and invite all the "power players," including the financial staff member who will be managing the budget. Before the meeting, prepare properly, and be prepared to make suggestions for projects as well as serve as the expert in the room. This meeting will give you all a chance to discuss the guidelines, brainstorm, and ultimately decide if your organization has a project idea worthy of many hours to produce and, more importantly, will yield significant results to the museum community.

Have multiple projects in mind? Pick up to three options that tie most closely to the mission of the funding organization and ask for feedback. This is when it is appropriate to connect with a program officer personally. Typically his or her contact information is listed on the NOF. Send an email and ask to set up a short call with you and your PI to introduce or reintroduce him or her to your organization and run the potential projects by him or her. Remember, agencies and their staff want your organization to succeed and are typically encouraging. They might not necessarily give you hard limits, but if your project is somewhat misaligned, they will guide you in the right direction. You can also schedule a meeting if you are local to an agency. If you attend the American Alliance of Museums conference, you can often find program officers from a range of agencies in the federal pavilion looking to make conversation.

Did you receive the green light? Then it is time to work on the application's infrastructure. When it comes to the narrative and abstract sections, you can usually take text from the general sections of past applications and copy/paste/update the new files.

In general, this can be an exciting time for any organization, and you may want to share that you will be applying for this award with board members and colleagues, but I recommend exercising restraint as you do not want to end up with too many opinions floating about your head.

SUBMITTING A COMPLETE APPLICATION

Submitting the application can be the most nerve-wracking part for any writer. There is something both thrilling and terrifying about pressing "Submit." Before you do that, though, ensure you are even eligible to submit by checking your SAM.gov registration has not expired and that you have a Grants.gov account—a requirement for all federal agencies.

Be sure to look at the attachments you will need to submit as part of the application package. Many of these attachments, such as key staff biographies and the budget justification, are not difficult to produce, but they need to be straightforward and consistent with your narrative. Reviewing for inconsistencies will take time and extreme attention to detail. Also pay attention to format. The majority of agencies are looking for certain fonts and margin settings and will not accept narratives longer than a certain number of pages.

Give yourself enough time! If you think the application will take at least eight hours, double it. Unplanned hiccups will occur and eat time. Keep in mind that most federal agencies are based in Washington, DC, so pay attention to the time zone. Applying on the last possible day is also never a good idea. Websites will crash and life can get in the way. Try to submit at least three days in advance. To keep on target, schedule monthly meetings with the PI to discuss ongoing changes to the project concept. Yes, the PI will become your best friend. Remember, your job is not to design the program but to sell the program. Ask the PI questions, point out red flags, and provide your own professional opinion when needed.

Make sure the PIs have the ability and time to review and edit each draft. I recommend using Microsoft Word's Track Changes feature to comment where you need more text. I have found that popping your draft into Google Drive gives the grant writer less control. You always want to be the one who is ultimately in control. Two drafts before the final draft should suffice; none of you want to go too far down the "rabbit hole" of finding perfection. It does not exist. The final draft should then go to the president and CFO of the organization for review, edits, and blessing.

BUDGET

Behold, the budget: the one document everybody is going to want to see. Because federal agencies can make six-figure grants that pay for salaries, payroll, supplies, overhead, and more, ears will perk up. These are the holy grails of grants.

The federal indirect cost rate (FICR) is the percentage your institution can apply to your final ask amount to cover overhead costs (if your institution does not have an FICR registered with the IRS, then use 10 percent). You may feel the pressure to pad the budget more if your institution has a higher FICR. Do not do this. Program officers and panelists will see through inflated numbers. Do your research and be realistic about actual costs, including how much effort you can apply to your PI and project staff. Do not sell yourself short either. State in the budget justification document and/or within the narrative if you think more explanation is needed regarding specific costs. Federal and some state agencies also require a 1:1 match or cost-share breakdown. I recommend not only meeting the match but also exceeding it by a few hundred dollars. Use whole numbers if you need to—make it easy for yourself. Once again, be realistic and stand by your numbers. For example, voice your concern if you see the PI, who is already spread too thin with other projects, has been written in for 50 percent effort toward the project (equating to underwriting a significant percentage of his or her salary).

The chances are that if your grant is approved, your organization will not receive the full amount, as competition is steep and the agency's "funding pot" can be reduced at any time depending on the political climate. Unfortunately, there is not any "rule of thumb" as to what reduced percentage the agency will award you. It is dependent on a number of ever-changing variables. It is always best to assume you will *not* receive the full ask amount and will need to address the gap with another funder. (Note: You will need to find other support regardless as most agencies require a 1:1 match.) The good news is that most reduced awards are substantial, ensuring the time and energy you spent on the application process was worth it. If you are awarded a reduced amount, the majority of agencies will tell you the amount and then ask for a new reduced budget equaling that number. In some cases, the agency will simply assign you an amount.

EVALUATION

Because there can be no issue of bias, the agency itself will not be reviewing your application. Yes, they will read through and ensure it meets the guidelines, but they will not evaluate or recommend it for funding. This is the job of a team of panelists. The federal agency determines the number of panelists. Panelists are often identified and asked to serve by the agency and do not receive compensation for their time or efforts unless travel is involved, and then they are given a per diem.

The team of panelists often consists of leaders in similar fields, such as higher education, museology, or creative place making. If given the opportunity to serve, I highly recommend being a panelist to see how it works from the "other side." Be warned, though, it can be quite a time commitment. Also note that the names of the panelists will never be publicly revealed to you or anyone else outside the agency.

Panelists are provided a strict scoring rubric and evaluate all facets of the application, even the attachments; however, remember they are people and being 100 percent unbiased is difficult. This is why the majority of agencies take the individual scores and then calculate the average—similar to grading on a scale.

DEFYING DISAPPOINTMENT

So you failed and now feel like you disappointed your institution? Well, do not forget that misery loves company and most organizations do *not* receive funding. For large government agencies, they can only approve a small fraction of the applications they receive. Just because your project was not selected does not mean it is not a worthy, important endeavor. It just means the competition was steep and 200+ organizations also had slightly more worthy and more important endeavors. My suggestion? Ask for the panel reviews and grow from this exercise. IMLS and NEH will send you the comments and the score sheets from each panelist while other organizations, such as NEA, will relay the comments via a phone call with a program officer. Yes, there have been times when I have not agreed with a comment or suggestion by a panelist, but remember, constructive criticism is a good thing, and these agencies want you to succeed. Take heed of their suggestions. If the project still adds value to your organization, try again the following year.

MANAGEMENT

So your organization received the award? Celebrate! But what's next? The job of the grant writer does not end when you receive the notice of award. In fact, your job is just getting started. Although the PI and the project staff are the ones conducting the work, it is your job and perhaps the job of the financial controller to manage all facets of reporting.

Your first task is to review the reporting guidelines that are typically included in the award paperwork. Some agencies will pay you the full amount up front and others will have you invoice either annually or quarterly. Smaller, state organizations, such as the California Arts Council, will pay you 90 percent up front, then pay the remaining 10 percent after the project has been completed and found in compliance. The majority will have you invoice yearly using a federal form provided on their website. The due date of the invoice or the federal financial report (FFR) and the narrative reports are typically the same. With the majority of funders, you will usually submit a progress report during each project year, then a final report within three months of project completion. Timely reporting is key to staying in good favor with these agencies and receiving the last payment.

TIPS

- Use an online calendar tool to schedule all reports for the year in the PI's, project staff's, and controller's calendar one month before the deadline. Upload an attachment to the calendar request indicating what content you need from the specific person. Remember, some budget items, such as salaries, should be privy to a select few. Keep that in consideration when making a blanket request.
- Regarding deadlines, move the reporting deadline up two to three weeks before the actual due date. This is the same thread of "moving up" the proposal deadline internally for your staff. Give yourself enough wiggle room to handle those staff members that may procrastinate.
- The FFR template is designed more for staff accountants or controllers than for the grant writer or PI. Please have the staff person who handles the finances for your organization fill this out and return to the grant writer for submittal. This form will then need to be signed by the organization's authorizing official (AO) who was identified within the application. The AO can be the financial controller, PI, grant writer, or even the CEO of the organization; however, it is best to list the financial staff person as the AO because he or she will be managing the expenses.
- Is your project off schedule? Did the PI resign? Did your contractors charge more than anticipated? Keep the program officers informed via email or a phone call. Need more time to complete the project? You can put in the request for a no-cost extension for an additional six months or year depending on the agency. This happens quite often and the agency will not fault you for it as long as you have a strong case as to why you need the extension.

Finally, get excited! Promote your project and recognize the federal agency for its support in newsletters, online, to the board, and among your peers. Securing federal grants is a sign that you and your institution are doing something right and ahead of the curve.

CONCLUSION

The key to success is proper preparation and being able to roll with the punches. Do the research, inform your team, and offer your professional opinions. Take into account how much time and effort will need to go into this project, if funded, and adhere to a realistic budget. Do not be afraid to introduce yourself to the agency and ask for clarification and/or guidance. Once you receive an award, ensure timely reporting. Share your successes with the agency and be honest about any challenges or obstacles. I promise you, the daunting application and management process is well worth it.

State-Level Grants and Grant-Seeking Strategies for Your Museum

Andrew J. Verhoff, Coordinator, Ohio History Connection

This chapter will succeed if it inspires you to look for new sources of state-level grant support or revisit known sources for new opportunities. For our purposes, "state grants" are those available from state government agencies and other state-wide granting institutions. While seeking such grants, keep in mind what Supreme Court Justice Louis Brandeis asserted, commonly summarized as "states are the laboratories of democracy" (Tarr 2018). Grant makers' priorities, museums' needs (as understood by grant makers), and historical circumstances vary from state to state.

Grants can be a lot of work. Before pursuing them, you should be able to explain to your board or governing authority that

- your museum is "grant ready." It has the capacity to pursue and administer grants, while simultaneously completing the day-to-day activities that enable it to achieve its mission (curating exhibits and managing collections, leading school and public programs, maintaining the facilities, etc.).
- grants in question will support projects directly related to your museum's mission.
- the size of the grant request justifies the effort spent pursuing it. In other words, apply for grants that will result in the greatest reward relative to effort required. Ask this question: Is it worthwhile to spend a cumulative total of X months to win a grant for $X for this project?

In Ohio, my state, we have approximately ten state-level grant or grant-like programs for museums. Some are grants for operating or project support from state agencies, such as the Ohio Arts Council. Some are regrants of money appropriated by federal agencies, such as those made by Ohio Humanities, the Ohio Arts Council, the Ohio Historic Records Advisory Board, or Library Services and Technology Act (LSTA) grants from the State Library of Ohio (LSTA grants can support museum activities undertaken by libraries). The Ohio History Fund, which I administer, is a grant program of the Ohio History Connection, our state historical society. The History Fund, made possible through voluntary donations of state income tax refunds, license plate sales, and private gifts, supports a range of museum activities: collections care, exhibits, digitization of archival materials, and small capital projects, to name a few.

Other agencies support a range of museum activities. Grants from Ohio Humanities can bring humanities scholars to museums as speakers and to develop exhibits and other programs. Awards from the Ohio Historic Records Advisory Board support preservation and digitization of archival materials in museum collections. Grants from the Ohio Local History Alliance support digitization initiatives for its members, most of whom operate community museums, while awards from the Ohio Perseveration Council offset the costs of staff training. In a related example, support from an automaker in Ohio enables the Statehouse Museum Center to make first come, first served grants to school districts. The grants pay districts' bus transportation costs for field trips to the state capitol, where students learn about their government.

Grants for historic preservation and state budget capital appropriations can also support museum projects. Certified local government (CLG) grants, part of an appropriation from the Department of the Interior's Historic Preservation Fund, are regranted by Ohio's State Historic Preservation Office (SHPO, pronounced "Ship-O"). CLG grants can support historic preservation-related projects museums undertake in municipalities that have earned the designation of "certified local government." Earmarks in Ohio's biennial state capital budget are grant like in that you must make a case for support, but whether you are funded is in part determined by the state's capital priorities for any given budget biennium (in the Buckeye State, the Ohio Facilities Construction Commission administers capital appropriations to museums).

Your state likely has versions of these grant-making bodies. The website of the National Federation of State Humanities Councils indicates that all fifty states and five US territories have humanities councils, and most have grant programs. The same is true of state arts councils and state historic preservation offices. Some state historical societies, whether departments of state government or private nonprofits, have grant programs. Search for them online using keywords such as "grants for museums in [your state here]" or substitute the kind of project for "museum"—for example, "grants for collections care in [your state]"

What should you know about grant making at the state level? The tenets listed here also apply, more or less, to grant makers and funders at the local and national levels:

- Round holes are for round pegs (and, maybe, depending on the funder, polygons). State-level grants are based on fields and subfields—history and humanities, art, historic preservation, archives administration, and digitization and access, for example. Your grant application must fit hand in glove with a funder's category for your proposal to stand a chance. Do not try to fit a square peg—your idea for a grant project—into the round hole of the grant maker's rules unless you have contacted the grant maker first and he or she, after hearing your idea, encourages you to apply.
- "State" means the "entire state." State-level grants are fair game for any eligible applicant within that state's boundaries. If your museum is in a traditionally underserved part of your state, according to the grant maker and your research, then your application could gain a competitive advantage compared to those from geographic areas that the grant maker thinks are overserved. If the application guidelines state

that "we seek proposals from applicants not widely served by us previously," make sure to emphasize that your area has not (if so), make sure other parts of your application are strong, and answer all key questions.

- Be creative. Be strategic. A variety of grants from state-, local-, or national-level grant makers can help your museum accomplish shorter-term objectives that will help your institution achieve its longer-term goals. If your museum's overarching goal is to create better storage and access for the collection, a grant from the Ohio History Fund will pay for the purchase of storage boxes and shelving (for example), while funding from the Ohio Historic Records Advisory Board will enable your archivist to arrange and describe the papers of historical personages represented in your collection. A grant from the Ohio Arts Council will help your museum develop a disaster preparedness plan (if you are an arts organization). A grant from Ohio Humanities will bring to your museum an engaging speaker to explain how the contents of collections—archival, three dimensional, and digital—enrich our understandings of the human condition and can raise public awareness for your museum's importance to your community. These are just a few ideas of how to deploy grants from state-level funders. A conservation assessment program grant, offered cooperatively by the Institute of Museum and Library Services and the American Institute for Conservation of Historic and Artistic Works, will bring experts to your institution to help you identity priorities for collections care. Preservation assistance grants from the National Endowment for the Humanities (NEH) will assist with the purchase of collections care equipment and supplies and support other collections-related projects. Think creatively and strategically about your grant seeking. Which of your museum's needs best fit state, local, or national grant makers' priorities? Which grants do you think you can win with the least amount of effort?
- Contextualize your project appropriately. When I pointed out to a colleague that writing this chapter challenged me to compare grant making on local, state, and national levels, she said that this is how she thinks of grants all the time! She teaches in a university history department that also operates a museum. She pursues grants for projects that will help the museum interpret aspects of communities shared within. The context into which she places a project depends on the funder. If her target is a national funder, such as NEH, she describes how the project will explicate subjects of national interest in a local context. If the proposal is for a state-level funder, such as the Ohio History Fund or Ohio Humanities, she emphasizes the state context. If the grant is to a local or regional funder, the local connections take precedence. She underscored that the project remains essentially the same, but the aspects she highlights depends on the funder, whether national, state, or local in scope. She pursues grants that help her accomplish her institution's goals and contextualizes accordingly.
- Remember that funding decisions are usually made by committees, depending on the grant program. Some members of a committee may love your application and want to fund it. Others may not. The administrator of the grant program may be your point of contact and may (or may not) be one of the deciders. I am not suggesting you lobby individual committee members on behalf of your application. That is unseemly and subverts the funder's review process. Rather, you should attempt to find out the

general qualifications of the reviewers and write your application accordingly. Is the committee composed of fellow professionals from the field, political appointees, or the board of trustees of the grant-making organization—or all the above? Target your application accordingly. Accept the challenge that your application must be specific enough to demonstrate to the experts that you know what you are doing and general enough to demonstrate to the entire committee that it matters. Explaining clearly and concisely the "so what?" and "how?" of a project should be every grant writer's goal because they are every grant reviewer's favorite questions.

- Walt Disney was right: "It's a small world after all." Assume grant program administrators at state, local, and national levels know each other—or that they can easily make each other's acquaintance—and that they talk about applicants. Administrators of different grant programs talk among themselves when they have questions or concerns about an applicant. A grant seeker's reputation can precede it, for good or ill. Do what you can to ensure your museum's reputation is sterling in the eyes of a grant maker, or, if you know it is not, contact a program officer and explain what you have done to right past missteps.
- Copy and paste with care. As with any grant, make sure your application addresses the requirements spelled out in the application guidelines. Different programs have different guidelines. Copying and pasting from one grant application to another can be a time saver, but cut, paste, and revise extensively to conform to the requirements of the application at hand. Grant reviewers spot sloppy cut and paste attempts quickly, to the detriment of the grant seeker. Ask peers to play the grant maker and review your work to make sure that you meet all requirements and that everything is crystal clear. The best reviewers are those who are not as close to the project as the grant writer but understand the project's purpose. Proofreading and budget math checking by another set of eyes ensures that careless mistakes will not compromise your hard-wrought proposal.

State-level grants exist on that middle ground between local grant makers, whose focus can be a wide range of projects within a geographic community, and national-level grant makers, whose purview is the whole country and who want to support projects that provide nationwide examples for innovation and implementation. Treading onto this middle ground, it can seem that grant making is rather "bureaucratic." Depending on the grant, application requirements may not take on the hue of red tape but can manifest ever-deepening shades of pink. A grant seeker in a smaller community who has enjoyed success by writing one- or two-page letters to local service clubs or foundations where the local museum is liked may find the length and requirements of state- or national-level grant applications daunting at first glance.

There is a reason for those requirements, however. Grant makers are accountable too. They must justify the good their grant programs do—to help you, after all. If you do not understand why a grant maker needs this or that bit of information, ask. There is likely a good reason why an application asks for your museum's "state nonprofit entity number" or the name and district number of your organization's state senator and representative (and if a grant maker does not have a good reason, maybe it is time to revise the application).

There is also the matter of distance. In a smaller community, a local museum's good reputation combined with the board members' and staffs' strong web of relationships can bolster the words in a letter of application to a local funder (given the letter addresses all application requirements well). In distant state or national headquarters (or a major metropolitan area), a grant maker receives tens or hundreds of applications from its service area. Your working assumption should be that your grant maker will come to know your organization and its needs mainly through the words you write and the budget you compile in your application. If your application raises questions, you cannot rely solely on your institution's good local reputation to bridge gaps in understanding. Blanks and boxes asking this and that on a grant application are a grant maker's attempt to bridge these gaps, give all applicants an equal shot at success, and remain accountable. (And at the state and national levels, you must build a good reputation too.)

Compared to the other grant and revenue opportunities described in this book, why should you consider state-level grants? Obviously, grants result in money that supports your museum's mission and makes your community a better place in which to live. State-level grants are also "tree shakers," as are counterparts at the federal and local levels. The receipt of a state grant, especially if competitive, can inspire local givers to take new looks at you. How many of us have heard this: "I've lived in town for thirty years, and this is the first time I've visited the museum." The same is true of funders. The Ohio History Fund, the program I administer, made a $14,000 grant to the Fayette County Historical Society in 2015 to repair the windows on the second and third floors of the Fayette County Museum, the 1875 Morris-Sharp House. The construction the public saw around the house as a result and the society's promotion of the grant generated local donations to make other repairs. Those activities snowballed into a $25,000 state capital appropriation to install central air conditioning in the house, making it a more comfortable place to visit and to volunteer and stabilizing the environment for the museum's collection.

The receipt of grant money and the completion of projects are important. So is the pride and confidence that result from a grant award! Winning grants on the state level demonstrates to local constituents that the museum is worth their (continued) support. Grant getting boosts a museum's faith in itself and gives it the confidence to ask for more. Winning grants from outside of your community, ironically, can also bring more of the community you serve to your door—more volunteers, more visitors, and more donors. What is true of investing is true of grant seeking: past performance is no guarantee of future results. Successful grant seeking, however, becomes a part of the museum's history and creates legacies to which future leaders can aspire.

BIBLIOGRAPHY

Books and Articles

Brophy, S. S. *Is Your Museum Grant Ready: Assessing Your Organization's Potential for Funding.* American Association for State and Local History Book Series. Lanham, MD: AltaMira Press, 2005.

Cilella, S. G., Jr. *Fundraising for Small Museums: In Good Times and Bad.* American Association for State and Local History Book Series. Lanham, MD: AltaMira Press, 2011.

Hruska, B. "Oh Just Write a Grant and Fix the Building: Landing Grants to Support Your Institution." In *Small Museum Tool Kit 2: Financial Resource Development and Management*, edited by C. Catlin-Legutko and S. Klingler, 57–80. American Association for State and Local History Book Series. Lanham, MD: AltaMira Press, 2012.

Tarr, G. A. "Laboratories of Democracy?" Paper prepared for Rutgers University, Camden, Center for State Constitutional Studies. https://statecon.camden.rutgers.edu/sites/statecon/files/publications/lab.pdf. Accessed April 2018.

Verhoff, A. "History Fund Recipient: Fayette County Historical Society." *The Local Historian* 33, no. 4 (September/October 2017): 5–6. https://www.ohiohistory.org/OHC/media/OHC-Media/Fayette-Co-Hist-Soc_HF_LH_Sept-Oct2017.pdf. Accessed April 2017.

Websites

Collections Assessment for Preservation Program (CAP), Institute of Museum and Library Services. https://www.imls.gov/grants/available/collections-assessment-preservation-program-cap. Accessed April 2018.

Federation of State Humanities Councils/Council Programs. http://www.statehumanities.org/program/ Accessed March 2018.

National Assembly of State Arts Agencies/About State Arts Agencies. https://nasaa-arts.org/state-arts-agencies/. Accessed March 2018.

National Endowment for the Humanities/Preservation Assistance Grants for Smaller Institutions. https://www.neh.gov/grants/preservation/preservation-assistance-grants-smaller-institutions. Accessed April 2018.

National Park Service/Certified Local Government Program. https://www.nps.gov/clg/. Accessed March 2018.

Ohio Arts Council/Grants. http://www.oac.ohio.gov/grants. Accessed March 2018.

Ohio Facilities Construction Commission. http://ofcc.ohio.gov/Services-Programs/Cultural-Facilities-Grant-Program. Accessed April 2018.

Ohio Historical Records Advisory Board/Grants. http://www.ohrab.org/grants/. Accessed March 2018.

Ohio History Connection/Ohio History Fund. https://www.ohiohistory.org/historyfund. Accessed March 2018.

Ohio History Connection/State Historic Preservation Office/Certified Local Government Program. https://www.ohiohistory.org/preserve/state-historic-preservation-office/clg. Accessed March 2018.

Ohio Humanities/Grants. http://www.ohiohumanities.org/grants/. Accessed March 2018.

Ohio Local History Alliance/What We Do. http://www.ohiolha.org/what-we-do/grants/. Accessed March 2018.

Ohio Preservation Council/Grant. http://opc.ohionet.org/opcjoomla/resources/opc-grant. Accessed March 2018.

Preservation Assistance Grants for Smaller Institutions, National Endowment of the Humanities. https://www.neh.gov/grants/preservation/preservation-assistance-grants-smaller-institutions. Accessed April 2018.

State Library of Ohio/Library Services and Technology Act (LSTA) grants. https://library.ohio.gov/services-for-libraries/lsta-grants/. Accessed April 2018.

21

Perseverance and Success

The National Endowment for the Humanities Sustaining Cultural Heritage Collections Implementation Grant

Zinia Willits, Director of Collections and Operations, The Gibbes Museum of Art

In 2014 the Gibbes Museum of Art (the Gibbes) received a Sustaining Cultural Heritage Collections (SCHC) Implementation Grant of $250,000 from the National Endowment for the Humanities (NEH) to relocate the fine art collection and purchase new space and energy efficient storage equipment as part of a major museum renovation. The Gibbes is dedicated to generating scholarship, exhibitions, and programs that promote a broad understanding of art in the south. The renovation (completed in May 2016) respected the original 1905 Beaux Arts building and introduced state-of-the-art systems for security, environmental controls, and collections care. As director of collections I was tasked with planning and executing the packing, storage, and return of ten thousand pieces of art during construction and facilitating the design and up-fit of a new collections storage center. Museum leadership instituted a capital campaign to fund the $15,000,000 renovations, but special initiatives, such as the purchase of high-quality storage equipment, needed additional support. I had a unique, once-in-a-career opportunity to create a quality space for long-term preservation of the collection; grant funds would be necessary. Three years (and many hours of work) later, art storage came to life by way of the SCHC grant. Achieving success with this grant was one of the most challenging projects I have tackled in my twenty-year museum career. This chapter contains anecdotes and lessons learned throughout the process.

I first applied for the SCHC grant in 2011. Up to that point I had written several small NEH preservation and access grants; my experience was not "none" but might as well have been given what I was facing. The SCHC grant offered up to $350,000 to "help cultural institutions meet the complex challenge of preserving large and diverse holdings of humanities materials for future generations by supporting sustainable conservation measures that mitigate deterioration, prolong the useful life of collections, and support institutional resilience" ("NEH Grants: Sustaining Cultural Heritage Collections," National Endowment for the Humanities, 2017, www.neh.gov/grants/preservation/sustaining-cultural-heritage-collections). This description fit our project and we decided to apply for the full $350,000 to offset costs related to storage of the collection during renovation and new equipment. We identified the grant as a possibility in September; the application deadline was December. In retrospect this was an extremely short window of time to adequately prepare a major government application.

I had two months to write a twenty-page narrative, prepare a complex budget, solicit bids from vendors, gather letters of support, and pull together all the parts of an NEH grant. As I outlined the project, contacted shippers, negotiated storage spaces, and secured bids, the narrative began to take shape. What I did not do during these initial weeks of preparation was talk to anyone at NEH. I had one brief conversation with the grant's senior program officer to let her know our intent to apply. She listened to my project, asked how it fit into our larger building campaign (which was just beginning), and peppered me with questions about plans for museum-wide "sustainability." My answers were vague and the program officer cautioned that it may be too early in the project to apply. However, she encouraged me to move forward (realizing I was going to do so anyway), advising that I fully develop the sustainability component, read all available narratives from successful SCHC grants (available on the NEH website), and send her a draft prior to submitting the application. I did none of that.

My first attempt to secure an SCHC grant was a categorical failure. We could not yet persuasively articulate how the storage project fit into a larger sustainability plan for the museum. In addition, my knowledge of "how things work" with regard to the application process was seriously lacking. Others who had dealt with these mammoth grants warned that first attempts are rarely successful. Ever the optimist, I shut my ears to all advice and soldiered on—not a good strategy. Federal grant funding is limited; project narratives, goals, and budgets must be airtight. One should plan to be overprepared on all fronts before attempting to apply.

I was humbled by the rejection but found a silver lining in the reviewer feedback NEH provided. Overall, the review panel considered our application to be strong but expressed uncertainty about the project timeline. They wished for more information about the building renovation and how the proposed project was one piece of the larger effort. Several were unsure if the museum was truly invested in the capital renovation. They required greater clarity on funding and when those funds would be in place. The narrative was admittedly thin on all these topics as it was early in the campaign. Many reviewers considered our application to be very long (perhaps it was the one hundred-page appendix) and there was widespread concern about the high cost to pack, transport, and store the collection; most wanted to see several bids to verify costs. I was curious about this review panel and asked the program officer for more detail on who they were. While she could not tell me names, she could reveal that the panel included a museum studies professor, a conservator, a museum director, and a curator. It was revealing that not one person on the panel appeared to work directly with collection packing and shipping, and most probably had limited knowledge about the high cost of art movement and storage. I realized the narrative must be written for reviewers who may have only basic awareness of the technical aspects of a project; detailed explanation of industry standards and associated costs was required. I had assumed the application would be reviewed by collections management experts; in reality, NEH review panels are composed of a broad cross-section of humanities representatives.

I was determined to resubmit the grant for the next cycle and got back to work armed with reviewers' feedback and better insight into the process. My preparation for the second try entailed frequent visits to the NEH website to read every posted example of successful SCHC grant narratives. I pored over each project description, taking notes, learning the language, and absorbing everything I could about current trends in sustainable preservation of museum collections. I watched YouTube videos of expert lectures on the topic and read reports from the American Society of Heating, Refrigerating, and Air-Conditioning Engineers on energy efficiency. I also called our program officer and asked to see successful narratives specifically from art museums, the first of many regular conversations I would have with her. While the NEH program officer does not participate in the review, he or she is in the room while debate takes place and may be able to convey nuances of the discussion. I learned a new panel would assess our next application and would not know we had applied before.

I revised sections of the narrative related to project phasing and better detailed the costs of art shipping and storage. I clarified each step and provided three competitive bids from national vendors for packing, shipping, and equipment. The second application contained specific information about the project costs based on industry standards. I was confident about the grant. The narrative was organized and concise, the capital campaign was farther along, and the language was correct and solidly anchored our project within current trends in museum sustainability. I did not have time to send a draft to the program officer but felt good about the final package. I had addressed all the reviewer concerns, established a relationship with the program officer, and found myself telling anyone who would listen about passive preservation techniques that would be implemented in our new storage center. As it goes, we found out a few months later that our second attempt to secure a $350,000 SCHC grant had failed. Again.

I was crushed. My first attempt to secure funds was premature; it took effort but was just work. However, I put my heart and soul into the second application and truly believed I had done everything required to achieve success. Reviewer comments came to me shortly after the rejection email. While all were positive about the project and its place within the renovation, this panel needed more detail about how it would benefit the humanities. They noted the museum's commitment to institution-wide sustainability did not appear to be present in the renovation campaign. One even wrote, "I was somewhat discouraged that the environmental sustainability element is not mentioned anywhere in the museum's plans, fund-raising information or other supporting documentation" ("Framing the Future: Collections Care and Storage Renovation at the Gibbes Museum of Art," Grant Review, 2013). I realized that reviewers had perused the Gibbes's website and supplemental information looking for any indication that the museum was committed to sustainability and that they found very little. At that point the Gibbes did not have a sustainability policy and the narrative and campaign information was still not persuasive enough to convince a panel that the collections project was part of a larger commitment to sustainability. I was hesitant to revise and resubmit the grant a third time. The idea of going through the process again (the writing, the letters of support, the editing, the forms, the index) was exhausting. However, I wanted to make art storage spectacular and still needed funding. Despite the latest rejection I also had a sense that the grant was close to success and resolved to give it one last try.

My strategy for the third attempt incorporated tactics from the second application and a few new strategies. I began by contacting my program officer to schedule a face-to-face meeting at the NEH offices in Washington, DC. She was very kind and assured me that phone conversations were sufficient and a meeting was not necessary. However, I was determined to meet her. People respond to people and even though she did not make the final decision, I wanted her to know me. I arranged a multipurpose day trip to Washington, DC, and told the program officer I would drop by. This meeting may have had little impact on our eventual NEH success, but it was beneficial for me to meet the program officer and personalize the Gibbes. During our time together she provided further helpful details about the reviewers' concerns with our application and helped me better understand the necessity of framing our project within the humanities, a concept I had struggled with. She gave me confidence to try one last time and was frank about weaknesses in the narrative and how to strengthen each point. I left feeling I had accomplished my goal of creating a personal touch at NEH and conveying my passion for our project in a different way.

For the final attempt we hired a professional grant writer to craft the introduction to the narrative. The project description was solid but we continued to fail at placing the Gibbes, the renovation, and the art collection into NEH's broad concept of "the humanities." I was too close to the narrative to address that weakness, but our grant expert, who was also the museum's capital campaign consultant, was not. She was familiar with the renovation goals and skillfully revised the introduction (the first impression of a project) to focus on the City of Charleston and its place in a national conversation about preservation and sustainability. She expertly weaved the Gibbes and its collections into Charleston's historic fabric and city-wide commitment to preserving the past for the future. This angle successfully aligned the storage project and museum renovation with the humanities.

Before final submission we decided to drop our "ask" from $350,000 to $250,000. The program officer did not feel that lowering our funding request would impact the application, but museum leadership was confident we could reduce the amount and supplement the project with capital campaign funds. We also created (and publicized) the Gibbes's first sustainability policy. It was basic and included practices already in place such as recycling, use of glassware for meetings instead of plastic water bottles, seasonal HVAC energy-saving setbacks, and use of "green" cleaning products. It also noted that the renovation incorporated Leadership in Energy and Environmental Design standards.

Figure 21.1   Glass Windows in the Collections Storage Center at the Gibbes Museum of Art
Courtesy of MCG Photography.

Figure 21.2   State-of-the-Art Painting Racks at the Gibbes Museum of Art
Courtesy of © James McGavick.

We submitted the grant and waited. I attended the American Alliance of Museums Annual meeting that spring and made it a point to attend every session related to NEH and introduce myself to panelists, noting the Gibbes currently had an application under review. The wait continued into the summer as capital campaign and other renovation activities increased. In July we finally received the email we had been waiting for: "NEH is pleased to inform you that you have been awarded a Sustaining Cultural Heritage Collections Grant in the amount of $250,000." We did it. The third time was the charm and the NEH support breathed new life into the capital campaign.

Managing the grant was relatively easy. A major goal of the project was to protect an important humanities collection during the museum renovation. NEH monies allowed staff to hire professional art packers and safely relocate ten thousand pieces of art to museum-quality storage. Likewise, the SCHC grant supported the implementation of an environmentally conscious preservation strategy at the Gibbes and was a true catalyst for long-term commitment to sustainability. Today the museum continues to develop art storage through smaller humanities grants that support collections care education; assessment of the preservation methods employed with grant funds is ongoing.

While the journey to secure the SCHC grant was long and at times overwhelming, it was an incredible learning opportunity. The following tactics were helpful to achieving final success. One must read the fine print of grant eligibility; descriptions can be challenging and a few words may tell you if you can apply. If a first attempt is unsuccessful, try again. Read all reviewer comments; they will provide clues about what needs to changed or added to a narrative. Introduce yourself to staff at the granting agency. These individuals will guide you through the process. If time allows, send a copy of the narrative to the program officer who can advise if there are major problems. Consider asking someone from outside your museum, such as a humanities scholar, to review the narrative. It is essential for NEH grants to clearly state how the project will benefit the humanities. Ask the program officer for information about the review panel; it is important to know who will be reading your grant. One area not detailed in this chapter is the letters of support; these are essential components of the application and should ideally be from local, state, or federal politicians in addition to project experts. Keep the appendix reasonable; executive summaries of policies and procedures are sufficient. Remember that the review panel will be looking at things other than your application to learn about your project. Is it mentioned on the museum website or in the strategic plan? If you've never traveled the government grant road, you don't know what you don't know. This chapter provides a basic framework of what to expect. Good luck!

22

The YAA ArtHouse Story

A Practical Guide to Managing an IMLS Grant

Marie Berlin, Director of the Young at Art
Institute and Community Initiatives

Young at Art Museum (YAA), now in its twenty-ninth year, opened its new 55,000-square-foot facility in 2012. The museum, located in Davie, Florida, a suburban area in west Broward County, received a $150,000 Community Anchor, Institute of Museum of Library Services (IMLS) Grant to open the YAA ArtHouse. The grant cycle was from October 1, 2013, to September 30, 2014. The vision for the YAA ArtHouse was that it would be a satellite community art, place-making space, in an urban area near downtown Ft. Lauderdale. The area called NW Gardens is owned and operated by the Housing Authority of the City of Ft. Lauderdale (HACFL), the local public housing division. HACFL renovates dilapidated duplexes into beautiful Gold LEED apartment homes and utilizes the museum's same architectural firm. These two- and three-story apartments are located within the Sistrunk Corridor, known nation-wide for high crime rates, poverty, blight, health risk factors, and unemployment.

The challenge was to bring a unified and destitute community together through art. IMLS matched money received from the Community Foundation of Broward (CFB), National Endowment for the Arts, Horvitz Family Foundation, Taylor Bryant Foundation, CSX Corporation, and HACFL to bring this initiative to life. The grant would support the opening and initial programming of the new YAA ArtHouse. The goals outlined in the IMLS grant were

> To create a strong relationship among residents, artists and YAA by engaging residents in meaningful art activities.
> To bring residents of diverse backgrounds into an ongoing dialogue about themselves and their community, using art to find a common ground and voice.
> To actively involve residents in all stages of creating highly visible community art, teaching them artistic skills that celebrate and brand the community and bond residents with each other and to their community.

The first challenge would be construction; fortunately the 1,600-foot duplex owned by the housing authority was due for renovation. The costs of contracting, permitting, project management, gutting the building, the architectural floor plans to open up the space, upgrades of new cabinetry, tiling, and flooring to the tune of $115,000 was all part of the Housing Authority's in-kind support.

Through a longstanding partnership with IKEA Sunrise, we were able to secure a donation of all new interior furnishing—tables, chairs, cabinets, shelving, framed art, wall hangings, and more—for the YAA ArtHouse. Jenny Bencomo, IKEA's interior designer, created a warm, colorful, and welcoming space for the community. Prior to the grand opening, residents painted the interior walls and assembled all the IKEA furniture. YAA also outfitted the ArtHouse with studio equipment and supplies. IKEA's donation was secured after submission of the IMLS grant, so it was not specifically mentioned in the grant. However, we included the value of this in-kind donation as part of our match; thus the $150,000 IMLS grant was matched by $170,595 from cash and in-kind donors.

The space was designed to YAA's specifications to resemble an open art studio/gallery space. Construction is pricey and there are always unforeseen costs that arise. Having a partner that absorbed that full burden was a blessing. However, I suggest you do your research if you are embarking on a construction or build out project. Include a person with similar experience on your team who has your organization's best interests in mind. He or she can serve as an advisor or liaison between you and the construction company. Unfortunately, we didn't have that person on our team. By the time the project was complete, I felt like an expert in renovations. I learned to ask a lot of questions and trust my instincts. The project took six months longer than expected, but it was a Godsend. It allowed us more time to develop relationships and build trust with residents and partners. The neighborhood was accustomed to organizations popping up and then leaving. Residents saw our genuine interest and that the YAA ArtHouse was there to stay.

The additional time gave us the opportunity to host ongoing open forums that connected neighbors, broke down barriers through art, and asked important questions adapted from the CFB's Sense of Community Test. We asked residents to respond with True or False to the following statements:

> *I think my neighborhood is a good place for me to live.*
> *People in this neighborhood do not share the same values.*
> *My neighbors and I want the same things from the neighborhood.*
> *I can recognize most of the people who live on my block.*
> *I feel at home in this neighborhood.*
> *Very few of my neighbors know me.*
> *I care about what my neighbors think of my actions.*
> *I have no influence over what this neighborhood is like.*
> *If there is a problem in this neighborhood people who live here can get it solved.*
> *It is very important to me to live in this particular neighborhood.*
> *People in this neighborhood generally don't get along with each other.*
> *I expect to live in this neighborhood for a long time.*

Each forum was standing room only, bringing together neighbors who had never met and residents who had seen the area change for the worse over the decades. The results of the survey questions reflected the following: residents were disconnected, aloof regarding impacts they could make, and viewed their residence as a short-term stop. We definitely had our work cut out for us. However, at the end of the grant period, *88 percent of those responding to questions in the Sense of Community Test responded favorably to feeling more connected to each other and their community as a result of their involvement with the ArtHouse.*

During the course of a year, YAA became involved, engaged, and invested in doing the groundwork to create community and conversation through the arts. In the nearby property management offices, YAA helped to form a resident committee that met monthly to discuss public art projects, programs of interest to residents, and any community issues. The information gathered in these meetings became the roadmap for the type of arts programming the community wanted and the optimal operational days and hours for the YAA ArtHouse.

Resident families took a community field trip to Young at Art Museum. The field trip took residents into a creative environment that promoted conversation with each other and artistic play. They visited the ceramics studio and created clay tiles with imagery that represented who they are or what they want their community to be. These clay tiles would later be used in the first public art project.

The first public art project was to beautify the neighborhood through a series of six mosaic benches. Residents of NW Gardens were excited to add color and meaning to their walking paths. The first workshop introduced Miami-based artist team Carlos Alves and JC Carroll to the community. They showed pictures of their mosaics and shared their story. We asked residents to paint on pre-fired tiles a message or symbol of hope for the future of their community. The resulting hundreds of tiles were then assembled onto the benches by residents and the artists during the first community block party. The party was organized by the property management offices to bring neighbors together. They had seen the success we had in our forums and decided to move in the same direction. A few weeks later, residents decided where the six benches would be placed. Using a large map of the area, they diagramed their walking paths, and in the highest traffic areas residents worked with the artist team and HACFL to install the benches.

The long-awaited Grand Opening on February 22, 2014, was a celebration of art, music, and food. Residents took part in ongoing art workshops in Japanese calligraphy, sculpting pots on the potter's wheel, painting, music, and drumming with YAA resident artist Chisseko Kondowe. Resident founding families unveiled the first of the six story benches in front of the YAA ArtHouse.

The achievements at the end of the one-year grant cycle were:

- 893 residents participated in YAA ArtHouse programs, public art creation, and events.
- 552 individual artworks were completed by residents.
- 165 art studio programs were provided to residents, ages four to seniors.
- 15 residents actively served on the YAA ArtHouse Resident Committee.
- 3 public art projects—Mosaic Tile Story Bench, Story Quilt, and African Batik Wall Hanging—were created during residencies with professional artists and installed throughout the NW Gardens community.

I believe managing a longstanding community-based IMLS project effectively requires adopting humility and practicing active listening. Here are my practical suggestions for this type of grant management.

- Help establish the goals, scope, and reach of the project.
- Research the organizations currently in place in the community and schedule meetings to talk with those on the ground floor. Ask about their successes and pitfalls. You can save planning and programming dollars if you don't have to reinvent the wheel.
- Document the progress of your project through pictures, surveys, evaluations, attendance counts, calendars, flyers, and any other data. IMLS required one final report. That report summarized the project, included descriptions of programs and events, restated the goals of the project, gave an overview of achievements (outlined earlier), included the results of the Sense of Community Survey, and explained our outcomes, results, and challenges.
- Gather the demographics and statistics of the area. These data will give you a general idea of the issues facing the population you are serving and how to plan accordingly.
- Establish the best way to communicate with your audience.
  - We learned that in NW Gardens the best way to communicate and market events was door to door. We added a canvasing day into our weekly staffing plan. Emails, websites, and calls were not effective because most families could not afford computers in the home and phone numbers were often changing or disconnected. A couple years later we added a community Facebook page and website.
  - Be flexible with your plans and be willing to change them.
  - For example, a partner organization was planning an event in the local park, but residents informed them that the park was used for drug dealing and solicitation. Organizers decided to keep the event there as an effort to clean up the park but had to arrange for extra police presence.
  - Partner with local organizations. You will go farther together.
  - When we first entered the NW Gardens community, we were the only arts organization in the area and the only institution that was working cooperatively to bring the neighborhood together. We now have joined forces with 40+ partners and become the Communities of Promise. The nonprofits in this group have learned to leverage their resources and eliminate duplicity for the common good. It's been a win-win for everyone. We've been able to plan an annual Holiday in Sistrunk community block party bringing 800+ residents together.
  - Pray and step out on faith.
  - This was a worthwhile but difficult journey. My organization is not faith based but I am, and I could not have done it without prayer. I soon found out that I was surrounded by a community of faith. We had a unified belief that God's plan was for a safe and happy community. YAA ArtHouse joined with nonprofits and faith-based organizations in a two-mile walk around the YAA ArtHouse to raise awareness and bring to an end human trafficking of our neighborhood children.
  - Allow the community to take the lead.

○ Embrace the old adage: "Give a man a fish and he will eat for a day, teach him to fish and you feed him for his lifetime." To make a lasting change you have to teach, empower, and then step back. The YAA ArtHouse has inspired residents to form grassroots arts and cultural events. These range from mural painting to beautify the community, poetry and film nights, monthly talent shows, and a permanent painted shipping container called the Megaphone for community pop-up events. We've inspired youth and young adults to pursue their artistic talents academically and in gaining an income. The YAA ArtHouse in addition to its own programming serves as host for many of these community events by partnering organizations.

In 2016, YAA was invited to talk about their IMLS-funded Community Anchor project at the Southeastern Museums Conference. IMLS hoped to encourage museums to work more closely with their communities so they could be funding sources for these initiatives. The future of museums is not inside their four walls but rather reaching out into the community at large. This is a belief shared by IMLS and several funders who want to see how institutions are reaching an ever-growing and vastly changing world. The YAA ArtHouse has helped the Young at Art Museum realize greater partnerships and more funding sources, but even greater is the legacy it leaves: a connected and unified community.

23

Demystifying Private Foundation Grants

Lily Williams, Director of Development,
The Fabric Workshop and Museum

Whatever your project, whether mounting an exhibition or building a literacy program, there's a good chance there's a foundation to help finance it. But knowing where to begin can seem overwhelming. While there are several types of grant makers (corporate foundations, government agencies, and community foundations), this chapter will focus on private foundations (usually independent, family, or corporate foundations) and provide useful tips to help you get your project funded.

DEVELOPMENT DETECTIVE

Before you can apply for a grant, you will need to identify which foundations might support your project. This can seem an impossible task, but there are a number of useful resources to help get you started. If your budget allows, invest in an online database such as the Foundation Directory Online or GrantStation. These subscription-based resources provide search engines that will allow you to sift through thousands of grant makers and find funders by field of interest, geographic region, and project type. They also offer additional resources for grant seekers, such as webinars, classes, and other training tools, some of which you can take advantage of without a subscription.

Don't lose heart if your organization doesn't have the capital for any of these. There are plenty of ways to get the information you need for free, it just involves a little more work. For example, your local library may have a subscription to a funder search database available for public use (usually on site). Web searches can also provide surprisingly valuable results. When I started writing grants in the 1990s, there was no internet as we know it. Today, search engines such as Google have made foundation research much easier.

Start by searching keywords that describe your project to find relevant news articles and foundation websites. Another approach is to search other nonprofits' websites for projects similar to yours. For example, if you want to fund an afterschool education initiative, looking at comparable programs at other organizations can reveal funders you may not have considered. Review online annual reports from organizations like yours for even more prospects. And don't just limit your research to the web; I make it a habit to take note of the funder plaques wherever I go—the library, the museum, even the hospital! This is especially valuable in identifying grant makers that fund in your community.

There are also a host of organizations and publications that provide advocacy for nonprofits and/or help grant seekers find funding. While some, like *The Chronicle of Philanthropy* or The Foundation Center's *Philanthropy News Digest*, serve nonprofits at large, many are field or location specific. These might target performing arts or social services sectors, for example, or a particular city, state, or region. Do your research to find out which ones best align with your organization's mission and avail yourself of their services. These often range from job postings and articles on funding trends to notification of upcoming grant opportunities. Subscribe to receive emails and newsletters from the ones that best suit you.

Finally, don't forget to tap your own board for leads. Most nonprofits select board members not only for their personal giving capacity but also for their influence and connections. Take advantage of these. Often development officers think of their board as being helpful only in identifying other individual funders, but your board members may sit on foundation boards as well, or they may be involved with other organizations that receive funding from grant makers you haven't considered. Contact your board members and set up one-on-one meetings to brainstorm about your project, who they know in the grant-making community, and how they might help you connect with potential foundation funders.

THE MATCH GAME

Once you've identified a list of potential funders, it's time to dig deeper. Visit their websites (if they have them) or contact them directly to ask for guidelines and funding priorities. Read these carefully. Matching your project with a funder is a little bit like online dating: you might start out with a broad group of possibilities that look good on the surface, but you need to get to know them better to see if they're a good fit.

All foundations have specific funding priorities, so it's imperative that you be sure your project aligns closely with them. Don't just assume that because a grant maker funds museums your museum will be a good fit; they may give only to a specific geographic area or project type. Funders are usually clear about their limitations, such as no support for capital campaigns or staff salaries, and many give only to preselected causes. It's no use spending weeks putting together a proposal for your early childhood education initiative only to realize a funder's goals revolve around high school students, or to submit a request to a foundation that funds organizations with budgets under $100,000 if you're a multimillion-dollar nonprofit.

Also pay attention to nuance. For example, a funder might state "preference given to" or "does not typically fund." In cases like these, if your project seems to align in every other respect, contact the funder—foundation websites will usually tell you if they prefer phone calls or email—and ask the program officer for guidance. Not only do these sorts of conversations help you decide whether or not to apply for your current project, they also put you on the foundation's radar for future or different initiatives.

Once you think you have a good fit, look at the projects the grant maker has funded in the past. This is especially true of smaller foundations, which may not even have a website. The best place to find this information is in a foundation's 990. These are publicly available tax documents and a basic free account at GuideStar will give you access. Understanding a 990 can seem daunting at first, but a careful read will provide not only the foundation's assets, amount of money they've recently given, to whom, and sometimes for what project but also a list of officers and directors. Understanding past behavior is useful to determining if your organization or project is a good fit for a particular funder.

BUILD A RELATIONSHIP

Now that you've done your homework, it's time to begin the relationship-building process. Many grant seekers skip this step, but that would be a mistake. While the guidelines and priorities of a foundation determine what type of projects it supports and precludes, it is ultimately human beings who make the funding decisions, selecting between many equally worthwhile proposals. And if the program officers, board members, and staff of a foundation are enthusiastic about your project, you have a much greater chance of going to the top of the list.

Even if you don't have specific questions about how suitable your project is for a given foundation, reaching out to a program officer is a great way to begin to build a relationship. Emails are probably the most effective way to begin. Write the program officer or other foundation contact and tell them a little (no more than a paragraph—you can always provide a link to your website) about your organization and its mission. Say that you have a project you think the foundation might be interested in and ask if you can arrange a time for a phone call to discuss it further. The response you receive will give you a lot of information not only about whether or not the funder is interested in hearing more but also how they like to communicate. Some will readily arrange a call, while others may say that all the information you need is on their website. Respond accordingly.

If possible, a personal conversation provides an unparalleled opportunity to learn more about the foundation's priorities and grant-making process. Foundation staff are often more candid one on one than they are able to be in print. Of course, be sure to have read the foundation's guidelines first and be prepared; you don't want to ask questions whose answers appear on their websites or other written materials.

Find out everything you can about their grant-making process, such as when grants are made and how often, and particularly who actually makes the funding decisions. This will help you develop a cultivation strategy. For example, sometimes the foundation staff reviews proposals and makes a first cut, then sends recommendations to a board or funding committee. In this case, getting the program officer excited so he or she advocates for your proposal gives it a much better chance of success. Other times, a single person has the sole authority to distribute funds. There are a lot of models, but there's one thing they share: the better you are at building personal relationships throughout the process, the more likely you are to receive a grant.

No matter what their reply—even if they say they're not interested in your project or supporting you at the moment—don't be discouraged. Play the long game. Cultivation—sometimes years of it—is key to success in receiving foundation support. Put grant makers on your mailing list (with their permission) so that they receive regular updates on your projects. Find opportunities to invite them to events, even (actually especially) when you're not asking for money. Talk to your board to see if they know someone in a leadership position at the foundation who they might personally invite to tour your organization. Be creative and find ways to engage the people behind the foundation. And remember those foundations that fund only preselected organizations? You may find that patient cultivation ultimately lands you on that list.

KNOW THE GROUND RULES

Now that you've identified the perfect funder for your project, you're ready to write, right? Not so fast. Have you carefully read the foundation's instructions? I can't tell you how many times I've seen grant seekers submit a proposal only to find that they've skipped a step or omitted an essential element.

Some funders, for example, require a letter of inquiry (LOI) before inviting you to submit a proposal. Depending on the grant maker, this can be something as simple as a brief letter describing your project to a form in which you answer preset questions. An LOI is not only valuable in helping you organize your thoughts and the shape your ultimate grant request, but it could save you the time and effort of writing a full proposal that isn't a good fit for a funder.

If your LOI is approved, you've gotten past a big hurdle and can move on to the full proposal. Even if it's declined, though, you should take the time to contact the program officer and ask if there is something that you can do to achieve a better result next time. It may be that even after all your research, your project just isn't the right fit (though hopefully this is something you would have figured out in the relationship-building phase). But it's equally likely that you have failed to present your case in a compelling way. Following up could provide valuable information and can help you succeed in the future.

When reading a foundation's instructions, pay attention to deadlines: While some grant makers accept proposals on a rolling basis, most have specific dates by which you need to submit in order to be considered during a particular funding round. Another thing to note is the format in which a foundation prefers your proposal be submitted. Some ask you to send it (often multiple copies) by mail, while others want you to submit it by email or through an electronic grant portal.

If using a grant portal, (which can be complicated and notoriously temperamental), I cannot overemphasize how important it is to thoroughly familiarize yourself with the site well before you begin writing. Sometimes you will find sections buried within sections. No one wants to hit the "send" button only to receive an error message. I strongly recommend you compose and save your narrative or answers to questions in Word before copying onto the online form. This may feel like an unnecessary step, but I have more than once thought the portal was saving my responses only to have my work mysteriously disappear. Additionally, Word has features like spell check and word count that most online forms don't. You may notice that when you paste your text into the form, you've lost formatting as some don't support bold or italics. This isn't uncommon, so be sure to reread your proposal in the portal to be sure it still makes sense. If a foundation uses word or character counts (and pay attention to which one—I've known people to write five hundred words when the response was limited to five hundred characters!), always scroll to the end of the section and be sure your response hasn't been truncated. Finally, it may seem obvious, but when you begin completing the form and uploading attachments, be sure to save frequently.

Whatever format, be certain you know all the required elements well ahead of time. These usually include a narrative, project budget, and supporting documents. Developing a project budget is one of the most important parts of any proposal. Pay careful attention to what elements a funder will and won't support. For example, some foundations won't support indirect costs, such as overhead, administrative costs, and salaries. Others may require your organization match the amount of their grant and will often ask you what other funders you have secured or plan to approach. Draft your budget accordingly.

Begin gathering required supporting documents as early as possible. These can include photos, videos, audited financial statements, proof of nonprofit status, letters of support from partners, and biographies of key staff. Be sure you are clear on what format these documents need to be in and, in the case of photos and videos, the number and length required. Sometimes you will be able to submit additional attachments of your choice, so be strategic with these and think about what will give the funder a more complete picture of your project. If your organization has recently been featured in a terrific article, for example, here's the place to include it.

TELL YOUR STORY

Now that you are finally getting down to the business of writing, remember the three Cs of a successful grant proposal: Clear, Concise, and Compelling.

Clear

Before you write a word, become an expert on your project. Talk to all the project stakeholders and take notes. Don't assume your reader knows all about your project or even your organization. A funder I know often says, "it doesn't go without saying." If you are able, share a draft of your proposal with someone who doesn't know much about your project. The questions he or she asks can reveal where your proposal lacks clarity. Some program officers will even offer to do a preliminary review of your proposal and provide feedback if you send it to them in plenty of time. Do it! This is an unparalleled opportunity to fine tune your pitch.

Concise

Once you've gathered as much information as you can, start with an outline to clarify your thinking and direct the structure of your writing. This not only allows you to identify areas where you may need more information to build a case for support, but it also makes the final proposal much easier for the reader to follow. And be as brief as you can while still making a strong case. Not only may you be constrained by word and character counts, but overlong narrative sections tend to lose readers.

Compelling

No matter how strong your mission or impactful your programs, you won't succeed if you don't present them so that funders relate to them. That's where storytelling comes in. Start with the facts, but be sure to add the human touch. Take the reader on a journey. Testimonials, anecdotes, and quotes can be effective when used sparingly. Read and reread what you've written not only for errors but also to be sure that you have built a persuasive case.

I always try to answer the questions:

- Why is this project important right now?
- What is its impact?
- Who does it serve?
- How does it align with the funder's priorities?
- How will this grant make a difference?

Of course, it's not only words that tell the story. Numbers, statistics, and analysis are key components of successful grant proposals. How many people does your project serve? Who are they? What outcomes do you anticipate? How do you know? If you are asking for funding for an ongoing program, this is where you want to highlight past successes and include evaluations.

Finally, build a day or two into your schedule to walk away and come back to your proposal with fresh eyes. You might be surprised at the odd typo you missed or a section that's not quite as clear as you thought. Once you've done this, it's time to submit your request.

FOLLOW THROUGH

Most funders' guidelines will tell you when to expect a decision on your request. If you hear that you haven't been funded, don't despair. Failure, more than success, is a learning opportunity. Try to have a conversation with the program officer about what you could have done better. Foundations usually have set budgets and many worthwhile organizations vying for funding. It could just be that your project or the case you made wasn't as compelling as theirs. Depending on your project and the foundation's guidelines, you may be eligible to apply for the next round of funding. You'll have a greater chance for success if you apply what you've learned.

If you receive the good news that you've been funded, congratulations! But you're still not done. First, be sure to send an acknowledgment, tax receipt, and any required forms (such as a grant agreement) right away. Nearly all foundations also have terms you will need to meet to actually get your check or qualify for future funding. These often include acknowledging the foundation in specific ways using approved language in project-related materials. Most also require narrative and financial reports throughout the grant period. Read the terms of your grant carefully and be sure to put any necessary follow up on your calendar. Finally, continue to strengthen your connection to the funder with good stewardship practices. Invite them to participate in events associated with your project and send materials and press related to it. Remember, you aren't just seeking a one-time grant, you're building an enduring relationship that will sustain your organization for years to come.

Expert Opinion: Building Relationships with Private Foundations

Gary N. Smith, President and Texas History Program Officer, Summerlee Foundation

What are the key factors that determine if you will fund or sponsor an institution?

The key factors are the quality of the proposal and the strength of the organization. A good proposal from an organization that we know has good governance and follows best practices in their operations will be a good candidate. Particularly for museums, we prefer (but don't require) AAM accreditation and clear indication that they work from a knowledge of best practices and have professional staff carrying out their operations. If they are a very small operation, we like some indication that they are working with or consulting with qualified people. We also need to know that the organization is already receiving support from their local community and that their board is being supportive. Finally, it is important that applicants read our grant guidelines carefully to make sure that they are submitting an eligible proposal.

How do you prefer to build relationships with institutions?

We ask that applicants begin with a telephone appointment to discuss a proposed project. If I don't already know the organization, I will spend time looking at their website and any other information available online. Whenever possible, I conduct site visits so that I can meet with applicants face to face and see their project and community first hand. I personally enjoy getting to know applicants and their organizations, and it helps me to work with them to craft the strongest possible proposals. I also enjoy hearing from organizations informally from time to time—whether they have a current ask in front of us or not.

What are the most common misconceptions that institutions have when they approach you for funding?

In general, it is difficult for applicants to understand that foundations have annual budgets, funding guidelines they must follow, and a board of directors that makes the final decisions on grants. Given those factors, and the large number of applications most foundations receive, no proposal, no matter how worthy or well presented, is guaranteed to succeed.

Some applicants are too inwardly focused when developing a funding proposal. What seems like the best and most compelling project to an applicant might still miss the mark without some objective vetting. Development staff and executive directors need to "think like a donor." An applicant should always ask themselves: "If it were my money, would I fund it?"

Have your funding preferences changed over the past five years? How often do you reevaluate funding preferences?

Our funding preferences have not changed significantly since we operate very closely to our founding donor's intent and will continue to do so. We occasionally launch an initiative of our own in collaboration with one or more organizations, but for the most part we respond to the grants that we receive. We believe that the professionals working in the field know better than we do what they need.

What goals, metrics, and/or indicators do you use to evaluate the performance of your funding or sponsorship activities?

Our foundation supports the protection of animals and the promotion and preservation of Texas history. Within those two broad categories we support a great variety of organizations which sponsor a wide range of projects. Because of these factors we do not have statistically based evaluations, but rather rely heavily on the progress reports we receive and our own site visits to evaluate the success of projects. Most of our history grants are for preservation or research projects, a museum exhibit, a seminar, or other public programs. These are fairly easy for us to evaluate for effectiveness and audience participation. We of course value projects that have lasting impact, but we realize that most funded projects have a more immediate, if still important, impact.

How do you use that information to develop future funding or sponsorship activities?

We do appreciate candid feedback in progress reports and final reports. If a project has been successful, we like to hear some detail of how and why it was successful. But it is also valuable to hear from people who share information about a project that did not work out as planned. Both kinds of feedback help inform future grant funding.

25

The Greenwood Fund

Using a Donor-Advised Fund to Support Small Museums

Alyssa Kopf, Vice President of Strategic Services; and
Kelly Purdy, Deputy Vice President, the Philanthropic
Services Group at the Denver Foundation

Colorado is home to all kinds of museums, big and small, proper and peculiar. While the major institutions receive the most attention and log the most visitors, smaller museums play an essential role in preserving our heritage and history on a human scale.

After years of working in large museums, Charles Patterson III has a passion for conservation and is helping to preserve the collections of small museums in Colorado and Wyoming. Mr. Patterson spent his career as a restorer, archivist, and curator working in range of institutions with a wide range of collections.

"I've worked in major museums and small museums do compare in importance once placed in the setting of that community," said Patterson. "In the history museums in Wyoming, every artifact in the museum relates to a person and family from that town." Patterson believes that the preservations of those small museum artifacts is central to the preservation of America's past (Kopf 2017).

The artifacts on display in many smaller museums are often the everyday objects of our ancestors made significant by the passing of time. Unlike written history and photographs, artifacts provide a tangible connection to the past and allow us to jump back in time to share the lives of families, miners, farmers, cowboys, and artisans from the nineteenth and twentieth centuries.

Patterson started the Greenwood Fund in 2010, a donor-advised fund of the Denver Foundation that provides small grants for artifact preservation and collection care to museums in Colorado and Wyoming. Currently, the Greenwood Fund gives between twelve and twenty grants per year, typically ranging from $500 to $1,500.

"I found out about the plight of small museums over a long period of time when I was paid to go out in the field and visit all sizes of museums for conservation assessments," said Patterson. "I saw that need was a common denominator, often for the basic materials like tissue paper, shelving, light filtering, and locks on the doors. The solutions are often right there and we are able to address them through Greenwood Fund support" (Kopf 2017).

A recent grant from the Greenwood Fund helped the University of Denver Museum of Anthropology safely preserve its collection of artifacts from the Ludlow Massacre, a tragic confrontation between striking miners, private security, and the Colorado National Guard. The artifacts from the broken and burned tent colony of 1914 bring to life the stories of the men, women, and children who died in the strike-breaking raids: an abandoned women's shoe, the tags and headlamps of the striking miners, and everyday household items such as children's toys, tins pierced with bullet holes, and a collection of colorful buttons.

"It is such a mixture of material," Patterson explained. "There are some solid items, other sensitive and fragile. Many times these types of items are kept in paper bags until the preservation can be updated" (Kopf 2017).

The collection will now be housed in museum-quality lockable cabinets with clear doors for display purposes. As a major teaching collection, there will be continued work organizing, archiving, and providing historical context for the remnants, while the artifacts prevent the past from becoming abstract.

Considering the fact that two-thirds of museums in the United States report generating less than $10,000 per year in revenue, small grants from the Greenwood Fund can play a big role in preserving the history of the Rocky Mountain West (Kopf 2017).

REMEMBERING THE LUDLOW MASSACRE

Colorado is home to one of the most violent and socially significant clashes between labor and capital in the history of the United States: the Ludlow Massacre.

In the early twentieth century, 10 percent of Colorado's workforce was employed in the coal industry, which was controlled by a small number of operating companies. Mining laws in Colorado were not consistently enforced and the pay structure for miners encouraged individual risk taking. The death rate in Colorado mines was more than twice as high as the national average.

Miners and their families often lived in company towns that dictated the quality and price of housing, groceries, and medical care. Demanding greater safety at work and more autonomy in their lives, workers in Ludlow, Colorado, unionized and went on strike. Evicted from their company-owned homes, striking miners and their families gathered in tent colonies from September 13, 1913, until the raging faceoff on April 20, 1914.

That morning, a mix of camp guards and members of the Colorado National Guard opened fire on the encampment, followed by looting and the burning of tents. Inside one tent, eleven children and two women suffocated while in hiding. Along with the up to two dozen people who perished on the day of the massacre, archaeologists and historians estimate as many as two hundred total people died in skirmishes before the strike ended in December 1914.

DONOR-ADVISED FUNDS AND COMMUNITY FOUNDATIONS

The Greenwood Fund is held at the Denver Foundation, the oldest and most experienced community foundation in the Rocky Mountain West. The Denver Foundation was established in 1925 and was among the first handful of community foundations established in the United States. At the time of their creation, community foundations

Donor-advised funds are incredibly versatile, allowing fundholders to recommend grants to a wide variety of organizations addressing their choice of causes and issues. The federal government has created some requirements regarding how donor-advised funds can be used to prevent potential misuse.

What types of organizations are eligible for grant recommendations from my fund?
The majority of donor-advised grantmaking is made to 501(c)(3) designated charities. Organizations may also be deemed as educational, charitable, scientific, or religious institutions by the IRS. Many Denver Foundation donors support religious institutions and other faith-based organizations through their donor-advised funds.

Are there geographic restrictions on my grants?
We will be happy to help you support nonprofits doing work in the United States, and abroad.

Can I be present when grants are awarded?
The Foundation mails all grant checks. It is not permitted for donors to deliver their grants personally. However, you can release the name of your fund to the organization as well as specifically highlight if a grant is made in honor of a person.

Can I request that a recommended grant be used for a specific purpose?
Donor-advised fund grants can be made to charitable organizations for general operating purposes or for specific projects or programs, with some restrictions.

What are the restrictions on uses of grant dollars?
Because gifts to your donor-advised fund qualify for a full tax deduction, the IRS does not allow grants to:

- Support political campaigns.
- Purchase silent or live auction items or raffle tickets.

- Purchase a table at an event if you or others plan to attend the event through the donation. You may recommend a grant from your fund to provide sponsorship for an event, as long as you personally purchase event tickets separately at full price.

- Assist or support a specific person or family. You cannot recommend grants to help specified individuals affected by a crisis event. Grants may go to 501(c)(3) nonprofit organizations providing disaster or emergency relief

- Support a nonprofit if the fundholder or anyone immediately related receives any monetary compensation or is in a position to direct financial decisions.

- Provide scholarship support designated to a specific individual. The IRS has separate rules for scholarship funds and we would be happy to discuss funding a scholarship with you.

- Receive additional or enhanced tax credits for a grant made from your fund.

- Provide loans, compensation, or similar payments, including expense reimbursement to fundholders, advisors, or any related parties.

Can I raise money for my fund?
The IRS also has rules about how people may raise money for their donor-advised funds. The Denver Foundation has additional policies on this issue. The only approved method of raising funds for your donor-advised fund is direct solicitation of your personal friends or family in person or in writing. If you are considering raising money for your fund, you must first discuss your ideas with a member of the Philanthropic Services Group.

Please call the Philanthropic Services Group at 303.300.1790 with any questions. We are here to help you achieve your philanthropic goals.

303.300.1790 | denverfoundation.org

Figure 25.1   Donor-Advised Funds: Flexible Tools with Firm Rules—Greenwood Funds Handout

were a solution to the thoughtful management of assets with charitable instructions that individuals had left through trusts and bequests. Community foundations were a means of stewarding those assets, growing them through thoughtful investment, and overseeing the charitable restrictions individuals had put in place.

Because this tool worked so well for testamentary giving, in the 1940s, the IRS approved the creation of the donor-advised fund at a community foundation as a means of managing lifetime giving. A donor-advised fund is a component fund held at a community foundation or other charitable institution. Sometimes referred to as "private foundation light," donor-advised funds allow the individuals, families, or businesses that establish the fund to recommend grants to other charitable organizations to meet their specific charitable goals. Individuals donate assets to their fund, receive a tax deduction in the year in which that donation is made, and then have the right to recommend grants out of that fund in the future. Donor-advised funds are a tax-wise means of managing philanthropy without the complexity and expenses associated with a private foundation.

Functionally, community foundations legally own all assets donated to the fund and have full authority over the grant making. The donor, and any advisory committee established by the donor, recommend grants that are then reviewed by the sponsoring organization. Like most community foundations, the Denver Foundation vets all grant recommendations for legal compliance. Specifically, the grant is vetted to ensure that the recommended organization is a 501(c)(3) nonprofit organization in good standing with the IRS and that the grant doesn't provide any benefit to the individual or family recommending it or is supporting any nondeductible activity (such as buying auction items at a charity event). Once reviewed, the sponsoring organization handles cutting the check and providing the award.

THE GREENWOOD FUND COMMITTEE AND GRANT PROCESS

Many donor-advised funds are managed by individuals without a formal process, but Patterson established the Greenwood Fund with an eye toward its perpetual management and a desire to make a specific impact in the narrow field of small museum collections care. To that end, he worked with the Denver Foundation to create a comprehensive process for managing the grant-making decisions from the fund. This process has been in place since 2012 and will continue long after the donor's lifetime.

The Denver Foundation worked alongside the donor to establish the criteria for grant making that is outlined in the request for proposals (RFP) that the Greenwood Fund releases each year. The RFP reflects Mr. Patterson's values and his careful analysis after a career working in artifact conservation of the challenges facing small museums. The Denver Foundation advertises the RFP each spring through promotion in its publications, through social media, and through the Colorado-Wyoming Association of Museums, an institution that has been an instrumental mouthpiece in ensuring that word of the grant opportunity reaches the smallest museums that are its target.

The foundation also worked with the donor to establish a review committee to evaluate the proposals and make funding recommendation decisions. This five-

THE DENVER FOUNDATION

DEADLINE AUGUST 31:
Small Grants for Conservation Projects in Colorado & Wyoming Museums through
The Greenwood Fund

(Denver, CO) – Please note that THE DEADLINE IS AUGUST 31, for grant applications to the Greenwood Fund. The Greenwood Fund is a donor-advised fund of The Denver Foundation that supports the conservation of museum artifacts and collections care projects within the museum community of Colorado and Wyoming. Grant size typically ranges from $500 - $1,500.

Eligibility: Grants are available to any museum with a permanent collection in Colorado and Wyoming that has current non-profit status (501C3) and that is open to the public on a regular basis. Grants are not available to individuals and cannot be used for endowments, routine building maintenance, events, or travel. Funds can be used to purchase equipment, archival supplies, and outside services.

Funds are not available for exhibitions, education, salaries, general operating support, building expansions (unless for conservation labs), endowments (except for conservation), marketing, public relations, travel, or scholarships. At this time, the grant will not cover collections management expenses such as computers, digitizing projects, or collections photography

Preference will go to legitimate museums that have permanent collections on exhibit to the public. In other words, *not* to galleries, children's museums without collections, science museums without collections, corporate collections, etc. or "museums" that are without 501C3 status.

Application Process:

The application process will consist of a letter/narrative no longer than two pages with a font size of 12 which:

1. Contains an Executive Summary clearly presenting the project and amount being requested
2. Demonstrates the need for conservation/collections care
3. Outlines the project and steps taken to address the need
4. Explains why conservation is important to your museum.

In addition to the two-page letter/narrative, applicants should include:
1. A cover sheet with all necessary information: contact, mailing address, phone number, full name of institution, and type of museum.
2. A complete description of any materials and supplies as applicable.
3. The names and credentials of personnel involved. All conservators and contractors should be identified. Please attach a resume if appropriate (not to exceed 2 pages).
4. Any treatment requests should include a treatment proposal which outlines procedures, costs and time estimates.
5. The project budget, including detail on expenses and income.
6. The organizational budget.
   a. Estimated collections and conservation budget for the year
7 A copy of their organization's IRS tax-determination letter
8. Final Report if previously funded.
9. Where possible, please contain all attachments and narratives in one file.

Applications are due on the close of business, August 31 of each year The committee will not consider late applications. If you have previously received funding, you are eligible to apply again. Notification will be mid-December Money will be available by the end of the year and must be within 9-12 months.

Figure 25.2   Greenwood Funds Donor-Advised Fund Request for Proposal

person committee is composed of individuals who have experience working in small museums, individuals with experience in collections care and art restoration, and lay persons who can bring the perspective of a museum's overall impact and impression on the community in which it is situated. The current committee meets annually to discuss the merits of each proposal and make the tough funding decisions. The committee follows the guidelines and values outlined in the RFP and gives preference to small museums and direct conservation and artifact restoration work.

The committee also provides expertise in the conservation process, occasionally meeting with applicant groups when there are questions about the proposed conservation plan or offering advice on the proper materials to use along with an approved application. This level of funder engagement is not common, but Patterson and the committee feel that it is an important added value given that many of the museums that receive funding have mostly volunteer staffs and meager budgets for this type of important work.

All grant recipients are required to submit a report on the work that they completed with the grant within one year of the grant award, earlier if the museum is submitting a proposal for additional funding in the next cycle. Given the size of the grants, the reporting requirements are relatively simple and straightforward—a simple narrative description of the work that was accomplished and an accounting of expenses. Many museums send in photographs of the restoration and conservation work, which is greatly appreciated by the committee.

Mr. Patterson's connection to Colorado and its historic treasurers runs deep. He has worked at, volunteered with, or consulted for many of the museums that the Greenwood Fund has supported and has conserved countless artifacts, large and small. The Greenwood Fund has allowed him to give back in the most personal and meaningful way possible, both through his lifetime and through a generous estate gift he has planned for the fund. Though the Greenwood Fund, Mr. Patterson will continue to preserve and protect the treasured objects of the Rocky Mountain regions for generations. For other institutions or communities, Mr. Patterson and the Greenwood Fund are examples of how committed preservationists and donors can productively support institutions and fulfill their own philanthropic goals for generations.

BIBLIOGRAPHY

Kopf, Alyssa. "Preserving History." *Give Magazine*, Summer 2017.

Donor-Advised Funds

Handle with Care

Martin Levine, Principal at Levine Partners Consulting

Donor-advised funds (DAFs) have become an attractive giving option for donors. Their growing popularity has attracted the attention of nonprofit organizations who see them as both a possible source of increased funding and a threat to their existing philanthropic base. While DAFs have been in use since the 1930s, only in recent years have they become a mainstream giving option, available to the "average" donor. Donors see them as offering some of the flexibility that was once only available to the wealthiest donor. Nonprofit organizations of all kinds recognize them as an opportunity to retain supporters and hope they will lead to increased giving. But all that glitters is not gold; along with the potential benefits come dangers. Every nonprofit needs a strategy for responding to the growing interest in DAFs: one that is sized and shaped for their organization and fits their philanthropic environment.

DONOR-ADVISED FUND: A DEFINITION

The IRS definition of a DAF is simple. It's a "separately identified fund or account that is maintained and operated by a section 501(c)(3) organization, which is called a *sponsoring organization*. Each account is composed of contributions made by individual donors. Once the donor makes their contribution, the sponsoring organization has legal control over it. However, the donor, or the donor's representative, retains advisory privileges with respect to the distribution of funds and the investment of assets in the account" (https://www.irs.gov/charities-non-profits/charitable-organizations/donor-advised-funds, accessed April 2018).

THE BENEFITS OF DONOR-ADVISED FUNDS
FROM THE DONOR'S PERSPECTIVE

From the donor's perspective, establishing a DAF provides an efficient mechanism to manage the pace and direction of their giving over an expanded timeframe; it allows a donor the ability to think about their giving over a multiple year timeframe in the manner of a philanthropic foundation, but with less overhead and cost.

Because the funds placed in DAFs are charitable gifts to the sponsoring organization, the funds are fully deductible in the year they are given, even if they are retained in the DAF and not distributed for years. While the donor no longer owns or legally controls these funds once this gift is made, their agreement with the sponsoring organization provides them with the ability to guide when and how these funds are finally distributed to charities of their choice; the governing agreement can also provide for the donor to guide how the funds are invested.

When funds are distributed from a DAF they may only go to a 501(c)(3) but, unlike foundations, there is no requirement that any portion of the DAF be distributed each year, allowing the donor to have a long-term capital appreciation strategy tied to their philanthropic goals. A donor can receive their tax deductions in years they contribute funds to their DAF but time the actual giving of these funds as they choose, spreading them out over extended periods of time. Donors can allow their funds to remain invested under the guidance of the sponsoring organization, hoping they will grow into a more substantial gift when finally distributed. The DAF can outlive the original donor's life and be transferred to their heirs. And DAFs are easier to manage than a charitable foundation because much of the cost and the burden of management is assumed by the sponsoring organization.

FROM THE SPONSORING ORGANIZATION'S PERSPECTIVE, THE ADVANTAGES ARE LESS CLEAR

A motivation for a nonprofit organization to become a sponsoring organization and take on the burden of managing DAFs is that donors are asking them to provide this option. There is a fear that important relationships and needed funding can be lost if donors turn to another organization to find the sponsor they need. As current donors raise the question of DAF availability, not saying yes risks alienating and losing needed support. Not including DAFs among giving options creates the risk that a hot new prospect will be lost.

Another motivating factor for organizations to sponsor a DAF is that they will be keeping up with their philanthropic competitors. As DAF benefits have become clearer to donors, more and more nonprofits have offered to serve as their sponsoring organizations, raising the pressure on all to keep pace.

While the demand and pressure to become a sponsoring organization may be high, there is no guarantee that there will be an actual benefit. While the funds that are given to establish and support the DAF are legally donations to the sponsor, how and when they will be released from the DAF are unclear. The formal and informal nature of the agreement that establishes the DAF will control this critical outcome for the sponsoring organization. As a widespread giving mechanism, we do not have enough experience to know how well sponsors ultimately do in capturing these funds for their own use.

Before jumping into the DAF arena, or getting deeper into it if you are already providing this option, some deeper thinking about the costs and benefits to the sponsor is critical.

BECOMING A DAF SPONSORING ORGANIZATION—A QUICK LOOK

Any 501(c)(3) organization is qualified to sponsor one or more DAFs. A specific agreement with each donor is needed and will specify the role that the donor may play in advising the sponsor on distributions from their DAF, including

- how often they can make recommendations about allocating funds to other charitable organizations;
- the ability of the donor to have input on how the DAF is invested;
- how the donor can request information about the status of their fund;
- any limits on where the funds can be directed beyond the need for the recipient to be a 501(c)(3) organization;
- any limits on the frequency, number, and size of distributions; and
- the fees (if any) that will be charged by the sponsor for managing the fund.

The detail of these agreements provides the mechanism for the sponsor organization to control their investment in DAFs.

The sponsor will need to allocate the needed staff resources to establish the accounting systems necessary to fulfill their agreement with the donor and the IRS's requirements for annually reporting the total number of funds and the value of their assets, the total amount of new donations received for their pool of DAFs, and the total value of grants distributed from these funds. With those systems in place, an organization can become a DAF sponsor.

A GUIDE TO ANSWERING A CRITICAL QUESTION: DOES BECOMING A DAF SPONSOR FIT YOUR ORGANIZATION?

Step 1: Assessing the Risk of Avoiding DAF Sponsorship

- Are donors already shifting their annual donations away from you to the DAFs they have already established and not advising these funds to make a gift to you? How many and what dollar loss have you seen?
- Are your donors actively asking you to become a DAF sponsoring organization? Are they finding other organizations to fill that role when you won't?
- What portion of your current donor base do you think is at risk if you don't offer to become a DAF sponsor?
- Are you presently receiving distributions from DAFs with other sponsoring organizations that you feel will be lost because you are not the sponsor?

Step 2: Checking Out Your Philanthropic Environment

Even if giving to DAFs does not appear to directly affect your organization, there may still be reasons to add them to your arsenal of fundraising tools. Consider other organizations with whom you compete for philanthropic support.

- Have DAFs become a larger part of their fundraising program?
- How successful are they in using DAFs to increase their philanthropic base?
- Are they just retaining current supporters or are they attracting new donors?

If your assessment of the internal impact of not providing a DAF option and a look at the philanthropic environment tells you that your organization faces a significant risk, there is reason to go further and consider what it will take for you to successfully add DAFs to your array of support mechanisms. If your risk is not great, there may be little reason to take on the burden of sponsorship.

Step 3: Building a DAF-Capable Organization

Looking at the risk you saw as reason to go forward, does the internal investment needed to manage DAF sponsorship still warrant going forward?

Each DAF must be set up in a way that you can discreetly and clearly monitor how these funds are received, invested, and disbursed. This requires having the management and accounting capability that will allow you to segregate the assets of your DAFs from those of your core operations and any other restricted funds you are already managing. Consulting with your auditor or other nonprofit accounting expert may be advisable if managing restricted funds is not already a significant part of your organizational DNA.

You will need to have the capability of negotiating a contract with each donor that clearly defines all the details of your DAF program and their specific DAF. The negotiations will need to have staff or volunteer resources capable of working through a process that will touch on several key features of the DAF, including

- the minimum size of a DAF your organization will support. This becomes an important decision related to your overall DAF strategy. A higher minimum will be warranted if your strategy is focused on retain "significant" current donors. A lower minimum will support a more broad-based strategy designed to expand your overall philanthropic base.
- how often funds can be received and disbursed to and from each DAF.
- the minimum amount of each distribution, if any.
- any limits on the number of distributions made annually.
- any fees that you will charge for the work you undertake as sponsor of the DAF.
- the mechanism you will create for each donor to advise your organization on how funds will be disbursed and any restriction you or the donor is placing on where funds can be given.

- the mechanism, if any, for the donor to advise you on how their fund is to be invested.
- any limits on where the funds may be given.

The staff/volunteers assigned to negotiate DAFs will need to handle these discussions tactfully but forcefully so that your organization's interests are protected.

Consult with other organizations in your community and with your legal counsel to ensure that your agreement is proper and includes all the key points that must be defined may be a needed investment.

If you are launching a DAF program, you need a system to monitor the process to ensure that you will be fulfilling the terms of each DAF agreement and staying within the bounds set by the IRS. Vetting each donor recommendation for a distribution from their fund is needed to ensure that they are a qualified nonprofit organization and that they fall within any limitations that were included in the DAF contract. There is also a need to ensure that distributions from a DAF do not personally benefit the donor. Staying current with IRS rulings related to DAFs is required as both changes in the tax law and guidance from the IRS can change the requirements and obligations for the sponsor.

A hard look at these requirements including a discussion with your auditor to ensure that your systems are being properly established is critical before beginning. Looking at the risk you saw as reason to go forward. Does the investment needed to manage DAF sponsorship still warrant going forward?

Step 4: Defining Your DAF Strategy

Before you can fully understand the cost of building a capability to handle DAFs, there is a need to decide if your approach will be passive or aggressive.

A passive approach looks to accommodate requests from donors to allow them to use your organization as a home for their DAF. It can be restricted to current donors and minimum size restrictions can be set to limit the number of donors who will be allowed to make this decision. DAF contracts can also narrowly restrict the scope of giving to only certain nonprofits and may build in a requirement that your own organization be on the list of distributions. Similar agreements can be offered to new donors if they present a major gift opportunity. No active marketing effort would be needed to support a passive strategy.

An active approach would see the addition of DAF capability as an opportunity to significantly grow your organization's philanthropic base. From this perspective any limitations on the size and scope of DAF funds would be minimized. The goal would be to use the establishment of DAFs as a tool to retain current donors and expand their giving while attracting new donors and using that new relationship to connect them to your organization's mission and value. Beyond the competent systems to manage these funds, an active DAF strategy requires an effective marketing plan and the staff needed to properly present and close with DAF prospects.

DOES IT REALLY MAKE SENSE TO BECOME (REMAIN) A DAF SPONSOR?

If your objectives for managing DAFs are minimal, for example, retaining a few key donors and being able to say yes when approached by a new major donor, the cost of getting there and the impact on your organization may not be very great. But if you see this as a significant need, either because you fear great losses or see great gains, then there are a couple of other necessary considerations.

Planning for a DAF strategy can give you a good understanding of the investments you will need to make. But it is much harder to predict the actual return your organization will achieve. The funds that are in DAFs are assets of your organization and not of the donor. But how and when they will be used remains unclear. Many DAF agreements give the donor great control of what their fund does. Because many of the largest sponsors of DAFs, community foundations or organizations specifically formed to manage DAFs, are not themselves operating nonprofits with service missions, donors may not be willing to agree to contracts that do not give them the latitude they wish. Organizations are cautious in overriding the donor's wishes, fearing the loss of reputation and, more critically, the loss of future funding.

While, by managing the DAF, your organization can deepen its relationship with the donor and make your organization's case for support from within this intimate connection, there is no guarantee that your input will be heeded. It is very possible that funds will remain unallocated over time as the donor sees their corpus grow and they prepare to transfer control to their family's next generation. It is very possible that their philanthropic objectives will not be in your direction and they will be advising funds to go elsewhere. To see DAFs as a growth opportunity is a bet placed on your organization's ability to sell your philanthropic and community value.

Thinking from the onset of how you will respond to finding that your DAFs are not resulting in greater return to your organization is important before you make an investment in building out whatever infrastructure growth you've determined you need.

Rather than going forward independently, a better strategy may be to partner with organizations that are more suited to serve as the sponsor. A discussion with your community's United Way or a community foundation about partnership options so that you can respond to requests from donors to form DAFs but not have to assume the direct burden of managing them may prove to be more productive than going down this path alone. This discussion can also include looking at how your philanthropic message can be shared with a broader array of DAF donors than might be possible only within your current sphere.

DAFs offer benefits that make them attractive to donors and nonprofit organizations. The popularity and increased availability of DAFs requires every nonprofit organization to consider if DAFs should be included among their giving options. Because the benefits of DAFs come at a cost, organizations should develop their strategy thoughtfully and cautiously. A strategy that integrates local philanthropic environmental conditions with a realistic assessment of an organizations capabilities and expectations is needed to avoid making an expensive mistake.

Section V

EARNED INCOME: MUSEUM SERVICES

Earned income is generated by providing goods and services to your visitors. In this section, we will focus on the earned income categories that are derived from activities that support an institution's mission: museum services. Those categories are 1) admissions, 2) programs and education, 3) exhibitions, and 4) collections/intellectual property.

Mission sets the parameters for museum services. Tensions can arise when financially successful programs stretch the boundaries of mission, but there is no reason why mission-driven programs cannot generate significant revenue. New scholarship

Table V.1 Programs, Education, and Tours Income as Percent of Total Revenue by Institution Discipline 2012

	All institutions	Museums	Historical sites	Zoos and botanical gardens	Nature parks and similar institutions
Admissions to live performing arts performances	2.9%	2.6%	2.9%	4.4%	10.2%
Traveling exhibits	3%	3.1%	2.1%	1.5%	4.8%
Guided tours and educative services	4.2%	2.4%	8.3%	4.1%	32%
School visits, children's parties, and programs	3.1%	3%	2.5%	2.7%	14.7%
Academic trips and tours	1%	0.7%	2.3%	1.2%	5.3%
Packaged tours, with a cultural, historic, or natural theme	1.3%	1.3%	8.7%	0.6%	5.2%
Admissions to film exhibitions	2.3%	2.4%	0.0%	0.0%	0.0%

Table V.2   Intellectual Property Licensing Income as Percent of Total Revenue by Institution Discipline 2012

All institutions	1.5%
Museums	1.8%
Historical sites	0.6%

or interpretative lenses can provide inspiration for new programs, too (Hughes 2010). Adult education programs are an opportunity to offer mission-based programs to working professionals or lifelong learners (Alvarez 2010). Foundations may be willing to underwrite new education programs (Butterfield 2010). Portfolio analysis can be used to assess your program mix by plotting your programs on a grid with one axis representing financial return and the second axis representing mission advancement (Roberts 2010).

As discussed in chapter 1, the US Census Bureau calculated the revenue by type (product line) in 2012. The following tables show the contribution of programs, education, and tours to the total revenue of institutions that earn such income types.

Neither zoos and botanical gardens nor nature parks and similar institutions had measurable intellectual property licensing income.

The National Center for Charitable Statistics (NCCS) reports the actual revenue generated from different types of earned income, and rates of change can be computed therefrom. However, the NCCS combines admissions, programs, merchandise, and other income into one category, per the structure of the Form 990.

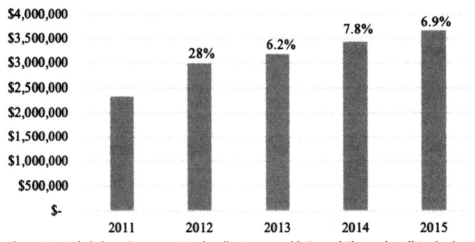

Figure V.1   Admissions, Programs, Merchandise Income with Rate of Change for All Institutions 2011–2015 ($1,000) in US$

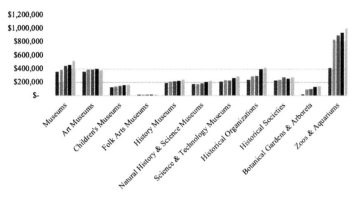

Admissions, Programs, Merchandise and Other Income by Institution Discipline 2011 - 2015 ($1,000) in US$

■2011 ▪2012 ■2013 ■2014 ▫2015

Figure V.2   Admissions, Programs, Merchandise, and Other Income by Institution Discipline 2011–2015 ($1,000) in US$

Even with these structural limitations, the rates of change, especially by institution discipline, can help institutions set realistic growth goals.

Royalties, in accounting terms and as reported on Form 990, are use fees for copyrighted materials or natural resource extractions, which are not exactly the same as the intellectual property licensing income category used by the Census Bureau and seen in table V.2 in this section. Logically, the preponderance of the income reported in this category for this industry are for copyright use fees.

Table V.3   Rates of Change of Admissions, Programs, Merchandise, and Other Income by Institution Discipline 2011–2015

	2011–2012	*2012–2013*	*2013–2014*	*2014–2015*
Museums	8.6%	13.8%	2.9%	14.2%
Art museums	8.7%	–0.1%	2.6%	–5.9%
Children's museums	4.7%	8.3%	7.7%	4.7%
Folk arts museums	3.6%	–2.9%	13.8%	–4.0%
History museums	11.4%	1.5%	3.4%	8.8%
Natural history and science museums	–0.2%	4.4%	12.1%	7.3%
Science and technology museums	8.4%	–0.9%	14.3%	10.8%
Historical organizations	21.3%	2.8%	33.1%	8.3%
Historical societies	2.7%	16.5%	–7.5%	8.1%
Botanical gardens and arboreta	289.3%	5.0%	35.1%	8.3%
Zoos and aquariums	101.7%	7.5%	4.3%	6.6%

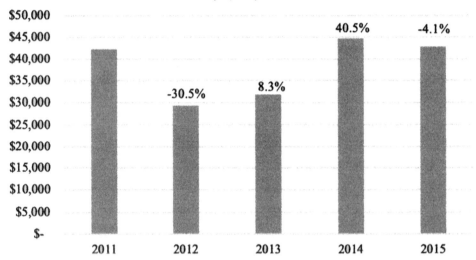

Royalties Income with Rate of Change for All Institutions 2011 - 2015 ($1,000) in US$

Figure V.3   Royalties Income with Rate of Change for All Institutions 2011–2015 ($1,000) in US$

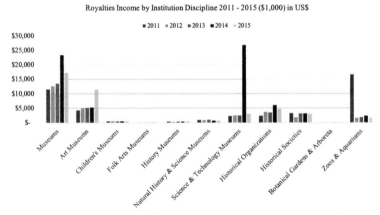

Royalties Income by Institution Discipline 2011 - 2015 ($1,000) in US$

Figure V.4   Royalties Income by Institution Discipline 2011–2015 ($1,000) in US$

Table V.4   Rates of Change of Royalties Income by Institution Discipline 2011–2015

	2011–2012	*2012–2013*	*2013–2014*	*2014–2015*
Museums	9.7%	6.4%	73.1%	−26.6%
Art museums	15.6%	3.4%	2.6%	116.1%
Children's museums	17.5%	−3.4%	−5.6%	−1.6%
Folk arts museums	−9.0%	−14.8%	24.6%	−70.9%
History museums	−4.9%	14.5%	15.3%	−12.8%
Natural history and science museums	−0.2%	16.8%	−29.7%	−12.9%
Science and technology museums	8.5%	0.2%	982.1%	−88.6%
Historical organizations	53.9%	−4.2%	72.9%	−23.0%
Historical societies	−42.4%	70.4%	−1.4%	−2.8%
Botanical gardens and arboreta	66.7%	−60.0%	125.0%	155.6%
Zoos and aquariums	−89.4%	8.1%	21.8%	−19.6%

The significant fluctuations seen in table V.4 are partly explained by the changing strategies toward monetizing copyrighted materials, which is discussed by the contributors to this section. As open access and digitization become more cost effective, the negative growth in royalties income should continue and eventually stabilize. If your museum is moving toward an open access model and has significant licensing income, then planning for the replacement of that income now is desirable.

CHAPTERS PREVIEW

This section begins with David M. Grabitske, site manager of the Landmark Inn State Historic Site, reviewing the concept of earned income and some of its key subcategories—following the structure of the Internal Revenue Service's Form 990. Grabitske explains fees, pricing, unrelated business tax income, and lesser known earned income categories. He also reminds us that earned income is critical to a successful total revenue portfolio. Without earned income, fulfilling your mission may be problematic. The next chapter is a "Roundtable" in which museum professionals discuss their earned income strategies and tactics. Strategies for funding and development of programs and educational activities, metrics, evaluation, and data are explained—including the contexts of governance structures, other funding sources, and community expectations.

The next three chapters focus on collections and intellectual property—sharing collections with the public, managing the potential commercialization of collections, and respecting sensitive artifacts. Rina Elster Pantalony, director of copyright advisory services at Columbia University, traces the history of museum commercialization of intellectual property. She reviews the different types of museum intellectual property and the different markets for licensing museum images, as well as the debate about the ethical concerns of commercializing collections that should be freely available. Open access to collection images is now becoming a norm because it is a public good. Your collection may include some sensitive items that require special considerations. Megan Bryant, director of collections and interpretation for the Sixth Floor Museum at Dealey Plaza, discusses how the museum manages access to and commercialization of its collection of artifacts from the assassination of President John F. Kennedy— including the Zapruder film. Obtaining the copyright for the visual items is critical to managing the collection; licensing fees can only be charged if the copyright is owned by the institution. In addition, the Sixth Floor Museum has established firm policies about the licensing and use of its collections, which are included in the museum's collections management policy and ethics policy. The revenue generated from the licensing that meets those restrictions must be spent on collection care, acquisitions, or public access initiatives, per the same policy. Michelle Gallagher Roberts, deputy director of the New Mexico Museum of Art, also evaluates licensing requests to ensure that they are compatible with the mission and values of the museum, as well as respectful to the original artist. The New Mexico Museum of Art publishes the images in its collections database online, which has spurred interest in licensing those images. Michelle explains how that interest falls into three main categories: licensing images directly, creating licensed merchandise for the museum, and creating products for off-site sale. Michelle explains the ins and outs for all three categories and provides a list of questions to ask before signing a commercial licensing agreement. Collections are the physical manifestation of an institution's mission. Intellectual property is a vehicle for expanding the audience and awareness for those collections. Per the contributors, you must understand the ramifications, ethical concerns, and possibilities involved.

RESOURCE LIST

Alvarez, Sarah E. "Putting Art to Work: Revenue-Generating Museum Education Programs for the Twenty-First Century." *The Journal of Museum Education* 35, no. 3 (2010): 267–77.

Butterfield, Anne. "Education: A Perfect Partner for Project-Based Fundraising." *The Journal of Museum Education* 35, no. 2 (2010): 153–60.

Hughes, Margaret W. "Bridging the Divide: Mission and Revenue in Museum Programming." *The Journal of Museum Education* 35, no. 3 (2010): 279–88.

Roberts, Laura B. "Assessment and Planning Using Portfolio Analysis." *The Journal of Museum Education* 35, no. 2 (2010): 181–86.

The Urban Institute. NCCS Core Files, 2011–2015. https://nccs-data.urban.org/data.php?ds=core. Accessed January–November 2018.

US Census Bureau. 2002, 2007, and 2012 Economic Censuses. https://www.census.gov/programs-surveys/economic-census/data/tables.html. Accessed January–November 2018.

27

Earned Income for Sustainability

David M. Grabitske, Site Manager, Landmark Inn
State Historic Site, Texas Historical Society

Earned income happens when people trade their money for something the museum produces. Other kinds of revenue depend on the motives of seeking compliant behavior (usually government) or an expression rewarding mission (membership, endowment, charitable gifts). Museums influence earned income potential by setting policies and prices, and seeking contracts.

Earned income, therefore, is a measure of strategic action. This chapter considers earned income as a strategic driver of mission. Pursuing mission with an eye toward the financial bottom line can find sustainability.

For convenience, this chapter follows Part VIII of Form 990, which the Internal Revenue Service monitors and sometimes foundations use in evaluating grant applications. Essentially there are three types of earned revenue: from self-generated content, from use of organization-owned property, and from trade items provided for convenience. All of the examples mentioned in this chapter are those with which I have firsthand experience either personally or as an adviser.

FORM 990 EARNED INCOME LINES

2a–g	Program Service Revenue
5	Royalties
6a–d	Rents
7a–d	Sales of Assets
10a–c	Sales of Inventory, aka "Museum Store"

PROGRAM SERVICE REVENUE

Program service revenue is revenues generated from ticket sales for self-generated content.

Admission

This is likely the most complex decision to get right for the institution and its community. "Ad-mission" derives from Latin, essentially meaning "toward purpose, calling, or aim." Admission is a deliberate act supporting the museum's mission. Charging admission creates a socioeconomic barrier for some, while free admission may diminish mission outcomes. Admission must strategically consider the mix of funding source expectations, needs of the community, and educational goals of the organization.

Admission creates value. Universal free admission may unintentionally signal a lack of value for what is offered. Economists study the choices people make between various opportunities. Choosing one thing means that other things cannot be done. The value of the choice can be expressed in terms of "opportunity cost": the value of what could not be done. For every person that enters there are opportunity costs—all those things that the person could have done instead of attending. Therefore setting admission prices must account for other opportunities. Consider what other museums, movie theaters, sporting events, and other such opportunities charge for admission to set your admission appropriately.

Nearly 40 percent of all museums are free or have a suggested donation (American Alliance of Museums 2013). In the early 2000s, one local history museum did not charge an admission. They conducted a small experiment with visitors that connected admission to mission. Staff studied the length of time visitors spent in exhibits while the museum was free, had a free will donation, suggested donation, and an admission. What they found, for their community, was that people who paid an admission stayed longer and learned more than any other group. Because the mission was to educate, admission would support mission as well as provide financial resources even though lower attendance could be expected.

Museums with solid total revenue often include government funding, which is meant to help the museum serve all equally. The choice to charge admission must consider a wide variety of solutions to the balance of income and access. Consider waiving or reducing fees for residents of zip codes taxed by the government partner. Another solution is to treat the government funding similar to corporate sponsorships and post regular free hours to grant more equitable access for all.

Programming

Many of the same ideas about admission should be applied to ticketed programming. Sources of funding supporting programming and the institution, needs of the community, and goals of the institution's mission will guide choices.

Here and in the discussion of museum stores later in the chapter, the museum must determine the return on investment (ROI). There are several ways to determine ROI. In all cases the materials consumed plus associated costs like insurance, rent, honoraria, and the like should be covered by ticket sales. Some museums include staff time and occupancy costs (for example, utilities) both in production and in execution of the ticketed program in ROI calculations. There needs to be a clear policy on how to calculate ROI and how to determine if the ticketed programming was worth doing.

Some institutions, particularly those owned by the government, may have "fee schedules" that govern what can be charged. Governing authorities (the "board") should always set these fees and categorize programs for consistency in its ticket prices. Carefully consider what makes certain offerings more valuable than others. Is the cost of material a factor? What about limitations in time or access?

ROYALTIES

Royalties are contractual payments to owners of intellectual property rights.

Publication

Museums—especially historical organizations—often have publishing associated with their activities. ROI remains a key factor in whether to publish or not. Publications contribute to earned income when they have great design inside and out, an index, an ISBN or ISSN, a good profit margin, and royalties for authors.

For most publications, retailers of all sizes will expect 40 to 60 percent discounts from the retail price in order to stock it and offer it at the same retail price. For example, a house museum on whose board I sat decided to publish a biography about the woman of the house to put in its museum store. Considering its audience, we knew the book had to sell for less than $20, which is essentially a meal ticket. The site paid $5.05 per unit to print the book, charged $14.95 retail, and $8.97 wholesale (40 percent off). Even at the wholesale rate, the house museum still made money from sales to local bookstores who sold it for the same price. Profits from the sale of these books then escrowed for use in defraying costs in publishing other works.

Royalties to authors vary. Museums may have a policy about staff-authored works. The institution may have right of first refusal to print the work. The institution may be due any royalties from the work if it was written on company time.

Reprographic and Use Fees

Many history and science organizations have research libraries as one of their business lines. Research libraries offer patrons an opportunity to go beyond the curated programs and exhibits to examine evidence for themselves.

Research libraries are noncirculating. The materials possessed must remain in the library during use. In many cases the research library may have the only surviving copy of a photograph, recording, manuscript, and so on.

Several earned income fees support funding preservation of these collections.

- **Daily entrance fees** might be waived if the patron is a member or lives in a certain place.
- **Research Fees**. One of the more challenging issues for patrons who are researching in contiguous areas is the variability of fees among research libraries. A regional coalition of history museums developed a common set of research fees covering

use of the library ($3 per day), the initial search ($30 for one-hour minimum charge), the hourly rate if staff did the work ($10), duplication fees, delivery charge (incurred even if the patron requested information electronically), and usage fees. Being consistent helped the earned income of all.

- Everyone pays **reproduction fees** to offset the cost of the copy.
- The "**use fee**" is established by policy as to what constitutes usage and who has to pay it. Often times the use fee will be waived for area publications (free marketing) and those with complementary missions (for example, libraries, nonprofits, schools). The general principle should be that if the user will be making a profit with the organization's intellectual property, then a use fee must be paid.

These sources of earned income should be escrowed and used to improve the research collection and maintain the duplication equipment.

RENTS

Rent is an exchange of money for exclusive use.

Facility Use

Facilities can be unique venues for all kinds of private events. However, the museum must consider both of its bottom lines when shaping policies for facility rental. While the income is attractive, is the fee collected sufficient to offset the real costs of utilities, janitorial services, security for the building and grounds, and potential damage? In terms of mission, how does renting out the facility further your mission? If rental is solely for income independent of mission, the museum may be subject to unrelated business income tax (UBIT).

When a governing authority allows rentals, the rationale for allowing it and museum standards and best practices need to be written into policies and agreements. All-purpose rooms, hallways, and lobbies are all rentable spaces. Access to collections storage must be limited to appropriate staff. Under careful supervision, there may be access to galleries, but only staff may move or arrange objects and exhibit furniture. Food attracts pests and therefore must be carefully controlled within the facility and quickly removed following rental events. Be sure to have legal counsel review all rental agreement templates prior to use.

One trend for museums is the use of historic properties as bed and breakfast operations. One organization worked with its IRS office to address IRS tests for UBIT. Once the museum satisfied its own requirements for quality programming and the UBIT tests, it was able to use all income generated for the bed and breakfast for the preservation of its historic property without having to pay UBIT.

Catering

Catering is a three-party rent: renter from a vendor from a museum. Some museums have agreements in place with a specific caterer granting the caterer exclusive rights in exchange for a percentage of sales or a flat fee. When the facility is rented, the renter must obtain all food and beverage service from the exclusive vendor. Having such a vendor can create a barrier for certain customers, but more often attracts paying customers drawn to the quality of the carefully selected vendor. The museum will need to determine whether it will perform set up and clean up (for an appropriate charge) or if the vendor will provide those services.

One museum with multiple venues had catering services for each site. Even though contracts with these vendors were uniform, the needs of the vendors varied. Seeking to reduce administrative costs, the museum put out for bid all venues as a single package. The winning bidder created a unique brand (store-in-a-store concept), lowering costs and increasing revenues for both the museum and vendor. A group of museums could easily do the same.

Parking

In urban cores, parking can be a premium both for operations and for adjacent opportunities. Museums can incentivize memberships through reduced fees or validation for parking. Museums located in common with other ticketed attendance (convention centers, performing arts, professional sports, etc.) can provide event parking. In rural areas where parking is more abundant and lacks the opportunity to charge for parking, agreements with departments of transportation to provide commuter park-and-ride lots, space for carnivals, staging areas for parades, and more can generate revenue.

SALES OF ASSETS

Sales of assets is a rare form of earned income. These might include disposal of real property acquired through bequests, or collection items might be sold as the scope of the collection changes. Whenever disposing of property, be sure to consult the *Code of Ethics for Museums* from the American Alliance of Museums. Above all, the museum must document its decision by articulating how the decision meets its mission and strategic priorities. Doing so should provide the basis for a publicly acceptable action.

SALES OF INVENTORY

Sales of inventory usually occur through a museum store—both online and physically. There are several numbers that a museum must track in real time in order to ensure success.

The most important numbers are net profit margin and volume. The net profit margin is calculated by (sales – costs)/sales. This ratio tells how efficient the store is from an input perspective. The Museum Store Association indicates that the average net profit margin in 2016 was 33.6 percent. That indicates that for every dollar in sales, the store has a profit of almost 34 cents. If the store sells $20 in a day, then the store earned $6.72. While the margin is very good, the institution now needs to explore ways to increase volume.

Two more numbers to track are conversion rate and net profit per square foot. Conversion rate is the percentage of those who buy something in the store divided by those who entered the store. The Museum Store Association guidelines suggest most museum stores convert 15 to 30 percent of those entering the store. One might also compare those numbers to all who enter the facility. Improving the number of people entering the store adds to volume. The volume of sales is best reflected in net profit per square foot, which is another measure of efficiency—this time from an output perspective. The Museum Store Association suggests that museum stores average $214 net profit (online and in person) per square foot.

Simply having a store does not guarantee success. Among the factors that impact success are selecting merchandise, pricing, design of displays, training staff for excellent customer service, marketing, and locations. The Museum Store Association is the place to obtain the most current information on effective practices. Some museums augment physical and online stores with additional outlets in facilities belonging to others (for example, co-locating museum merchandise in travel centers, airports, malls, and other locations earns income in a way that is accessible to customers). Co-locating merchandise is not for everyone as there is much to consider from a strategic viewpoint, including additional expenses for operation, dilution of brand, how to count visitation, how money is handled, inventory maintenance, and more.

MISCELLANEOUS EARNED REVENUE

Not all earned income neatly fits in the categories established on Form 990. Of all the miscellaneous earned revenue, though still exceedingly rare, these are two I have found a number of times.

Contracts

Museums might enter into contracts to provide a service. For example, a company observing its centennial may find it more efficient to pay a history museum to provide materials (books, exhibits, events, etc.) than to create these things themselves. Contracts could cover any number of specialized services such as regular meeting spaces, training for employees, parking, and much more.

Mitigation

Although mitigation is a rare occurrence and must meet federal guidelines, it is worth mentioning. Under federal regulations for federally funded projects (and sometimes mirror state legislation for state projects), when a cultural loss cannot be avoided, the government may choose to offset the loss by enhancing something related. For example, rebuilding a historic bridge to accommodate modern safety requirements resulted in contracts to document the bridge prior to and after completion of work. Mitigation also included historical markers and books about the natural environment of the crossing prior to renovation.

FINAL THOUGHTS ON EARNED REVENUE

Earned income is a measure of strategic action. The IRS requires nonprofits to report earned income on Form 990. Using Form 990 as a guide can lead to remarkable opportunities to earn income vital to the museum's mission, whether it is for

- access to created intellectual property (books, exhibits, tours);
- use of property (royalties, rents, disposed assets); or
- enhancing experiences with trade items (museum store).

Sustainability means earned income has balance. Above all, earned income must balance among its "business lines." When one business line is 73 percent of the total or higher, that level of reliance puts the organization at an elevated risk of vulnerability. Champions of earned income are well-meaning people who insist organizations can live entirely off earned revenue without "begging" donors or "living off the public dole." Colleagues within the field likewise can be equally misguided when considering themselves above earning revenue or considering this crucial and essential work of earning income "a necessary evil." Debate on how much one might rely on a given revenue stream is healthy, but insistence on elimination entirely of any revenue stream is organizational suicide. Relying too greatly on earned revenue puts at risk balance of equality or affinity considerations equally crucial to success.

A successful total revenue portfolio enhances mission, meets the needs of those it serves, and creates a level of predictability. Do all that, and sustainability becomes more possible.

BIBLIOGRAPHY

American Alliance of Museums. *Annual Condition of Museums and the Economy.* Washington DC: AAM, 2013.

Genoways, H., L. Ireland, and revised by C. Caitlin-Legutko. *Museum Administration 2.0.* Lanham, MA: Rowman & Littlefield (American Association for State and Local History), 2016. See chapter 5 on sustainability.

Greenlee, J. S., and J. M. Trussel. "Predicting the Financial Vulnerability of Charitable Organizations." *Nonprofit & Management Leadership* 2, no. 10 (Winter 2000): 199–210.

Museum Store Association, ed. *Museum Store: The Manager's Guide: Basic Guidelines for the New Museum Store Manager,* fourth edition. New York: Rutledge, 2016.

Oster, S. M., C. W. Massarsky, and S. L. Beinhacker. eds. *Generating and Sustaining Nonprofit Earned Income: A Guide to Successful Enterprise Strategies*. San Francisco, CA: Jossey-Bass, 2004.

Robinson, A., with contribution from Jennifer Lehman and Terry Miller. *Selling Social Change (Without Selling Out): Earned Income Strategies for Nonprofits*. San Francisco, CA: Jossey-Bass, 2002.

Roundtable: Programs and Education

What is your program mix (that is, lectures vs. food/drink events vs. book clubs vs. music vs. art vs. dance vs. holiday)?

Christina H. Arseneau, Director, Niles History Center
We try for a balance of traditional programming ([like] lectures) with newer, non-traditional programs. We are willing to try anything once.

Thaisa Bell, School Programs Manager, Nashville Zoo
For our school-aged audiences, we offer a mixture of classroom programs, self-guided excursions, informal chats, and camps.

Barbara Hogue, Executive Director, Christ Church Preservation Trust
We have a diverse mix: farmer's market, special themed tours, after hours tours, regular tours, performances and gallery exhibitions, archival and material culture exhibitions, musical concerts.

Lauren Malloy, Program Director, Historic Congressional Cemetery
We have weekly, free docent-led tours that are offered every Saturday, April through October. Outside of that, we generally have one [to] two small special events a month: these events could include a lecture, a special tour, or a movie night during the summer. We then focus a large spring event (as of now, it's our Day of the Dog festival), and one large fall event (now, Soul Strolls).

How do you develop programs and/or educational activities that are on brand, on mission, and of interest to the community?

Christina H. Arseneau, Director, Niles History Center
[W]e draw from popular culture a bit to develop programs and activities. Our exhibits are mostly themed to local history. We have a historic house which is a part of the history center. We broadly interpret the house to offer events on magic, mystery, arts and crafts—to appeal to people who may not be drawn to history.

Thaisa Bell, School Programs Manager, Nashville Zoo

Since our programs are primarily geared toward a school-aged audience, we use our local education standards first and foremost as a guide for the content of our programs, and then look for ways to connect what the students are learning in the classroom to wildlife or conservation-related issues. Then we show the students how they can take simple action steps in their school, home or community to help protect wildlife and their homes.

Barbara Hogue, Executive Director, Christ Church Preservation Trust

In developing our programs and exhibitions, we try very hard to connect our history with our current events and issues that folks are grappling with in the city of Philadelphia. We have developed a series of evening burial ground tours that connect the history of the burial ground and a variety of topics: beer, the yellow fever epidemic, death and taxes, and founding mothers. These late-night tours have a relaxed vibe and allow patrons to visit the burial grounds when they are not typically open to the public.

Last year, with our Neighborhood House arts program, we help to commission a new work by Philadelphia-based artist Mary Tuomanen entitled "Peaceable Kingdom" and was a contemporary approach to describing William Penn's vision of religious tolerance in colonial Philadelphia.

Lauren Malloy, Program Director, Historic Congressional Cemetery

I'm sure there's a better answer somewhere, but the honest one is that we came to our current schedule of events through quite a bit of trial and error. There was also a lot of soul searching as an organization, and some hard cuts were made a few years ago to some beloved programs that were on brand and of interest, but were not on mission, and ultimately, were not fundraisers either.

The program I am speaking about is a program called Ghosts and Goblets. I inherited this program, and during the early years of my time at Congressional Cemetery, we tried to build it as a larger affair. The event itself was structured to be a Halloween party, and guests were also given the option to take tours of the cemetery and hear "first-person" accounts of some of the people buried here. By the time we decided to restructure the program, it was still an enormously popular program, as the 2014 iteration brought in almost 400 guests. That being said, due to high overhead and other costs, it was not a fundraiser, and ultimately, was not on mission, as it was largely focused on the party, not on interpreting the history of the cemetery.

[O]ur organization did some soul searching and I looked to other cemeteries and historic sites for ideas about what they were doing. Oakland Cemetery in Atlanta has a highly successful program called Capturing the Spirit of Oakland, which essentially used the stories aspect of our Ghosts and Goblets event, and eliminated the party. Their staff was enormously helpful and generous with information, telling me exactly how their program worked and how we could restructure it for Congressional Cemetery. So although Ghosts and Goblets was beloved, we decided to transform it into Soul Strolls, which is four nights of tours featuring the stories of our "residents."

We have many more attendees at Soul Strolls, but it is spread out over four nights. Our largest Ghosts and Goblets brought in around 400 attendees, and each Soul Strolls night brings in around 300–400 attendees (we have a few more tours on the Saturdays). However, it's more manageable for a small staff: tours are timed, so 400 people don't come all at once, as they generally did for Ghosts and Goblets.

We did receive push back when we cut Ghosts and Goblets, as people loved attending a Halloween party in the cemetery. Frankly, the general public didn't respond to our reasoning about mission alignment of programs but did understand changing the program due to financial constraints—even though the decision was a combination of those factors. There are still some people who want us to bring back Ghosts and Goblets, but we've incorporated some of its better elements into Soul Strolls, which is a highly successful fundraiser for our cemetery. Moreover, it aligns with our mission and interprets the history of Congressional Cemetery.

We definitely still do events that aren't completely on mission, and I think that every museum struggles with that. But Soul Strolls is a program everyone generally feels good about: it brings in revenue, communicates the history, and engages a new audience for us. Again, I give many props and thanks to Oakland Cemetery in Atlanta, as they have perfected this particular program and gave us a great deal of encouragement when we were considering transitioning to this format.

What criteria do you use when reviewing potential programs?

Christina H. Arseneau, Director, Niles History Center
With a small staff, we try for the biggest "bang for the buck." Potential audience size is important.

Thaisa Bell, School Programs Manager, Nashville Zoo
Before implementing a potential new program, we identify our target audience (the broader the reach, the better), determine the strength of the takeaway message (something more impactful than "animals are cool"), make connections to the standards (we always strive for cross-curricular connections), and engage the students in new ways. Next, we pilot test our new program and evaluate the participants on their experience so that we can assess the effectiveness of the lesson, messaging, presentation techniques.

Barbara Hogue, Executive Director, Christ Church Preservation Trust
When reviewing potential programs, we always ask: Does it fit with our mission and does it fit with the history of the church? The church has been in Philadelphia since 1695, so that covers quite a long list of potential stories to tell and themes to focus on. That being said, there is a rich mix of programmatic areas that we work in: exhibitions, educational tours, a robust arts and cultural program, and a farmer's market. We are fortunate enough to have a rich history that allows all of those different brands to fit [under] a single brand or umbrella.

Lauren Malloy, Program Director, Historic Congressional Cemetery
Since we already have a fairly set calendar of programs that work for our organization, one of the biggest questions we use to evaluate new programs is: Do we have

enough staff time/resources to devote to making this a valuable addition? We also ask: How is this program sustainable in the long run? Specifically, is it worth the time and effort invested if it may be a one-off program, especially considering that program development can be time intensive?

How do you typically fund programs and/or educational activities?

Christina H. Arseneau, Director, Niles History Center

We seek private funds and grants to "grow" our budget for special projects or additional programs.

Dorothy Asher, Director, Lizzadro Museum of Lapidary Art

An initiative is generally a plan initiated by the board of directors, trustees, or executive staff. Initiatives are not developed without a budget. For example, larger, more expensive exhibitions require all departments work together to form a cohesive plan including programs, special events with members, and related merchandise in the museum shop. Funding that exceeds the general operating budget will come from contributions, grants, in-kind donations, and program fees to help offset any additional cost.

If the program is beyond the scope of the budget some type of extra support is solicited. We are always looking for grants that will fund general operating and/or designated programs, exhibits, and events. After that, exhibits will be in the works for a couple of years. During that time we look for project-based funding through grants, corporate or foundation support that will help offset the cost.

Thaisa Bell, School Programs Manager, Nashville Zoo

Our programs are designed to utilize the resources that we already have to minimize upfront costs. We do, however, have some operating funds available to purchase any needed supplies, and cover the costs of staff. In addition, most of our educational programs are fee based to help offset the incurred expenses.

Barbara Hogue, Executive Director, Christ Church Preservation Trust

We have two ways of funding program, exhibition, and educational activities. The first is through straight admission fee that covers the cost of presenting the program. The second way is to secure grant funding to support the special programs.

Lauren Malloy, Program Director, Historic Congressional Cemetery

Our programming is allotted a portion of the annual budget. Annual income is generated in part by interest from our endowment, but that money is restricted and cannot be used for programs. Programs ideally fund themselves, if we're doing it correctly, and our general fund also comes from donations, our K9 Corps dog walking program, and grants.

If you have a museum store or restaurant, how do those departments work with exhibitions and programs? Do you help them develop products or services to complement your programs and/or educational activities?

Dorothy Asher, Director, Lizzadro Museum of Lapidary Art

[L]arger, more expensive exhibitions require all departments work together to form a cohesive plan including programs, special events with members, and related merchandise in the museum shop.

Thaisa Bell, School Programs Manager, Nashville Zoo

Service System Associates (SSA) is a separate company that manages the restaurant, gift shop, and various kiosks throughout our park. In the restaurant, food is served with environmentally friendly tableware, and in both the restaurant and gift shop messaging is provided about conservation-related issues and how guests can take action to help.

Jennifer Gritt, Associate Director, Pittock Mansion

The educational component of museums, and then by extension museum stores, makes it a little easier to balance the commercial expectations with mission. Visitors want to keep the experience going and, in the museum store, they can touch and handle and feel similar objects to the ones they were not allowed to touch and feel in the museum. As long as the store's inventory is a relevant extension of the museum experience, the two go hand in hand.

Barbara Hogue, Executive Director, Christ Church Preservation Trust

We have a gift shop that works with the tourism department. There have been minimal efforts to develop products or services to complement our program. Though in the future, we'd like to move in that direction.

What goals, metrics, and/or indicators do you use to evaluate the performance of your programs and exhibitions?

Christina H. Arseneau, Director, Niles History Center

Attendance numbers, cost vs. donations received (most often in the form of sponsorships).

Dorothy Asher, Director, Lizzadro Museum of Lapidary Art

Evaluation of an exhibit is based on improved attendance, news and media coverage—free press, museum shop sales, memberships, tours, and program attendance related exhibit programming.

Thaisa Bell, School Programs Manager, Nashville Zoo

The annual budget, monthly ledgers, and the reporting system from our website are the primary tools used to evaluate the financial success of our programs.

Barbara Hogue, Executive Director, Christ Church Preservation Trust

Goals are measured more intuitively than numerically, simply because we have a small staff that holds a majority of the responsibility for creating program components and implementing them. There are no staff members dedicated solely to analytics. Financial programs are evaluated as to whether or not program revenue covers the cost of mounting the program. As such, we try to not add too many programs and focus on the ones that we know are successful from a programmatic and revenue perspective. For us those programs are: annual arts residency, special evening tours, and our farmer's market.

Lauren Malloy, Program Director, Historic Congressional Cemetery

This type of evaluation is only extended to our larger programs at this time, although slowly we're starting to develop a rubric to extend to all of our programs. But for now, I draft budgets for our fundraising events and set financial goals, mostly based on past performance. I write recaps and evaluations of these events based on these budgeting goals and number of attendees, but I also evaluate qualitatively, assessing with information from informal visitor feedback.

How do you use those performance evaluation data to develop future programs and exhibitions?

Christina H. Arseneau, Director, Niles History Center

We are more willing to repeat or try programs which will bring in a greater attendance. Number of people served is important since we have stable operational funding. For new program, we try to find sponsors or private donations.

Dorothy Asher, Director, Lizzadro Museum of Lapidary Art

We see what is popular or of interest to the public and what is not. Or how we can change something to attract a more diverse group of people. We also look at what age group did the exhibit or program attract and how many people were members or became members as a result of the exhibit or program. If a program is successful, we always run it again!

Thaisa Bell, School Programs Manager, Nashville Zoo

This information can help us identify trends in pricing, ideal times of the year to offer programming, [and] to maximize registrations.

Barbara Hogue, Executive Director, Christ Church Preservation Trust

One of the most important indicators that we use to develop future programs and exhibitions is can it be funding through grants or admission income? As a relatively small institution with an approximately $800,000 operating budget, we must ensure that special programs can fund them.

Lauren Malloy, Program Director, Historic Congressional Cemetery

If a program is consistently not meeting financial goals (which happens), we evaluate as a team as to whether that program should continue at all. As far as program development goes, it's still an informal process. We receive ideas from the community and feedback about our current programs, and we try to direct the specific feedback ("I wish you had more scary movies," or "I really want to learn about . . .") into programs that both align with our skill set as a staff, but also with the mission of Congressional Cemetery. It's a fluid and by no means formal process, although we someday hope to have more sophisticated evaluation and development criteria in place at our organization.

Museums and Intellectual Property

In Support of Good Museum Business Practices

Rina Elster Pantalony, Director, Copyright Advisory Services, Columbia University Libraries

Since the early internet years, museums have evolved their approach to intellectual property significantly. In the 1990s and into the dotcom era of the early 2000s, museums flirted with the idea that licensing access to museum images, if managed efficiently, could provide a good source of revenue. Museums were eager to experiment with their content and developed for-profit websites devoted to the discovery of culture and art, thinking that if they built them, audiences would flock to these sites and pay access fees for the content. The Museum of Modern Art, together with the Tate, as partners (Museum of Modern Art Press Release 2000), and the Guggenheim Museum (Bohlen 2002) were intent on creating dotcoms in part for this purpose, only to shutter both these initiatives two years later (Museum of Modern Art Oral History Program 2001).

Museums were not alone in this thinking during this era because universities also experimented in developing for-profit online learning websites as well. Columbia University, together with a number of academic partners that included the London School of Economics and Political Science, the University of Michigan, the British Library, and other academic institutions, attempted to create a dotcom devoted to revenue generation associated with online learning (Tomsho 2003). By 2002, however, these experiments failed, as did many dotcom experiments in that era, due to technology and business concepts that required more thinking and maturity. In short, business models of that era in the online space needed significant redevelopment and retooling in order to become successful.

These early experiments by museums, universities, and library partners, however, may now provide us with significant food for thought. Why did they fail, apart from the general lack of understanding about market development and audience attraction online? Were there inherent and underlying reasons for failure? The purpose of this chapter is to, once more and within a contemporary context, examine the potential that intellectual property plays in creating revenue streams for museums as a way of sustaining their programmatic activity.

Museums hold many different forms of intellectual property. In the early dotcom era, emphasis was placed on the intellectual property associated with collections, that is, museum images. While a full assessment of the types of museum intellectual property is not within the scope of this chapter (Pantalony 2013), generally speaking, museum intellectual property is often categorized as being either collections or institutionally based. Institutional intellectual property includes a museum name, logo, trademarks, and the goodwill associated with them. Collections based intellectual property instead relate to the objects in a museum's collection, including the photographic reproductions of collections.

With images of artworks driving the discussion in the early dotcom era, interest was generated at that time in what we define as collections-based intellectual property.

Photo stock agencies, such as Corbis Corporation and later Getty Images, were formed and took to the internet, and questions arose as to whether museums could do the same to generate revenues to fuel their programmatic activities. The first known assessment of commercial opportunities for images of objects in museum collections was published in 1999, when museums in Canada, with the assistance of the Canadian Heritage Information Network (CHIN) (Canadian Heritage Information Network 1999), considered the revenue opportunities associated with the practice of licensing out images of museum collections. At that time, digital images of objects in museum collections were considered primary intellectual property assets of the museum.

CHIN's study determined that there were five potential markets for the licensing of museum images: advertising, broadcasting, corporate, multimedia, and publishing (Canadian Heritage Information Network 1999). The study concluded that museum images held the greatest value in markets where consumers were willing to wait for a museum-branded image with the requisite precision and color correction. The study concluded further that where consumers required quick turnaround and cared little for image provenance or origin, museum images could likely not compete with the efficiencies presented by image stock houses (Canadian Heritage Information Network 1999).

While this study represented an initial environmental scan, it did not, however, take into account the complexities of managing underlying rights in images of artworks in museum collections. In order to carry out a licensing business, museums would have to license in the rights to the copyright-protected artworks captured by photographic images of their collections, because these underlying rights were still held by the artists or their heirs who had created the artworks and not, in most cases, held by the museums trying to generate licensing revenues. In addition, if museums did not hold the rights to the photographs of the artworks in question, they faced the prospect of licensing these rights as well. None of these licensing requirements were assessed, either in complexity or financially, in any great detail in the CHIN study of 1999.

In 2004, the Mellon Foundation commissioned a study concerning image licensing activities by American art museums that examined the actual revenue potential to be derived from image licensing of artworks in collections based on costs and revenues earned (Tanner 2004). Simon Tanner, professor of digital cultural heritage at Kings College London, the principal investigator of the study, concluded that, at best, and only with significant effort to centralize its licensing activities, museums can earn modest revenues in licensing images of their collections. In fact, Tanner concluded further that the overall purpose of licensing access to museum reproductions of its collections was carried out not for the purpose of generating revenues. Instead licensing activities were carried out by museums so as to serve particular commercial markets whose expectations were based on the licensing model (Tanner 2004). These markets are identified as being found in primarily the film, television, and publishing industries. Thus, the licensing model did not originate from the museum but instead was imposed on museums by entities asking to license their content.

The question remained, however, whether museums should be using the licensing model and charging fees to provide access to reproductions of its collections regardless of who made the reproduction request or the purpose for which the request was being made. From the outset, certain members of the museum community were highly critical of museums' early commercial dotcom experiments that extended to activities in charging access to photographic reproductions of objects in museum collections. The primary criticism was that museums had "sold their souls" by placing revenue above intellectual pursuits more commonly associated with museums, such as academic research. In 2001, Kirk Varnedoe, the Museum of Modern Art's then departing chief curator of painting and sculpture, voiced his concerns in an interview with Calvin Tomkins, published in the *New Yorker*. While acknowledging that the Museum of Modern Art had resisted, until then, the trends, he was concerned about their intentions to create a website with the Tate that had a commercial purpose at its core to sell merchandise and other services (Tomkins 2001).

Stephen Weil, an intellectual property lawyer and former deputy director of the Smithsonian Institution's Hirshhorn Museum and Sculpture Garden, in his highly respected and now classic treatise *Making Museums Matter* (Weil 2002), argued that a museum of quality will be driven by purpose, that is, its mission and mandate. Efficiencies of operation or revenue opportunities, while important, should not drive the institution. With respect to intellectual property, Weil pleads with his readers to reconcile the potential conflicts inherent in the educational, scholarly, and public purpose pursuits of museums with those that generate revenue. Specifically, he highlights the conflicts that appear in licensing access to museum reproductions of public domain artworks, thereby limiting scholarship on works no longer protected by copyright or licensing access to museum reproductions of collections to patrons carrying out scholarly or fair uses (Weil 2002).

In 2005, Ken Hamma, former executive director for digital policy and initiatives at the J. Paul Getty Trust, was critical of museum licensing activities, specifically those that were collections based and represented reproductions of artworks in the public domain. He stated,

> Placing these visual reproductions in the public domain and clearly removing all questions about their availability for use and reuse would likely cause no harm to the finances or reputation of any collecting institution, and would demonstrably contribute to the public good. (Hamma 2005)

What of the public good? What can the earlier studies, including CHIN's market study, provide to further an understanding of the revenue potential of museum intellectual property? If the 1999 CHIN study is reexamined, there may still be room for discussion about revenue generation concerning museum intellectual property, notwithstanding the significant criticism about its commercialization. The CHIN study highlighted an important facet of museum intellectual property. Arguably, it is the first study to recognize the value of museum goodwill, authority, and integrity in a commercial context. As mentioned, the study found that there was greatest opportunity in markets in which consumers valued origins or provenance. Goodwill, authority, and integrity are elements in museum intellectual property associated with the institution itself, its name and reputation, and have little to do with the collections-based images of artworks themselves.

Museums are now making the pivot in their treatment of collections-based intellectual property by providing open access to images of collections online as a means of discovery of collections. The Smithsonian Institution (Smithsonian Institution 2018), the Metropolitan Museum of Art (Metropolitan Museum of Art 2018), the Victoria and Albert Museum (Bailey 2006), and, most recently, the Wellcome Trust (Scott 2018), to name a few, have moved away from the licensing model as a means of providing access for research, study, discovery, and other noncommercial activities. Open access to collections, it is believed, contributes to the overall goodwill associated with their institutional intellectual property, such as their name and marks, and provides the public with a much better understanding about the breadth and scope of collection. This represents a win-win for the public good, for the museum in fulfilling mission and mandate, and, at the same time, provides an opportunity to increase the museum's bottom line. And, arguably, any activities that support the primary mission of the museum that also contributes to the public good support good museum business practices too.

BIBLIOGRAPHY

Bailey, Martin. "V&A to Scrap Academic Reproduction Fees." *The Art Newspaper*, November 30, 2006.

Bohlen, Celestine. "Retrenching Guggenheim Closes Hall in Las Vegas." *New York Times*, December 24, 2002. https://www.nytimes.com/2002/12/24/arts/retrenching-guggenheim-closes-hall-in-las-vegas.html. Accessed June 18, 2018.

Canadian Heritage Information Network. "Like Light Through a Prism: Analyzing Commercial Markets for Cultural Heritage Content." Public Works and Government Services Canada, Ottawa, 1999.

Hamma, Kenneth J. "Public Domain Art in the Age of Easier Mechanical Reproducibility." *D-Lib Magazine* 11, no. 11 (November 2005). http://www.dlib.org/dlib/november05/hamma/11hamma.html. Accessed June 18, 2018.

Metropolitan Museum of Art. http://www.Metmuseum.org. Accessed June 18, 2018.

Museum of Modern Art Press Release. April 19, 2000. http://dhhumanist.org/Archives/Virginia/v13/0542.html. Accessed June 18, 2018.

Museum of Modern Art Oral History Program. "Interview with Kirk Varnedoe by Sharon Zane." November 28, 2001, 148–57. https://www.moma.org/momaorg/shared/pdfs/docs/learn/archives/transcript_varnedoe.pdf. Accessed June 18, 2018.

Pantalony, Rina Elster. "Managing Intellectual Property for Museums." World Intellectual Property Organization. 2013. http://www.wipo.int/copyright/en/museums_ip/. Accessed June 18, 2018.

Scott, Tom. "We're Making the Most of Our Image Collection." *The Art Newspaper* 27, no. 300 (April 2018).

Smithsonian Institution. https://library.si.edu/image-gallery/faq. Accessed June 18, 2018.

Tanner, Simon. "Reproduction Charging Models and Rights Policy for Digital Images in American Art Museums: A Mellon Foundation Funded Study." 2004. https://kclpure.kcl.ac .uk/portal/en/publications/reproduction-charging-models--rights-policy-for-digital-images -in-american-art-museums(95d04077-f8ec-4094-b8c1-d585c6b16d9b).html. Accessed June 18, 2018.

Tomkins, Calvin. "The Modernist: Kirk Varnedoe, the Museum of Modern Art and the Tradition of the New." *New Yorker Magazine*, November 5, 2001.

Tomsho, Robert. "Columbia University to Close Fathom.com E-Learning Service." *Wall Street Journal*, January 6, 2003. https://www.wsj.com/articles/SB104188231770411424. Accessed June 18, 2018.

Weil, Stephen E. *Making Museums Matter*. Smithsonian Institution, Washington, DC, 2002, 3–23, 239–72.

The Sixth Floor Museum at Dealey Plaza

A Case Study of Rights and Reproductions Licensing

Megan Bryant, Director of Collections and Interpretation,
The Sixth Floor Museum at Dealey Plaza

Rights and reproductions are probably not thought of frequently by many in the museum profession as a potential source of revenue. In fact, a Mellon Foundation–funded study conducted in 2004 concluded:

> It is clear from the results of this study that the level of revenue raised by museums through imaging and rights is small relative to the overall revenue earning capacity of the museum from retail, ticket sales, membership and fundraising. A museum does not carry out image creation or rights and reproduction activity because of its profitability. (Tanner 2004)

Rights and reproductions programs are a mechanism for providing access to a museum's collections through images and use permissions. As such they are a key aspect of the public service mission of museums. Images from museum collections are everywhere these days—online, in magazines and books, on television, in films, even on stage—reaching audiences most of us have never considered. Usually the charging of fees for rights and reproductions services serves primarily to cover a museum's costs in providing those services—if that. However, in some institutions there may be specific circumstances at play that allow for the potential to generate revenue from rights and reproductions licensing that exceeds the recouping of costs. In these situations, rare as they may be, it is worth considering what the appropriate use or designation of such revenue should be. While our situation at the Sixth Floor Museum at Dealey Plaza is unique in many ways, a look at the development and growth of our rights and reproductions activity over the past twenty years may provide some insight into one way to manage these matters.

RIGHTS AND REPRODUCTIONS LICENSING AT THE SIXTH FLOOR MUSEUM AT DEALEY PLAZA

The assassination of President John F. Kennedy in Dallas, Texas, on November 22, 1963, was one of the most momentous events of the twentieth century; it dominated broadcast and print journalism and helped to create the modern news era. It precipitated the creation of a vast store of audiovisual documentation at both the professional and personal/individual level. As the history museum at the site of the assassination, the Sixth Floor Museum at Dealey Plaza (TSFM) has become the repository of much of this material. TSFM is fortunate that most donors of these materials over the years have transferred copyrights along with the donation of the objects, leading to the museum holding an extensive collection of—as well as copyrights to—film, video, audio, and photographs that constitutes the primary visual record of President Kennedy's visit to Dallas, the assassination, and its aftermath.

The collection includes still photographs from local newspaper coverage, video and film footage from local television stations, audio recordings from local news radio, bystander still photographs, and home movies—including a number of key eyewitness films and images, chief among these being the Abraham Zapruder film. A twenty-six-second, silent, 8mm color home movie, the Zapruder film is perhaps the most famous—infamous even—home movie ever taken; to put it simply and bluntly, the Zapruder film is a graphic depiction of the murder of a president. Shot by Dallas businessman and home movie enthusiast Abraham Zapruder, the film is the only known visual record of the entire assassination sequence. It has been relied on by all major investigations into the assassination to answer questions about how the shooting happened and has been the source of a significant amount of controversy and speculation regarding what did—or did not—happen in Dealey Plaza on November 22, 1963. Given its iconic status as the most widely recognized record of the Kennedy assassination, it is unsurprising that the film has inspired countless works of art and fictionalized retellings of the event both in print and on screen.

The Zapruder film and its copyright had a somewhat complicated ownership history, culminating in 1998 when the camera-original film was officially declared an "assassination record" under the President John F. Kennedy Assassination Records Collection Act of 1992 and was transferred to the President John F. Kennedy Assassination Records Collection at the National Archives and Records Administration (NARA). Zapruder's heirs retained ownership of the copyright, which they directly assigned to TSFM in 1999. This put the museum in the interesting position of controlling the copyright to the film, while the physical film itself is under the care and protection of NARA. In addition to the transfer of the rights, the Zapruder family further gifted to the museum an extensive collection of copies of the film in various formats, including an important first-generation print made the day of the assassination and frame-by-frame transparencies made from the camera-original film in the 1990s.

Due to the film's notoriety, the acquisition of the Zapruder film copyright brought a whole new level of awareness and interest in the audiovisual collections at TSFM, serving as the impetus for the museum to formalize a professional rights and reproductions program. The confluence of copyright ownership in most of the collection with this high level of interest and demand for its use by a wide variety of external parties has given TSFM the fortunate ability to generate revenue from rights and reproductions licensing.

There is an ongoing, seemingly never-ending, worldwide fascination with the Kennedy assassination that has led to the production and publication of countless films, documentaries, books, articles, theatrical productions, and multimedia projects in the decades since the assassination; and the extensive audiovisual collections at TSFM have provided a wealth of imagery and sound to support many of these projects.

The museum receives requests to license its collections from all over the world for a wide variety of use types, ranging from nonprofit to highly commercial. The type of use as well as the extent and breadth of the use rights granted in a license agreement determine what fees are assessed. In general, for a commercial project, the more extensive the package of rights granted, the higher the license fee will be. It should be noted that while our licensing program is quite active, fees are regularly reduced or waived entirely, allowing for nonprofit or purely educational or instructional uses and fair use considerations. License fees are always based on the specifics of any given request, using our licensing history as a guide to ensure that no fee is assessed in an arbitrary manner.

License fees are not assessed for uses that are purely nonprofit—such as research, school projects, lectures and presentations, and even museum exhibits. However, we see a much higher demand for uses of a more commercial nature, such as television— and, more and more frequently now, streaming—productions; independent and the occasional feature film; publications of various types, with an increasing number of self-published books every year; multimedia and web-based projects and apps, etc. The museum also provides licenses for uses that tread the line somewhere between nonprofit and commercial, such as theatrical productions, often staged by a nonprofit theatrical organization (for example, the Stephen Sondheim musical *Assassins* and the Robert Schenkkan play *All the Way*). License fees are assessed accordingly in all instances.

None of this licensing activity would be possible if the museum did not own the copyright to these popularly requested collections. License fees are only charged when the museum controls the copyright to the collections material being licensed. Similar to most museums, we also hold materials in our collection that are in the public domain or for which rights are unknown or held by another party. While access to these materials can be provided, they are not appropriate for revenue generation.

RESTRICTIONS ON LICENSING AT THE SIXTH FLOOR MUSEUM

Not all license requests are granted at TSFM. Collections stewardship plays a priority role in assessing whether some proposed uses are responsible or congruent with the museum's mission and policies. Due to the level of continuing emotion and ongoing controversy associated with the assassination of President Kennedy, TSFM chooses not to engage in certain types of highly commercial uses that might exploit or sensationalize the violence and trauma of the event. For example, we do not license our collections for promotional or advertising uses, and the Zapruder film is never licensed for any kind of merchandizing. While we do consider uses of collections media in fiction-based projects, these license requests receive a higher level of scrutiny to ensure that the context of proposed use aligns with the museum's concerns regarding respectful treatment of graphic imagery, does not alter the content of the historic images, and is not solely being used for sensationalistic purposes.

Examples of requests declined for the reasons outlined here include use of the Zapruder film in a popular first-person shooter video game, promotional use in the opening credits sequence for a television science fiction series, and a request to digitally alter several eyewitness films to change their outcome for use in a streaming mini-series.

BUDGETARY DESIGNATION AND INSTITUTIONAL IMPACT OF LICENSING REVENUE

TSFM is in the fortunate—and somewhat unusual—position to be able to generate some revenue from licensing that goes beyond administrative costs. Since the early days of the museum's rights and reproductions program, the general institutional philosophy was that revenue earned from licensing collections images should be directed back into support of collections. In 2010 this philosophy was formalized with the establishment of a board-designated collections/licensing fund and enactment of the collections/licensing fund policy. The purpose of the fund is to capture revenues generated by the licensing of historic images, films, and footage from the museum's collections; the policy directs that expenditures from the fund must be "dedicated to acquisitions for the permanent collection and special activities or projects that directly further the care and support of collections or increase public access to collections." The policy is also stated in brief in our collections management policy and ethics policy.

The ethical standard regarding appropriate use of funds from the sale of deaccessioned collections, limiting their use to new acquisitions and/or direct care of collections, serves as the foundation for this approach. While in the case of licensing of collections images the objects themselves are not being removed from the collections and sold, the revenue comes from the reproduction and use of collections items—this can be considered a form of "sale" of collections. In outlining the policy for use of licensing revenue, we determined that, due to the nature of the collection and licensing activity, it would be most appropriate to direct any revenue earned from the collection back into the growth, development, and support of the collection.

This revenue stream is not substantial, nor is it wholly predictable on a year-to-year basis. It is entirely dependent on external interest, and the licensing activity we see can varies greatly from year to year with peaks and valleys often influenced by significant anniversary years, as well as unanticipated world news and events. Due to these external influences and unknown variability, it would be a mistake for the museum to rely on this revenue stream in perpetuity or even in the short term. However, since its establishment, this special fund has allowed us to undertake activities and acquire collections that we would not otherwise have been able to under the general operating budget. For example, we have added significant depth to our collections by successfully acquiring several key artifacts related to the Kennedy assassination at auction and by direct purchase from collectors. Because licensing serves as a form of collections access, we have also tied use of funds from licensing to projects that broaden the ability of the public to access collections—including funding the initial set-up of an online collections database in 2011 and ongoing digitization projects for audiovisual collections.

FINAL THOUGHTS

While in general museums have many of the same concerns and issues to face when it comes to rights and reproductions and licensing, policies and practices will vary widely depending on institutional perspectives, philosophies, mission, and collection type. Significant revenue from rights and reproductions licensing is not the norm, but if a museum is fortunate enough to hold copyrights to materials in its collection, it would be a beneficial exercise to examine the potential to monetize those assets for licensing revenue. Regardless of the specific circumstances to be considered, museums with the potential to develop a robust licensing program should still be bound by their missions, industry standards, and legal and ethical considerations. As a form of public access, licensing—whether it leads to a revenue stream or not—should be governed by the same philosophies that guide other forms of collections access. While not all museums choose to have a designated fund like the one TSFM has put in place, it was the best solution for us because it allowed for public use of collections, ethical protection of funds generated, and additional specialized support and development of collections as long as licensing continues.

BIBLIOGRAPHY

Abraham Zapruder Film. http://emuseum.jfk.org/view/objects/asitem/items@:32274. Accessed May 14, 2018.

Tanner, S. *Reproduction Charging Models & Rights Policy for Digital Images in American Art Museums: A Mellon Foundation Study*. King's Digital Consultancy Service, 2004.

31

Harnessing Rights and Reproduction Licensing at the New Mexico Museum of Art

Michelle Gallagher Roberts, Deputy
Director, New Mexico Museum of Art

Opening its doors in November 1917 as the state art museum, the New Mexico Museum of Art is located on the historic plaza in Santa Fe, New Mexico. For one hundred years, the New Mexico Museum of Art has served as a catalyst and showcase for creativity and the enjoyment of art. The museum's collection encompasses over twenty thousand works dating primarily from the introduction of the railroad into New Mexico in 1879 to the present day.

Like most museums, the New Mexico Museum of Art is reliant on a mix of financial support. The museum is a division of the Department of Cultural Affairs, State of New Mexico. The New Mexico state legislature, through the general fund, provides financial support for the building and twenty-five staff. Funds for exhibitions and programs must be raised through the museum's affiliated 501(c)(3) foundation, the Museum of New Mexico Foundation (MNMF).

With eighteen museums in the Santa Fe area, competition for donations and admissions is steep. The MNMF must raise funds for four state museums, eight historic sites located throughout the state, and the Office of Archaeological Studies.

While the Museum of Art is fortunate to be financially supported by the state legislature, this backing is not sufficient to fully fund the building, staffing, and general programmatic needs. The Museum of Art must also support its activities through earned income. In addition to earning revenue through admissions and renting the building for events, the museum also supports itself through licensing images. Some of these licensing pursuits are handled directly by museum staff and others in collaboration with our foundation.

The museum has taken a three-pronged approach to licensing images: licensing images directly, creating our own licensed merchandise, and working with for-profit companies to create products sold in other locations. Each approach has its advantages and challenges.

Licensing images from the collection through any avenue requires the museum staff to evaluate the copyright status of each work. The artworks in the museum collection fall into three categories: works in the public domain, copyright owned by the museum, or copyright owned by a third party. Licensing images in the first two categories is relatively easy. The final category of works requires more investigation and usually partnering with the copyright holders to license these works.

The Museum of Art actively seeks the ownership of copyright to works in our collection. We currently own the copyright to many of our most requested images. Many museums may find managing copyright to be burdensome. This should only be pursued after fully evaluating the associated advantages and costs. (For a thorough examination on how to determine the copyright status of an object, see Young 2015.)

LICENSING IMAGES DIRECTLY

The Museum of Art directly licenses images from the collection to scholars, publishers, movie and television production companies, and other museums. We have occasionally directly licensed images for specific products after being approached by commercial companies. These products have ranged from limited edition playing cards to calendars aimed at small targeted audiences. For these, we charged set image fees rather than royalties. This type of licensing is the most frequent for which a museum might be involved.

Our fee schedule is available on our website and covers the most regular types of requests. Also included on our website is an application form that must be completed and submitted. Turnaround time for requests is usually under two weeks, with rush requests subject to an additional fee. Any new photography required must be paid for by the requestor. As the museum doesn't have a photographer on staff, an outside contractor must be hired, and those direct costs are passed on.

Museum staff evaluates all reproduction requests to ensure the use is compatible with the museum's mission and values and doesn't denigrate the artist's work. Conditions for use are clearly spelled out in our reproduction agreement. These include no cropping, overlay of text, or bleeding to the edge. The provided credit line with appropriate artist attribution is required to be prominently displayed. If applicable, at least two copies of any publication must be submitted to the museum for inclusion in our library. Payment of fees along with a signed reproduction agreement are required before any high-resolution images are sent to the requestor. In this way, the museum can exert some control over the use of images from our collection.

As the museum is dependent on others to contact us to license images, there is relatively few ways to actively increase revenue from this type of endeavor. The most effective is by making our collection readily available to a wide range of people. Some museums work with distribution partners to license images, such as Art Resource, Getty Images, or Bridgeman Images. While the New Mexico Museum of Art doesn't currently work with an outside partner, we have increased access to our collection by publishing it online via a web interface with our collections database. The images on our online collections database are published at no more than 600 pixels on the longest edge. Larger image files can only be obtained by licensing the image.

We have seen an on average increase of 54 percent since the introduction of our online collections database. Because other cultural institution can also see the breadth and depth of our collection, the number and diversity of items requested for loan has also increased. We have also seen a more diverse selection of works from our collection being licensed. This has also assisted in disseminating the art of New Mexico to a much wider audience, a central ambition of the museum's.

For works in which the copyright is owned by a third party, such as the artist or artist's estate, the Museum of Art has been seeking nonexclusive licenses, agreements by which the owner of intellectual property rights gives another party the nonexclusive right to exploit the specified intellectual property rights in accordance with the specific terms and conditions specified in the license. Unlike permissions for one-time specific uses, a broad nonexclusive license can allow an institution to reproduce a work on an ongoing basis for any of the uses covered by the license, ideally for the entire duration of the term of copyright. These licenses specifically grant the museum the right to sublicense the same rights granted to us to third parties. These licenses usually exclude the right to create commercial products though. So if the Museum of Art has the right to publish an image in a scholarly book, then we have the right to grant another the same. If the work isn't in the public domain, the Museum of Art doesn't own the copyright, or the museum doesn't have a nonexclusive license with this sublicense, we will provide the image with the condition that any external requestor seek additional permission directly from the copyright holder. All external licensors must assume the risks associated with clearing any required copyrights. This requirement is explicitly stated in our reproduction agreements.

CREATING OUR OWN LICENSED MERCHANDISE

There are many reasons to have items for sale in a museum gift shop, including creating a memento of a visit and a lasting memory for our guests. An institution can leverage the strengths of the institution and its services, building(s), and collection(s) to strengthen its brand identity. These products can support the museum mission and exhibitions goals. These products can also generate earned income.

The MNMF operates the gift shop at the Museum of Art. Museum staff work directly with MNMF staff to identify items from the collection that will be on exhibit in upcoming exhibitions or will be highlighted in programs. Shop staff also work to create branded materials for the museum. Products range from notecards to hats and bags to posters and many others.

These products are best when they are very specific to our institution, collection, and regional identity. Tourists from around the world visit Santa Fe, New Mexico. They want items they can't find anywhere else and that remind them of their trip to our museum. Products illustrating collection items that showcase New Mexico's unique culture and landscape perform the best. It is our guests' opportunity to take a little piece of New Mexico and our museum home with them.

By working directly with our shop staff to create products, curators can highlight works in upcoming exhibitions. Lead time for creating these types of products can be relatively short, usually four to six weeks. This allows our shop to be nimble in changing products in the shop in response to the museum's needs. However, all the risks associated with the creation of merchandise are also borne by our shops. If a product doesn't sell as anticipated, those costs must be absorbed. In addition to a physical store, the MNMF also maintains an online presence, selling most of our museum products there. This additional effort requires staff, IT support, and infrastructure to store and ship products around the world.

Licensing images from the collection to create unique products is handled by MNMF staff in combination with Museum of Art staff. Images that need to be licensed from copyright holders must have written agreements. These agreements may include the payment of royalties or fees to the copyright owner, which requires staff to manage. All details related to the creation of these products must be clearly articulated so there are no misunderstandings. Often a certain number of the product is reserved for the artist's or copyright holder's use. In addition to copyright concerns, artworks that depict a known or potentially living person should be carefully evaluated to ensure any additional rights of privacy or publicity are considered before creating merchandize. (For a thorough examination of this issue, see chapter 3 in Young 2015.)

Product creation and merchandizing require specialized knowledge in order to maximize returns. For better or worse, the museum and MNMF have complete control over the merchandise and the production schedule. We keep all net profits earned from these efforts. Because the museum is prominently located on Santa Fe's historic plaza, our museum store also has high visibility. With its own external exit, visitors may patronize our store without necessarily visiting the museum. Not all museum stores will have these advantages.

The benefit to this approach is that you can scale your efforts. Creating a small run of a product or limited types of merchandize can be accomplished with a minimum initial capital investment. While these efforts might not create a large return, other benefits might be gained from having unique museum-branded items available to visitors.

WORKING WITH COMMERCIAL PRODUCT DEVELOPMENT COMPANIES

The Museum of Art, through the MNMF, also licenses images from our collection to commercial product development companies. These products are sold in the Museum of Art's store, in other types of stores around the world, and online via the product development companies' website. It would not be unusual to find products featuring Museum of Art collection items in the gift shops of other museums.

The New Mexico Museum of Art has licensed images from our collection to create calendars, notecards, puzzles, coffee table books, postcards, address books, and coloring books, as well as many others. We have also worked with furniture companies to create works inspired from our collection. The Museum of Art has the benefit of working with a product licensing consultant on staff at the MNMF, as finding commercial companies and pitching products can be a full-time job. For these products, we waive any upfront image or licensing fees in exchange for recurring royalties and a set number of the final product for our use.

In contrast to the products the museum and MNMF develop for our own gift shop, items created by a commercial company need to have a broad demand. Regional images or works with too specific a reference point are passed over in favor of the universally appealing. Artists with a wider reputation are also sought by these companies.

Commercial merchandizing companies also typically work twelve to eighteen months in advance of product hitting the shelves. This is to accommodate design, production, and marketing, often at trade shows. Given the lead time and resources required to bring these products to market, it is not worth it to invest in an item only saleable for a short time or at a limited venue. These companies are typically not interested in creating product for a nontraveling exhibit.

The commercial company assumes the risks associated with designing and producing products for a wider market. While the museum won't see any royalties if a product doesn't sell as anticipated, the direct costs are absorbed by the commercial company. The Museum of Art relies on the expertise of the commercial company for product development, packaging, and marketing. For this expertise, we give up some control over what is selected for production. While we have final veto power, a work or artist that is important to our museum or location may not make the final cut. On one point the museum does not waiver: proper artist attribution and credit lines are required to be clearly displayed. The museum's logo must also be prominent.

Primarily these products are based on items for which the museum owns the copyright or which are in the public domain. Artworks in which the copyright is owned by a third party can be licensed but require more consideration. Copyright holders must be consulted and be brought into the process. This may entail the copyright owner being party to the licensing agreement with the product development company or having a separate contract with the copyright holder in which he, she, or they have agree to have the museum act on their behalf. These agreements should be reviewed by a knowledgeable legal advisor. Before entering into a commercial licensing agreement, you should consider the following:

- Does the contract bestow any exclusivity to the licensing company?
- What is the final product?
- Who will own the copyright to the final product?
- What are the terms of the contract?
- What are each party's responsibilities?
- Does the cultural institution have final approval of the product?
- What is the agreed upon schedule for approvals and deliverables?
- What is the payment schedule?
- Under what circumstances can the contract be canceled?
- Will use of the images be assignable by the commercial production company to third parties?
- Will the commercial production company be able to create derivative uses?
- Will the institution take on additional liability under the contract?

OTHER CONSIDERATIONS

The Museum of Art staff has final approval of all products, regardless of who creates them. We are involved throughout the process to ensure the image being licensed and the underlying artwork are properly respected. When we decide to license an image, we must consider an artist's vision and philosophy about the commercialization of his or her work. This can sometimes be difficult to determine for a deceased artist, but the museum must act in the best interests of not only itself but also the artist and his or her legacy. We have declined to license images in which we felt the final product would be disrespectful to an artist's work regardless of the revenue we could have generated.

Any products created should not be mistaken for an original work by the artist. This can be guarded against by making any products in a different medium from the original and in very different size. Copyright symbols, artist attribution, and credit lines should be clearly visible and not easily removed from the final products. Any third-party logos or trademarks associated with a particular artist, manufacturer, or other brand that may be included will also need to be cleared.

There are a variety of ways to harness the rights and reproduction licensing power of a museum's collection to earn income for the museum. These licensing activities can also support a museum's overall mission and reinforce its brand. Every institution should review their capacity and resources before undertaking any or all of these activities, but they can be a valuable resource for increasing earned income.

BIBLIOGRAPHY

Theobald, Mary Miley. *Museum Store Management*, second edition. Nashville, TN: Rowman & Littlefield Publishers, 2000.

Young, Anne M., ed. *Rights & Reproductions: The Handbook for Cultural Institutions*. Indianapolis, IN: American Alliance of Museums, 2015. (Second edition to be published in 2019.)

Section VI

EARNED INCOME: RETAIL SERVICES

Similar to section V, "Earned Income: Retail Services" refers to income generated by providing goods and services to your visitors. In this section, we will focus on the retail services that museums may or may not provide, and on the earned income categories that are derived from retail activities: retail services. Those categories are 1) food services, 2) facility rentals, and 3) museum stores. Each institution varies as to the types of retail services offered. A small historic house museum may not have the space or equipment for food services or facility rentals. A large art museum may have multiple museum stores, on site and virtual, a destination restaurant, and multiple spaces available for rent.

All of the categories in this section may also be outsourced to vendors. The institution still receives income; the vendor also receives income and fees from the service provided. The categories in this section may also be subject to unrelated business income tax (UBIT). Nonprofit organizations are exempt from taxation; their revenue is generated to fulfill their missions rather than to generate profit. If a nonprofit organization generates income from products or services unrelated to its mission, that income is taxed as unrelated business income. If a nonprofit organization generates too much income from unrelated businesses, the nonprofit organization may lose its nonprofit status. Facility rentals and museum stores are two departments that may generate unrelated business income. Your institution's accountants and attorneys can guide you through UBIT issues.

Hewing to mission reduces UBIT exposure. The food in a museum restaurant may reflect the cultures or time periods represented in the institution. The restaurant can also serve as a classroom, a program venue, or a conduit to the larger community (Haight 2017). For example, the Children's Discovery Museum of San Jose completely revamped its café after recognizing the disconnect between selling processed food and sugary drinks versus the programming emphasis on healthy eating and physical fitness (Jennings and Weiden 2016).

As discussed in chapter 1, the US Census Bureau calculated the revenue by type (product line) in 2012. The following tables show the contribution of programs, education, and tours to the total revenue of institutions that earn such income types.

Table VI.1   Meals and Beverage Services as Percent of Total Revenue by Institution Discipline 2012

All institutions	6.8%
Museums	5.4%
Historical sites	9.3%
Zoos and botanical gardens	8.7%
Nature parks and other similar institutions	11.8%

Table VI.2   Facility Rental Revenue as Percent of Total Revenue by Institution Discipline 2012

All institutions	4.1%
Museums	7.3%
Historical sites	19.8%
Zoos and botanical gardens	6.5%
Nature parks and other similar institutions	12.3%

Table VI.3   Merchandise Sales as Percent of Total Revenue by Institution Discipline 2012

All institutions	9.1%
Museums	8.8%
Historical sites	14%
Zoos and botanical gardens	8.7%
Nature parks and other similar institutions	10.9%

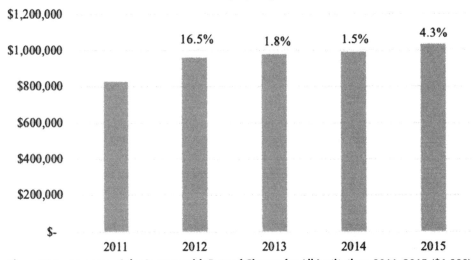

Figure VI.1   Inventory Sales Income with Rate of Change for All Institutions 2011–2015 ($1,000) in US$

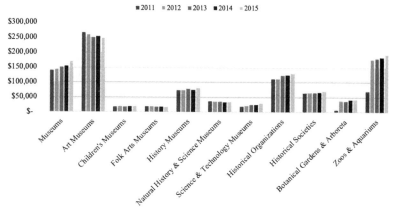

Inventory Sales Income by Institution Discipline 2011 - 2015 ($1,000) in US$

■ 2011 ■ 2012 ■ 2013 ■ 2014 ■ 2015

Figure VI.2 Inventory Sales Income by Institution Discipline 2011–2015 ($1,000) in US$

Table VI.4 Rates of Change of Inventory Sales Income by Institution Discipline 2011–2015

	2011–2012	*2012–2013*	*2013–2014*	*2014–2015*
Museums	2.29%	4.77%	2.52%	10.74%
Art museums	–2.67%	–3.49%	1.30%	–1.65%
Children's museums	8.73%	–8.30%	4.01%	3.48%
Folk arts museums	–0.19%	–6.84%	3.89%	–7.15%
History museums	0.48%	6.02%	–4.14%	8.09%
Natural history and science museums	–5.41%	–0.17%	–6.84%	6.17%
Science and technology museums	13.29%	20.46%	–1.61%	18.59%
Historical organizations	–0.37%	10.21%	1.70%	2.94%
Historical societies	0.59%	0.53%	2.08%	4.71%
Botanical gardens and arboreta	443.53%	–3.26%	14.28%	1.98%
Zoos and aquariums	152.03%	1.82%	1.93%	5.70%

The National Center for Charitable Statistics (NCCS) reports the actual revenue generated from different types of earned income, and rates of change can be computed therefrom. Per the structure of Form 990, income from facility rentals and food services can be included in the admissions, programs, merchandise, and other income category; those data were included in section V. Museum store income may be included in the admissions, programs, merchandise, and other income category or the inventory sales category. The data for the inventory sales category are shown in figures VI.1 and VI.2 and table VI.4.

CHAPTERS PREVIEW

This section begins with Tracy Lawler, president of JGL Food Service Consultants, discussing how museums can generate revenue from food services via restaurants and/or catering services. Tracy reviews the pros and cons of launching a destination restaurant. She also shares the metrics and benchmarks that she uses to evaluate food service income, as well as walking you through pricing models for facility rentals. Sara Kennedy, the events manager at the Crocker Art Museum, then explains how facility rentals can help you engage with new audiences. Sara collaborates with her curatorial and education departments to incorporate their work into the design elements of her events. Sharing the uniqueness of your museum should be the touchstone for your facility rental marketing initiatives. Facility rentals do pose challenges, especially in immersive spaces. Rennae J. Healey and Sara Schultz present the difficulties in protecting collections and spaces during facility rentals at the Ford Avenue Piquette Plant. Detailed policies and contracts, along with supervision during events, are critical. Healey and Schultz also recommend teaching renters about your institution's mission and collections. A ten-minute introduction to prospective renters educates them on the uniqueness and fragility of your collections and building—the uniqueness may become a key factor in their choice of your institution for their event. Positioning the rental fee as supporting the ongoing preservation and mission of your institution also alters the prospective renter's perspective.

The remainder of this section is devoted to museum stores. Stores have the potential to continue the education journey of visitors, as well as provide a physical reminder of a memorable visit. Stores should be integrated with your institution's collections, exhibits, and programs. Christa Dyer, the director of retail for the Country Music Hall of Fame and Museum, begins by describing how she has worked with other departments throughout her museum career and translated their work into the merchandising of the museum store. Store staff is then continuously trained to relate store products to the museum's exhibitions, programs, and galleries. Blue Anderson, the manager of visitor services for the Columbia River Maritime Museum, also emphasizes the importance of training the museum store staff. When store staff engages with visitors, they obtain vital feedback about visitors' impressions, likes, and dislikes, which can be shared with other departments. Blue discusses how to increase sales per visitor, to buy merchandise that sells, and to "turn" slow-moving inventory. The challenges of broader retail competition and potential outsourcing of the museum store are examined too.

Michael Guajardo, the director of retail operations for the Virginia Museum of Fine Arts, explains how museum stores can use their ability to develop unique and artisanal products based on their collections to meet the competitive challenge of other retailers. Michael details the entire product development process from research to manufacturing to ordering to pricing to packaging to launching. Throughout the process, he reminds us that the main responsibility is to authentically represent cultures, artists, and works in store products. The institution's mission should guide decisions too. In an "Expert Opinion," Jennifer Gritt, the associate director of the Pittock Mansion, describes how the Pittock Mansion store was revitalized by refocusing on products that directly related to mission and the mansion's collections and narratives. Stuart Hata, the director of retail operations for the Fine Arts Museums of San Francisco, the de Young and Legion of Honor, closes this section by demonstrating how and why museum stores contribute to the success of their institutions. Stuart lists and defines the general objectives and strategies that all museum stores should attain. Like our other contributors, he links the store products with the mission of the institution. Museum stores, facility rentals, and food service all play a role in generating revenue. Savvy institutions also use these retail services to engage new communities and educate about mission.

RESOURCE LIST

Andoniadis, Andrew. *Museum Retailing: A Handbook of Strategies for Success*. Edinburgh: Museums Etc., 2010.

Haight, Andrew, and Rebecca Reilly. *Case Study: Museum Cafes: Integrating Food, Money, and Mission*. St. Louis: American Alliance of Museums Conference, 2017.

Jennings, Marilee, and Wendy Weiden. *Food as Discovery: Curating a Culinary Experience for Mission Alignment—A Case Study of* FoodShed *at Children's Museum of San Jose*. San Jose: Children's Museum of San Jose, 2016. Available at https://www.cdm.org/wp-content/uploads/2016/10/FoodShed-Case-Study-Final.pdf.

Manask, Arthur M., and Robert D. Schwarz. *Restaurants, Catering and Facility Rentals: Maximizing Earned Income*. Edinburgh: Museums Etc., 2012.

The Urban Institute. NCCS Core Files, 2011–2015. https://nccs-data.urban.org/data.php?ds=core. Accessed January–November 2018.

US Census Bureau. 2002, 2007, and 2012 Economic Censuses. https://www.census.gov/programs-surveys/economic-census/data/tables.html. Accessed January–November 2018.

32

Food Services

Models and Metrics

Tracy Lawler, President, JGL Food Service Consultants

Food services in a museum usually generates two distinct revenue streams; visitor food service sales represent the museum café or restaurant, while catering revenue is generated from special events that are often held after hours. Special events typically garner rental fee revenue, which is retained in its entirety by the museum and catering commissions, which represent a percentage of catering sales. Many museums generate a healthy six-figure return from their food service; this income stream is renewable once the food service program is developed. A successful and income-producing food service program requires clear identification of institutional goals, analysis of metrics and comps, willingness to adjust program elements, and an entrepreneurial approach to event rentals.

METRICS AND THE PER CAPITA SALE

When evaluating the potential for a museum café or restaurant to generate earned income, the per capita sale is an important measure to analyze. This measure reflects gross café or restaurant sales divided by museum attendance. We typically deduct catered event attendees and off-premise attendees from the attendance count. We do not deduct school groups or other users who might not utilize the café because their lack of participation is accounted for within the genre comparison. A science museum, as an example, typically has a lower per capita sale due to the higher percentage of institutional school group attendance. In our consulting practice we have encountered per capita sales ranging from $0.75 to $14.50. To put this in context, the $0.75 per capita sale is a small coffee cart operation while the $14.50 per capita sale is a successful daytime destination restaurant. The average science museum in our practice has a per capita sale of $2.00 to $5.00. The average art museum has a per capita sale of $3.00 to $5.00 for one outlet and $6.00 plus for two plus outlets. As museums seek to improve their earned income from visitor food, focusing on gross sales and the per capita spend can be productive. Efforts to increase the per capita sale can include relocation close to the primary museum entrance, directional signage in the museum, strong website presence with photos and menus, front line staff who serve as ambassadors, improved

229

menu variety, enhanced merchandising, pricing modifications, aligned customer service, and offerings that reflect the collection. Most museums generate between a 3 percent and 10 percent return on their visitor food. A museum with five hundred thousand visitors who can improve their per capita sale by $2.00 might stand to earn an additional $30,000 to $100,000 in earned income annually.

DESTINATION RESTAURANTS

The destination restaurant is a category unto itself. By destination, we mean a restaurant that is open for lunch and dinner five to seven days a week and is open independent of museum operating hours. Examples of well-known museum destination restaurants are the Modern at the Museum of Modern Art, Flora Bar at the Met Breuer, Esker Grove at the Walker Art Center, and In Situ at the San Francisco Museum of Modern Art. In our consulting practice we have coined a new term, the daytime destination; this represents the museum restaurant that seeks outside traffic when the museum is open to the public but does not attempt to be open for dinner when the museum is closed to the public. Examples of the daytime destination are Verde at the Perez Art Museum Miami and Fika at the American Swedish Institute in Minneapolis. Destination museum restaurants that "speak to the street" frequently achieve a per capita sale of $10 and above as outside diners are not typically counted in museum attendance. In the past ten years, virtually every museum expansion or new build project we have worked on has contemplated a destination restaurant. The destination restaurant can generate significant earned income, be noteworthy, activate the facility, and forge a deeper connection with visitors and donors; however, it is also a risky endeavor. The chance of success is heightened when the destination restaurant has a separate entrance, operator control over menu and operations, ample kitchen space, street front presence, and a name or well-known chef.

SPECIAL EVENTS AND CATERING

Catering sales and special events are frequently the more meaningful source of revenue for museums. In part this is due to the fact that events generate two sources of income. The rental rate is a fee charged by the cultural institution and is kept in its entirety by the organization. In approximately 90 percent of US markets, the food and beverage sales associated with catering generate a percentage commission back to the cultural institution. Success in the special event market requires an entrepreneurial mindset. Fifteen or twenty years ago, museums were the only "alternative rental venues" in most markets. Today every market has multiple "unique venues" such as converted bank lofts, foundries, art studios, or warehouses that serve as rental venues. These venues frequently have advantages over museums in that they are dedicated to rentals, frequently provide all day access, are run by a sales-oriented team, and do not have mission-based constraints.

Museums run the gamut with respect to how actively they seek external third-party rentals. We have met many museum directors who welcome these events not only because of the earned income they generate but also because of the potential exposure to new visitors or potential donors. We have also met a number of museum directors who are quite clear that they would never do another event again if budget constraints did not require them. Museums frequently hold their own internal events within the facility, and these events can create inventory challenges for the event sales team. The most successful museum event rental programs are those in which the mandate and rules are clear and understood by all.

EVENT PRICING MODEL

Developing the pricing model for rental events demands some analysis. Some museums charge a flat rental fee (that is, $5,000 for use of the space from 6 p.m. to 11 p.m.) and allow anyone to rent the space. Some museums allow rentals only as a perk of membership. We generally do not recommend charging a nominal membership (such as a $99 individual membership for a bridal customer) because customers perceive it as a nuisance fee. Quite a number of museums require membership at a reasonably high level to host an event. We have worked with major museums across the country who require a corporate membership of $15,000 to $50,000 to have the privilege of hosting an event. Some of those museums do not charge an additional rental fee but instead just pass along their incremental expenses such as security, janitorial, and event staff. Others charge a rental fee in addition to the membership requirement. There is no one universal model that is right. Important elements to consider when developing the pricing model are 1) the institutional goals, 2) what other museums in the market charge, 3) how unique the museum spaces are, 4) the capacity, and 5) the volume of demand in the market. Museums that have recently expanded or constructed a new facility can typically anticipate a honeymoon period following the opening. During that initial period, demand will be quite high and the museum may be able to command a higher rental price. When the San Francisco Museum of Modern Art reopened in 2016 following their expansion, as an example they charged inaugural rates for the first thirteen months post-opening.

SUCCESS IN THE EVENT RENTAL MARKET

Once a pricing model is developed, success in the event rental market depends on several factors. The number and type of rental spaces, their size, and their usability and attractiveness are important. In most markets a space that can seat 150 to 200 people is in high demand as is a space that can accommodate more than 300. Availability is very important. Each market has its most popular event months, but generally spring and fall are more popular for special events, as is December. Saturdays are popular for brides while corporate events tend to fall on Tuesday through Thursday. If as an example the museum is open late on Thursday nights and special events are precluded, that will limit corporate events as many corporate events are held on Thursday nights. Many museums struggle with availability for daytime events as those can typically only be held in dedicated event spaces or when the museum is closed. The further in advance a space can be booked, the more success the institution will have in the event market. Once a client makes an inquiry, he or she generally does not want to wait to confirm the space. The social market usually books further in advance with most weddings booking one year ahead. While we have seen the booking window shortening in many markets across the country, we still advocate for a one-year booking window.

EVENT RENTAL AMENITIES

Each event type looks for different amenities. The bridal market seeks a bridal suite (think conference room with adjacent restroom), backdrops for photo opportunities, and ceremony space. The conference market seeks a large keynote address space and breakout rooms. Corporate dinners might desire a separate pre-function space for cocktails. Having the right amenities for the type of events booking at the facility can improve special event volume.

EVENT SALES RESPONSIVENESS

Sales responsiveness is also important. Every museum handles the sales process differently. Some have a venue sales team and some look to their caterer to manage the sales process. In general we find that catering teams are typically more sales oriented while the venue team may know more about the building and the institutional mission. We recommend to all our clients that their venue sales team be compensated on a salary and commission structure. A venue sales team on a straight salary may have limited motivation to book another wedding, particularly if it means they have to work on a Saturday night with no additional compensation. We have worked with many institutions across the country where the venue sales team was slow to respond. The digital environment we live in has resulted in an expectation of immediate feedback and response. We advise an automatic response to all emails with follow up in, ideally, less than twenty-four hours. Museums frequently have long list of regulations regarding use of the space, which are to be expected given that they contain often priceless collections. The entrepreneurial competitors, however, do not have stringent facility guidelines and as such museums can be perceived as difficult to work with. One of the biggest challenges in a museum relates to early set up. Most museums close at 5 p.m. and many do not allow set up to begin in advance. A lucky few have dedicated space so set up can begin any time; for those who don't, creative measures are needed. Early set up (after 3 p.m.) can often be a real determination in whether an event books at a museum or at a competitive venue.

CATERING COMMISSIONS

The third food service revenue stream is commissions from catering. In most markets across the country, caterers pay a percentage known as commission to the museum. The starting commission nationwide is 10 percent of food and beverage sales. The nationwide average for our clients is 13 to 15 percent. These commissions are frequently tiered (so the first $500,000 in sales is 10 percent, the next $500,000 is 12 percent, and the balance is 15 percent, as an example). While we have seen and negotiated contracts with commissions as high as 25 percent or more, it is important to remember that the consumer ultimately pays the price. If commissions are so high that catering is not affordable, the end result will not benefit the museum. Similarly we sometimes see contracts with 25 percent commissions resulting in the utilization of substandard products to execute catering. Ultimately this will hurt the museum because visitors do not differentiate between the museum and its food service vendor.

CONCLUSION

Development of a successful food service program within a museum can serve to engage visitors, deepen ties to the institution, generate buzz, and create a dependable earned income stream. A well-executed program can generate six figures and be an important component of museum funding. While visitor food service in smaller museums may not generate significant income, we still advocate for it, as most museum visitors no longer ask "do you have a café" but instead "where is the café?" A well-thought-out plan with respect to food services that includes clear goals, measurable metrics, and flexibility is the blueprint for success.

33

The Opportunities in Facility Rentals

Sara Kennedy, Events Manager, Crocker Art Museum

Facility rental programs offer a great opportunity to increase a museum's earned income revenue while creating a new audience for that institution.

As museums continue to seek more funding and new ways to keep relevant in the changing political and digital landscape, future income requires engagement of the next generation and new ways to expand engagement. Private facility rentals offer a different way to add a successful and new revenue stream while increasing the museum's audience through appealing to a younger and more diverse groups of visitors. These event rentals can directly translate into leads for future donors to the museum.

Facility rental programs can help create a new audience. Art museums can come across as stuffy and elite institutions. Private facility rental events can shed a new light on that perception. If someone who's never been to a museum or was intimidated by that type of institution comes to a holiday party or wedding at a museum where he or she can have the chance to view artwork, have a cocktail, and spend time mingling or dancing in honor of a special occasion, not only will he or she have a fun memory of that museum, but it may encourage him or her to want to come back and delve deeper.

Facility rentals can come from all different areas. In my experience, I've found the greatest increase of revenue comes from pleased return clients. Those clients come back year after year, and sometimes after they have one event they discover additional events that could be held at that museum. A positive event experience with great customer service can multiply earned revenue in several ways.

Word-of-mouth can be your greatest asset for growing your facility rental revenue. If clients have a positive experience at your museum, they will share with others and recommend your venue to anyone looking for a unique location with impeccable customer service. Not only can your client help you by recommending more business, but all those event attendees can also help spread the word by telling their work colleagues and friends.

In addition, vendors can also help with word-of-mouth. If they have a positive experience at the event or have a good working relationship with the onsite contact, they too can spread the word. Having a great vendor team can improve the caliber of your events and help provide a consistent experience for event attendees.

Marketing and social media are another great way to increase revenue and event rentals. Museums offer a beautiful backdrop to any event. With image-focused Instagram, photos alone can help sell the museum as a venue for a wedding or corporate reception. Belonging to event associations and organizations can also help market your facility rental program. Attending mixers where you have the opportunity to grow your network and learn new trends will help keep your private events fresh.

Facility rentals can help expand the impact of fundraisers and internal museum events. Rental clients can lead to partnerships and donations. Often museums are primarily focused on growing their collection and endowments through corporate donations, grants, membership levels, and fundraisers. Event rentals offer a lucrative way to increase the earned revenue and expand the appeal of the museum.

Private events can help the institution stay up to date on event trends that can fuel that organizations own fundraising events, not just with tablescapes and linens but also with décor and entertainment. Staying current on event trends can infuse new life into museum events and programs. Conferences, associations, and mixers can all help forecast new trends. Events like fashion shows and couture brand collection launches, magazines, and other intuitions' gala events can all provide inspiration and trends. Social media can also provide inspiration—seeing what other museums, venues, or celebrity event planners are creating can be beneficial.

Treating fundraisers and donor recognition parties like weddings can put the emphasis on the guest experience and fun, making those guests feel like they are supporting a good cause but are also involved in a deeply special, one-of-a-kind experience. Done right, they feel taken care of and want to continue to support and be involved with the organization.

Another way facility rental programs can help capitalize on new revenue is creating engaging education-based programs that infuse learning and art making with live music and cocktails. I think facility rental events have really forged the path for this type of museum revenue. Take cues from private events to create more dynamic internal events for your institution. Facility rentals can help museums explore new engagement opportunities. By working collaboratively, education and events departments can curate unique and fun educational programming. I personally love working with colleagues from other departments on events. Infusing their programming with my design elements is really rewarding.

Weddings, though not always permitted at museums, can yield great return on investment. Weddings can be a tricky beast. They are a special kind of private event with a lot of pressure on the line. But they welcome the broadest appeal, as it's a happy occasion and typically everyone is in a festive mood. That unique event can open guests up to being very receptive to a unique venue. A positive experience translates in a multitude of ways. You can get multiple additional events based on that one wedding. A positive experience at a wedding can translate into weddings and events from those attendees, or the couple may choose to have their anniversary party back at the museum. Word-of-mouth is a wonderful marketing tool for the institution. While weddings can be time consuming, and stressful, and require endless attention to detail, with great customer service they can be a lucrative addition to a facility rental program. In addition to wedding events, there can be welcome and rehearsal dinners or day after brunches.

Figures 33.1-4 Crocker Art Museum Ballroom, Friedman Court, Tablescape, New Courtyard

While the museum is never technically an official venue as it will always be a museum first, it is a great opportunity to expose the institution to a new audience of potential members and donors.

It is key to have strong policies in place to protect the organization from potential harm that private events could create. From unwanted damage or simple wear and tear, it's beneficial to be as detailed in that policy as possible, including items such as not permitted décor and insurance ensure the safety of the museum for years to come. It's important to be firm and explain the rules thoroughly in advance to make sure clients are aware of the policies. Always be consistent about the policies and procedures, as exceptions can create issues down the line such as repeat clients or staff turnover.

There are an astounding amount of different types of events that rental programs can offer. They range from weddings, holiday parties, conference opening/closing receptions, lectures, concerts, and adult birthday parties to anniversary parties, rehearsal dinners, cocktail parties, conferences, board and corporate retreats, board meetings, luncheons, business meetings, wine/beer tastings, and concerts. Some museums also allow child and teen events like bar/bat mitzvahs and proms as well as other nonprofit fundraisers and religious organizations' events.

In terms of marketing, it's important to play on what makes your museum unique. In my experience, I've found success targeting marketing materials and collateral to corporate (holiday parties, conference receptions) and life celebrations (weddings, engagement parties, or anniversaries) separately. It helps to have several images of each of your spaces that show the diversity of options for your future clients. For example, if you have just one space, it's important to show that space as a wedding reception venue, a cocktail party, or a lecture hall. Social media can also help show your range of options, whether it's image-focused Instagram or Pinterest. Museums often can't compete with hotels and other venues for certain items, so it's important to play up what makes your museum special!

In closing, museum leaders should prioritize private rental programs as an important addition to their earned revenue. It is a great tool to find a diverse audience, additional revenue, and potential future donors.

34

Museums and Events Rentals

A Balancing Act

Rennae J. Healey, Assistant Events Manager;
and Sara Schultz, Museum Coordinator,
Ford Avenue Piquette Plant

As the demand for nontraditional sites for weddings, meetings, and corporate parties steadily increases, organizations that never intended to rent out their facilities are now jumping onto the event rental bandwagon. From rustic barns and fruit orchards to modern art galleries and theaters, unique rental facilities are in popular demand. Museums and historic sites, many of who fall into the category of underfunded non-profits, have also begun to open their doors to rentals as an important source of revenue. For museum professionals, it has become a balancing act: maintaining integrity as a museum while generating revenue through event rentals. With the resulting influx of nontypical museum visitors that comes with rentals, museums come up against new challenges and opportunities. These challenges include translating their story and mission into something meaningful and understandable to this new audience and also protecting and preserving their collections while balancing the expectations of their rental clients. At the same time, museums will also be presented with an opportunity to invite this new audience of visitors to take a personal stake in their mission and gain support from a group of people who may not have been previously inclined to take an interest in their cause.

One of the most important ways of working toward achieving this balance is to educate the renters about the organization's mission and convey to them why it matters. It can be foolhardy to assume that because renters are interested in holding their event at your museum they are therefore knowledgeable about your museum's purpose and mission. They may have only chosen you based on the attractiveness of the photos found online from someone else's wedding. Potential renters may have many misconceptions about your organization. They might assume that the museum's main mission is to collect as many rare objects as possible or that the museum is simply a storage facility for antiques. Connecting the museum to the idea of serving the public will have a significant effect on their overall outlook and attitude toward the space. When renters understand the importance of the museum's collections and mission, it can make their event feel even more special and unique, becoming something they'll want to share with their guests as well! An introduction to the space can make for an ideal element of their programming. Starting a meeting with a ten-minute welcome from a museum staff member can connect guests to the space and inspire them.

An important part of speaking with potential renters is to let them know how the museum is funded. This develops in them an understanding of the reasons why, as a nonprofit, the museum has chosen to use event revenue as a source of supplemental income. Educating your renters on the museum's reasoning for offering event rentals will also make them feel good about choosing you. Renters may have unspoken misconceptions about why the museum exists and how the museum is funded. They may assume that your museum is owned and funded by a wealthy individual, is run by the local government, or even that your museum is fully funded by the federal government because it is on the National Register of Historic Places. They may not understand the difference between a nonprofit organization and a for-profit business. Directly explaining that the organization does not operate to create a profit but that profit is put back into the care and growth of the museum can dispel many of these misconceptions and create goodwill.

Again, it's important to note that the renter's understanding of the philanthropic nature of your museum will have a large effect on their treatment of collections, the space, and even staff members. When the museum becomes something the renters and the community are part of, the renters often undergo a change in attitude. They become more generous, more understanding of the rules, and more apt to be satisfied with their overall experience. The particular verbiage used by museum staff can also be important in educating renters. The renter's expectations and viewpoint can be dramatically changed by choosing to use one word over another. Using the term "museum" or "historic site" instead of "venue" can subtly remind them of the museum's primary purpose. Using the term "exhibits" rather than "display" implies permanence and discourages requests to move cases and artifacts. Using the term "artifact" rather than "statue," "car," or "historically dressed mannequin" implies the item's underlying value. All of these things can be easily achieved within the first few interactions with potential clients.

Beyond the education of renters, there are other practical means of addressing preservation concerns that result from event rentals. One of the biggest sources of damage to the building and to artifacts is not necessarily the renters or their guests but the vendors they bring in for their event. Careless moving of rental equipment such as chairs and tables can gouge wood floors, tip over interpretative signage, and bump into fragile artifacts. Caterers can bring in open flames, overload electric circuits with appliances, or allow ice coolers to leak. Vendors who are unfamiliar with the museum can require almost constant vigilance, which can be overly taxing on staff or volunteers. One solution is to limit the number of vendors who enter the museum's doors.

Museums can hand select a small number of vendors to be on an "approved list" and only allow renters to choose from vendors on this list to work at the museum. This is common practice among traditional rental venues as well, often because of profit sharing. In the case of museums, however, limiting vendors is primarily for the sake of preservation. By having a small list of approved vendors, it makes it easier to thoroughly educate the vendors on the museum's rules and regulations. It also provides an incentive for vendors to closely follow the rules because vendors who violate them can lose their standing and be removed from the approved list. Developing a close relationship with your approved vendors can make them your greatest supporters, especially when it comes to seeking sponsors for your own special events.

In regard specifically to the renters, the rental contract is perhaps the most important tool in protecting the museum both legally and physically. An addendum to the rental contract can outline clearly to renters what rules must be followed in order to protect and preserve the building and collections. Reading the contract in its entirety with the renters will ensure that renters understand the museum's rules and limitations. It provides an opportunity for them to ask questions and for the museum staff to offer practical advice on how to make their event museum friendly.

Rules may protect the site and collections; however, rules may also make the space less marketable and can result in resentful renters. This is why educating renters is the most important first step in this process. These rules and regulations are meant to keep everyone safe and happy and protect not only the institution but also the renters and their guests.

Some items that renters wish to bring in will cause outright damage to collections or the building. For example, at the Ford Piquette Avenue Plant, a National Historic Landmark and automobile museum, candles, fog machines, glitter, confetti, bubbles, or other thrown objects such as rice are strictly banned. The Ford Piquette Avenue Plant also does not allow events with children to give out stickers or to host craft activities that involve painting or gluing. In order to maintain control over the space, a clause can be included in the contract that allows museum staff to reject decor or activities that they deem unfit for the building. Other rules regarding objects brought into the museum are for the sake of safety, such as banning items that block fire escapes.

Supervision during event set up is an effective form of damage prevention. Even though you may go over the rules with your renters, it does not mean they will remember them all or, more rarely, that they won't just blatantly attempt to push the limits. On one occasion during an event at the Ford Piquette Avenue Plant, an unapproved six-foot-tall dinosaur model standing in a bed of damp mulch was clandestinely constructed in the museum entrance in mere minutes! Supervision will catch potential hazards like a florist bringing in centerpieces with tea light candles. It is best to catch a potentially negative situation as soon as possible rather than at the last minute so that your renters have a chance to find a satisfactory substitute or solution. A quick interception can provide the renter time to switch the candles out with approved electric candles. Additionally, supervision during the event will prevent misplaced drinks on top of rare artifacts or guests wandering into restricted areas!

One of the most significant preservation concerns with event rentals will be fire safety. While a museum's current layout may already be fire inspector approved, event rentals have the potential to change that situation. Renters may choose to restrict their guests' movement rather than have them use the free flow space museum visitors experience. For example, a renter may select one room to host a cocktail hour or a workshop. In that situation, attention will need to be paid to enforcing room capacity. With new objects coming in, it also becomes necessary to make sure that fire exits aren't blocked by event set up. Providing renters with preset floor plan options will take a load of planning off their hands and have the added benefit of preventing fire safety violations.

Not only does preservation need to be a concern in regard to event rentals, but the overall visitor experience associated with the museum also needs to be maintained. Renters can design detailed events that involve constructing lounge areas with couches, hanging paper lanterns, draping curtains, or using other themed decor. These can create distractions and obstacles for museum visitors. Physically, they can block visitors' view of the exhibits, restrict what areas visitors can explore, and create a sense of disconnect with the site. This can be especially prevalent with themed weddings. For example, during the early days of bringing in event rentals, the Ford Piquette Avenue Plant hosted a wedding that turned out to be circus themed. Tour groups learned about the history of the early auto industry in Detroit as they were led past clown decor, a faux ticket booth, and a red-and-white striped tent. To make matters worse, the wedding was picked up by a major bridal magazine. While the resulting article was free advertising, it also created renter expectations that the museum desperately had to change.

The obvious solution is to allow renters to set up only after the public has left; however, this isn't always possible, and for some organizations, it's unavoidable that rental set up begin while the museum is still open to the public. Setting clear limitations on decor in the contract will help prevent disruptive event set up while the public is inside the building. Providing the renters with acceptable examples of event set up will help as well. The Ford Piquette Avenue Plant summarizes its decor policy to renters by using the line, "Only tabletop decor is allowed." These solutions are just a number of ways museum staff at the Ford Piquette Avenue Plant over the years have improved the overall experience at the museum for everyone from visitors to renters and guests and valued vendors.

With this new source of income for museums comes new concerns: challenging the institution to a balancing act between preservation, maintaining visitor experience, and collecting revenue through rentals. The tools and solutions previously discussed will hopefully provide a means to continue that balance of hosting event rentals and maintaining preservation standards. Because every museum is unique, museum staff should feel empowered to create effective event rentals policies for their specific situation. With sound policies in place, museum staff can ideally turn an event rental into a sense of partnership between the renters and the institution.

Establishing Roots to a Successful Museum Store

Christa Dyer, Director of Retail, Country Music Hall of Fame and Museum

Building a successful store is like planting a tree and watching it grow. Many believe that to run a successful museum store one must have an eye for innovation, keen management, and outstanding customer service. But what if your successes strive more from your relationship with other departments from within the museum itself? From my past successes building two museum stores, I am ready to share my wealth of knowledge with you. I have learned a lot along the way, have had wins and have had losses, but through those strides I have developed a key understanding to running a successful museum store. Let's dig in and see how by planting a tree, your store can flourish.

Every museum store has one thing in common: it can't be a museum store without a museum! Think of the museum as your tree's roots. Each root tells a different story about the museum's history and accomplishments. These roots are ever growing with the museum's milestones, donors, and past staff members—the list goes on and on. These roots are established within the museum's soil, or the city in which the museum resides. Think of the trunk of the tree as your museum's mission with each branch representing a moving part within your organization or departments. Branches will continue to grow and diminish over time as will your organization's departments. The leaves are objectives; leaves constantly come and go, and once an objective is reached, a new leaf appears in its place. Think of sunlight to be what makes your tree grow. Sunlight is your museum's attendance. Without people walking through your doors, your museum won't live; your leaves won't turn, your branches won't grow, and the tree that you've worked so hard to establish has become a stump. A stump that only leaves its roots and history.

Let's get started. You have your soil, your roots, your trunk, and now it comes to branches. Each museum's branches will be different from others', but how do these branches impact the store's success? You need to intertwine these branches by doing research for your store's merchandise plan. Your store's branch will grow and inter-twine among many different departments within your organization. For me, running two successful children's museum stores, my store branch mingled with education and exhibits. By doing so, my store was able to connect very strongly with the products sold within the store and their connection to the galleries and programming within

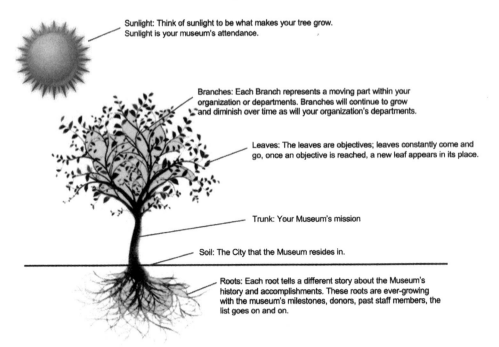

Sunlight: Think of sunlight to be what makes your tree grow.
Sunlight is your museum's attendance.

Branches: Each Branch represents a moving part within your
organization or departments. Branches will continue to grow
and diminish over time as will your organization's departments.

Leaves: The leaves are objectives; leaves constantly come and
go, once an objective is reached, a new leaf appears in its place.

Trunk: Your Museum's mission

Soil: The City that the Museum resides in.

Roots: Each root tells a different story about the Museum's
history and accomplishments. These roots are ever-growing
with the museum's milestones, donors, past staff members, the
list goes on and on.

Figure 35.1   Museum Tree

the museum. Your research will be never-ending as with new programing and camps commencing every quarter, you must find out what products you can bring into the store so that those visiting the museum only for a special program or camp can take their experience home with them. Meet up with your exhibits team often to find out what is happening and changing within the galleries. Your store product needs to be an extension of the museum—it is where your guests can continue their learning and exploring at home.

Merchandise your store to match that of your museum. Intertwine the museum galleries and the store branches. I've found that by merchandising by gallery, your store becomes more shoppable and easier to manage. Eliminate the craft section, science section, boy section, and girl section. Mix your product by gender, age, and price point all within the category of the gallery. This helps you extend the museum into your store and makes it easier on you for product selection and merchandising. Just think about it: a family comes to the store and your staff welcomes them and asks them what their favorite part of the museum was today. Both kids yell, "Innovation Station" (a science-themed gallery)! The store staff member directs them to that area of the store and within that area, the guests can find something for both kids, aged under five and over eight. Maybe it's a science kit geared toward kindergarteners and a chemistry set for the older child. They have a wide variety to choose from as you select product that will fit the needs of all different kinds of financial backgrounds. Maybe the family can purchase the $100 chemistry set or maybe they choose the $30 set. Either way, your product selection was prepared for their purchase and their shopping experience was enjoyable because you merchandised your store appropriately to the museum.

When it comes to running and staffing a successful museum store, the museums of tomorrow must pay close attention to their amenities and intertwine the store staff with neighboring department branches. The store staff must know the galleries, programming, camps, and special exhibits—the list is never-ending. Your store staff must know the product and how it relates to all aspects of the museum, otherwise they won't be able to sell it. I've created two wonderful activities to get to know the store's product and how it relates to the museum. They get my staff to interact more with other staff and other areas within the organization they might not be familiar with. Both activities are like scavenger hunts, one through the store and one through the museum. The museum activity is what I have all new store hires conduct within their first day. It gets them familiar with the museum galleries. The second activity is a scavenger hunt for the store. Now that they have discovered the galleries, they get to become detectives and really dig into why we carry the products that we carry within the store. Put your store staff through gallery training with the education team as well. I've found that this helps your sales associates "talk the gallery" when selling a product to a guest. Don't be afraid to meet with fellow departments. I met monthly with our exhibits team and education team to know what was happening in their areas so that I could relate their happenings to the store. This helped us be in the know of certain products education was using in programing and camps so we too can sell the item in the store. It also helped us mirror props that are used in the galleries.

Your tree's leaves are what happens every day. Maybe one of your branch's leaves this week is a special promotion. Work with your vendors! You'd be surprised how many vendors will pay you—you read that right, *pay you*—to hold special promotions within your store for their product. The best way to get involved in promotions like these is to ask. Make sure to ask, and ask often, your sales representatives and vendors. Make sure you heavily promote any sales promotion you conduct within your store via store signs, social media pushes, and e-blasts. Although vendors will not provide any additional marketing for your promotion or event, they will often provide a marketing kit. If one is not provided for you, you are more than welcome to request one. Another leaf is hiring and another leaf is merchandising: these leaves will change every day, month, and year, but you get to create them.

Another branch that will interweave will be marketing. Your store must mingle with marketing's branch! You need guests to visit the store that aren't necessarily there to visit the museum. Get yourself out there, get billboards and magazine ads, and market yourself. In the past I developed a holiday marketing campaign that ended up driving a lot of walk-in business. We played off being an educational facility and an educational toy store and told San Antonio that we are "The Smartest Toys in Town!" We invested in five billboards around town promoting fun shoppable sayings like, "Stuff Their Stockings with Brain Food"—get fun and creative with it! A lot of people came into our store and said that they saw our billboard and were glad they did as they didn't think of our children's museum gift shop as a place to find stocking stuffers. Sometimes you have to think outside the box! Marketing feeds into the sunlight that makes your tree grow. People will know about or visit your museum or its store without marketing and promotion out in the community.

Figure 35.2   DoSeum Billboards Example 1

Figure 35.3   DoSeum Billboards Example 2

Have a tight budget? Remember that trade can be your best friend. Team up with a local paper or shopping mall, put an ad up (whether it be a print ad or a poster), but trade admission passes, meeting space, or a basket of goodies from the store for a gala auction. The possibilities of trade are endless and always seem to work out for the best. Team up with local mommy bloggers too! They will write reviews on product and on the museum too, all for free! Mommy bloggers will promote their blog post on all social media platforms too, at no cost to you. Don't be afraid to send press releases for the store. Many times, marketing departments will sway away from sending a press release for store promotions, but in my experience, it's a great tool! I have created a top ten gift guide each year for the store and send it to local mommy bloggers and media outlets. It's how I've been invited to be on some morning news shows to highlight product from the store for holiday shopping. We've done it for the summer too: ten items to keep your kids entertained this summer was a great theme. It's great exposure for the store and a segment for the local news stations to have some fun with.

Figure 35.4   DoSeum Top 10 Holiday Gift Guide

This is a great pick for a long car trip with the kids. They can be entertained for hours with the games included. The secret decoder can then be used to write secret messages throughout the trip. I remember car trips with my brother and we'd create a secret language and pass messages to each other. It was a fun way for us to actually get along when spending hours together. This decoder allows kids to take that to the next level. It's a neat way to build creativity, ingenuity and analytical skills.

Secret Decoder Deluxe Activity Set
Meredith Doby
Director of Exhibits

DISCOVER   EXPLORE   CREATE   LEARN

Figure 35.5   DoSeum Summer Toy Recommendation Example

If you see missed revenue opportunities from areas within the museum, don't be afraid to reach your branch into those areas! I saw a decline in sales from our museum's field trips as many schools didn't want their students visiting the store. This of course hurt our bottom line as each student was considered part of our sales per visitor goal. So what did I do? I created a preorder form for our educational department to send out to schools when they book a field trip. Now schools can preorder $1.00, $5.00, and $10.00 museum souvenir kits and they never have to step in the store.

It's a win-win, not only for the store but also for the teachers. Now it's up to the teachers as to when they want to hand out the merchandise to those students that ordered. I've found that most teachers wait until the end of the day to distribute so that the students aren't distracted at school. Find out what items are being used in a program or camp and carry those items in the store. Your tree's branches should constantly weave in and out of exhibit's branch, education's branch, and more as you see fit.

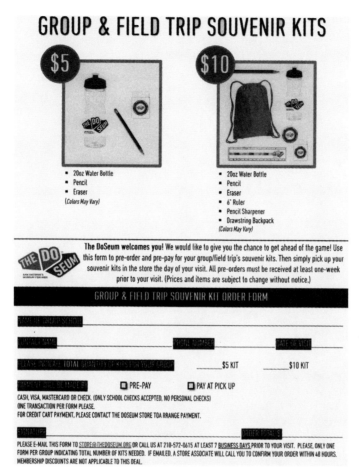

Figure 35.6   DoSeum Group and Field Trip Souvenir Kits

Every organization wants their tree to flourish and thrive. Some museums may only have a few branches while others have hundreds. No tree is the same, as goes for museum revenue. By planting a solid tree with intertwining branches with new leaves growing every day, your store will be set for success.

36

Why a Museum Store?

Blue Anderson, Manager of Visitor Services, Columbia River Maritime Museum

Souvenir: from the French, twelfth century, meaning "to remember, come to mind."

Souvenirs can be dismissed as trivial, and a museum store's stature can land near the bottom of a nonprofit institution's hierarchy. A nonperforming store could be looked at as an albatross around an institution's neck, the space put to better use for education, meeting rooms, or additional office or storage space. Why, then, a museum store?

MUSEUM STORES SERVE MANY PURPOSES

The primary reason to devote space and resources to a museum store is to have a reliable source of cash flow into the general fund. But extending the visit, as well as surprising and delighting the visitor, can be just as important for your long-range goals and brand loyalty. The museum store is the optimum venue to provide that connection.

Museum stores are often the last stop for visitors, and that stop can garner vital feedback on what they loved about the museum as well as what objects might need to be expanded on or added to your collections. Great store staff listens to visitors' personal stories and encourages them to give feedback of their impressions. Well-trained staff also note not only what visitors are taking with them but also what comments they hear about what items might be missing from the store's selection that would help visitors fondly recall your museum well into the future. At the same time, your visitors feel good because they are buying a special item that will delight either themselves or a gift recipient, while knowing that the proceeds of their purchase will support the institution to which they are loyal.

SALES PER VISITOR AND HOW TO INCREASE IT

Whether you are starting a retail presence, expanding it, or correcting a nonperforming store, the easiest indicator of success is your sales per visitor (SPV) number. Knowing

251

your SPV can be the strongest tool in planning and growing your store sales and can be easily understood by seasoned staff as well as volunteers.

To get your SPV, divide your store sales by the number of paid visitors for any period of time—daily, monthly, or yearly. For the best results, count the visitors that come to your site while the store is open; but the important thing is to be consistent with your method of counting.

The average SPV can vary widely depending on museum type, region, population, and institution size. The Museum Store Association (MSA) publishes a Retail Industry Report every two years that breaks down national data by specific categories and is invaluable to any nonprofit executive or retail manager. (Contact the MSA for the latest Retail Industry Report.) The natural inclination is to want to know what other institutions are doing and meet or exceed the industry average, and that is a great goal; however, knowing your own numbers and your own visitation trends can be quite effective. Hiring a professional museum store consultant who can take your data and trends and offer concrete ideas and solutions to help you improve your performance can also be particularly useful, especially if you have stagnant sales and staff and management that have long-embedded buying habits.

Museum stores often rely on special exhibits to increase their sales, but you can grow your sales and increase your SPV *without having to grow your attendance numbers or stock levels*. Say you are a historic house with a steady forty thousand visitors a year, and your store sells around $125,000 a year, which is a respectable SPV of $3.13. However, you'd like to increase your sales to $135,000 a year, or an SPV of $3.28. One way to naturally pop an increase to your SPV is to look at your pricing structure. If your store has a tradition of pricing small items at $2.50, and these items sell well, repricing them at $2.95 will most likely not result in a slowdown in sales. If your store keystones prices (doubles the cost) on larger items, look at implementing a 2.2 or 2.4 *basis* in your pricing. For example, if you increase the price of a $40 item to $44, it is unlikely that you will receive pushback.

Knowing your projected SPV can also help in your store budgeting. For example, let's say you are that same historic house and you will be hosting a traveling exhibit called "Tea Sets that Stirred the World." Past institutions that showcased this exhibit saw an increase of ten thousand visitors, and you believe you will have the same turnout and that half of them will go through your store. Your $3.38 SPV times forty-five thousand visitors (an increase of five thousand over your regular yearly visitation numbers) will give you a sales projection of $152,100. Your store manager might rightfully argue that those extra visitors won't shop in the store because you don't carry tea sets, and so in order to set a more realistic budget, you will need to add tea or tea sets and tea accessories to your mix of merchandise or plan for fewer tea exhibit visitors.

BUY WHAT SELLS

Museum store managers can get into trouble when they buy for their own likes and tastes or that of a key board member, especially if the core visitation has different interests and demographics or are looking for items in another price range. If you draw a large amount of children, for example, and they are allowed to shop, some of your merchandise needs to be child friendly. Have a good range of products under $10 and include any state or local sales tax into your pricing to make the transaction go faster. If you have, say, a 5 percent sales tax, price your $5 item at $4.75 so it will round up to an even dollar amount.

This concept can also work the opposite way, with staff buying "out of their own pocket" and afraid to bring in larger ticket items because their circle of influence can't afford the merchandise. High-end jewelry and original art sales can suffer if staff has an aversion to the price points. It can also be the reason expensive items lie in a case, untouched for months or years, and not displayed to their advantage, which then creates "proof" that your visitors aren't interested in higher-quality goods. Inviting the artist into your store to talk about the piece can help your staff understand why the item is priced as it is.

Logo items and proprietary goods can take your institutional name literally around the globe, opening up conversations about your museum, where it is, and what the visitor saw there. Supplying reusable and environmentally friendly bags can last long past the initial purchase. Putting your logo or image on both sides of a bag will ensure maximum visual exposure to your brand, offering a long-lasting embrace of your museum's story.

TURNING HARD-TO-SELL INVENTORY

"Turn" is a store's ability to sell merchandise quickly so that more products can be brought in to sell. Although having merchandise that sells quickly makes this a desirable goal, sometimes you need to have a slower selling item in your store because it is the right thing for your store to stock. For example, a historic house that is famous for its collection of gold leaf tea sets might be expected to carry very expensive gold leaf replica tea sets. The good news is that big ticket items can actually help sell less expensive items in the same product line. In the case of the tea sets, this could include gold-toned tea sets and budget-friendly add-ons such as packaged tea, teaspoons, and honey.

Museum publications offer a similar challenge. They are an important part of most institutions, but even a well-researched manuscript may not be a best seller and can become a major inventory issue. Beware both the allure of printing in mass quantities to obtain discount pricing and the unrealistic belief that there will be a high interest in the subject matter. Print, at the most, half of what the author thinks will sell; you can always reprint if you find you have a hit on your hands. Smart strategies like this will ensure that you will have a lot fewer boxes to store in your building and less inventory weighing down your store's profits.

OTHER INTANGIBLE "PROFITS"

Museum stores can be a resource for your library, curatorial, education, membership, volunteer, and fundraising departments as well. The museum store is where these departments should all feel comfortable researching books, logo items, executive gifts, educational resources, and other items they may use in their work. Museum store best practice would have no department making money on another department in the same institution. Departments should be charged wholesale price (that is, what the store paid) plus shipping, whenever possible.

Some museums combine the visitor services manager with the store manager position, thus saving payroll costs. Another benefit to combining the two areas is that it gives you the ability to use the staff interchangeably between the store and the admissions desk. This makes staffing very flexible, with either area being able to cover for the other during vacations, sick calls, and emergencies. It can also make for a happy staff, as they can have a more flexible schedule or add extra hours on when they are available.

KNOW YOUR RETAIL NEIGHBORS

Being aware of what your neighborhood stores stock and what they specialize in helps your store staff give exceptional customer service to visitors, fills in gaps of merchandise needs, and keeps staff abreast of the pricing trends in your area. Don't compete, complete. The goodwill toward your merchant neighbor can't be bought and will go a long way in promoting your institution to the tourist who might not normally visit a museum.

Your neighborhood merchants might also recommend local artisans as they fit into your museum's mission and special exhibits. Local consignment artists are a great way to get merchandise into the store without paying for it up front, creating a unique place to shop that isn't a cookie cutter of other stores in your area. Sourcing unique jewelry, art pieces, and local books are sure ways to help deter your customers from buying from online sources or the large national retailers.

BIG BOX STORES

"Big Box" fright is prevalent in the retail world, and nonprofit retail is not immune to some effects of their low-cost pricing. Selecting items that are not sold in national chains requires knowing what these large stores are carrying and usually requires you to visit these stores to be sure. Your local sales rep might not know a selection is placed in a mass-market setting because some manufacturers hire two sales representatives for the same area—one for specialty retailers and another for large distribution.

Internet sales are another hot topic in both regular and nonprofit retail, and a web presence is a positive objective. However, according to the MSA's 2018 Retail Industry Report, the average museum website produces less than 2 percent of the institution's brick-and-mortar store sales. The cost of running a lucrative web store requires dedicated staff for the five Ps: promoting, proprietary, posting, processing, and profit. To be successful, you must be able to create items that are not available on other retail websites that can, and do, undercut your prices. This is not to say you shouldn't sell items available at other museums or stores; these could be add-on sales, but not the driver to your website.

OUTSIDE MANAGEMENT GROUPS

There are pros and cons to consider before an institution rents its store to a for-profit company that specializes in institutional retail stores. Outsourcing the retail store can be a viable option for some of the larger institutions and can mean a regular income flow from rent, as well as no staffing or merchandise costs. While the elimination of payroll can be enticing, it also means renting out your space to management that doesn't report or answer to your museum board or management. Be sure to have a clear picture as to what this means for your product mix.

MUSEUM STORES VS. GIFT SHOPS

A nonprofit museum store differs from an independently owned for-profit gift shop because museums adhere to the code of ethics of their institutions, and the MSA requires its members to follow (in part) these guidelines:

- Fulfill our professional responsibilities with honesty and integrity.
- Stay informed of, and comply with, institutional policies, as well as all relevant local, state and national laws.
- Support and recognize the need to preserve and protect our cultural and natural heritage.
- Support and recognize socially responsible practices such as Fair Trade, environmental conservation and the integrity of product components, function and safety.
- Uphold the importance of quality sources, educational value and relatedness of all products sold in the retail operation.
- Ensure that all reproductions and replicas of cultural and natural artifacts are clearly labeled as such.
- Adhere to institutional policies regarding proper disposal of deaccessioned materials.
- Treat all business affiliations with respect.
- Do not conduct business with organizations or individuals with whom we have a conflict of interest.
- Never use our position for personal gain.
- Use MSA's Knowledge Standards to educate and encourage high standards of professional competence and conduct.
- Champion the retail operation as an important asset of the organization and a benefit to enhance the visitor's experience. (MSA Code of Ethics Adopted 1984, Revised 2014)

WHY A MUSEUM STORE?

Watching a kid's eyes light up when you hand him or her a spyglass and show him or her how to use it. Talking with that World War II veteran about his days as a flying ace. Having a merchant neighbor call to say he or she saw a great sail cloth handbag from a local company that we may find perfect. Getting an email from the development officer asking if we can gift wrap six shirts with our museum logo for visiting VIPs. Listening to different accents and languages and asking those visitors what brought them to the museum. Collaborating with all of the museum departments to make your institution the best it can be for visitors of all ages and from so many places. Sending the visitors home with a tangible memory of what might be their only visit to this country. And sending them home with a little piece of ourselves too.

That's "why" a museum store.

Edited courtesy of Kristen Daniels

Unique and Exceptional

Product Development for Museum Stores

Michael Guajardo, Director of Retail Operations, Virginia Museum of Fine Arts

Today's increasingly competitive retail environment requires a museum store to distinguish itself from its traditional retail brethren. Creating unique, exceptional, and artisanal products that relate to the museum's holdings or exhibitions is one of the best methods for enhancing competitiveness in the retail market while also reinforcing the museum's mission.

The basic principles of product development are the same for museum stores and traditional retail stores. However, there are some challenges that museum stores will have to consider that are not often encountered by traditional retail. Navigating these challenges requires innovation and creativity. In this chapter, I discuss these considerations and provide a basic blueprint for product development, drawn from my experiences as the director of retail operations for the Virginia Museum of Fine Arts.

CONSIDERATIONS FOR PRODUCT DEVELOPMENT IN MUSEUM STORES

A museum store functions principally as an extension of the museum, promoting and generating interest for the museum's mission, collections, and exhibitions. In contrast to the traditional retail store, which has the flexibility to create its own theme and product mix, the museum store must work within the confines of the museum's mission, reflect its collections, and garner curatorial support. Managing the heightened responsibility to authentically represent works and culture, and sustain artist integrity heavily influences what is appropriate to create. These unique challenges, along with inventory management, are key considerations.

Consideration 1: The Value of a Product

For museum stores, the value of a product is not solely defined by its marketability or its profitability, although both are important considerations. Products must also be mission driven and related to the museum's collections or its exhibitions. Curators are an important resource in that regard, as they can help shape and guide product ideas that speak to the museum's collection. Involving curators in the conversation at the beginning, middle, and end will help create buy-in and avoid any surprises from both sides. Custom products offer an opportunity to educate visitors about the museum's mission and to enhance their experience of its collections and exhibitions. Curatorial guidance will ensure that the educational component is on point and that the product idea is in keeping with the museum's mission.

Consideration 2: Collection Sensitivities

Museums already have a heightened responsibility to ensure sensitivity in regard to their collections and the way they are presented. Work with curators, focus groups, and peers to navigate these pitfalls. Stay away from projects that might be culturally or religiously insensitive or be too provocative for your clientele. Creating a product that you can't put on your sales floor, for whatever reason, would result in a waste of time, money, and resources. Depending on the type of museum, your challenges, in regard to product development, might be monumental. Holocaust museums, memorial museums, and museums dedicated to unpopular historical events might find it hard to venture into developing products that pass public scrutiny while still holding true to the mission and their heightened responsibilities. The museum store and the museum would suffer, both publicly and financially, without considering the importance of collection sensitivities.

Consideration 3: Inventory Management

Inventory management for a museum store is more difficult because the rate of turnover and the business cycle differ from traditional retail. The rate of turnover is slower for museum stores. As a result, profit margins on average need to be higher than for the traditional retail store, if only to account for these greater challenges. Creating a product or line to coincide with an upcoming exhibition can be tricky. There is always a risk that the product will not sell once the exhibition has departed. Moreover, even if the product was developed for an exhibition, it should blend with and complement the existing inventory. Gauging the right mix and number of products is another key aspect of inventory management. Carrying too much of a particular product, especially a slow-selling one, is detrimental for many reasons, not the least of which is that it consumes valuable retail space in the museum store, where space is often at a premium.

Use historical sales data to help determine your desired inventory level. Also consider whether the new products need special packaging and will be sold in store, online, or through wholesale channels. Addressing these issues in the early stages of a product's development will determine order quantities, space allocation, and turnover goals.

Managing all three considerations is key to a museum store's success in product development, a venture that is inherently fraught with risk. But it is also a venture that rewards innovation and creativity of spirit. Speaking from personal experience, developing a new product is one of the most challenging, but also gratifying, parts of my job. In the next section, I explain the process my team and I use to develop a product from initial research to developing the concept to sourcing vendors and, finally, to manufacturing and production.

A BLUEPRINT FOR PRODUCT DEVELOPMENT IN THE MUSEUM STORE

The first step in developing a product is compiling research about your particular store. Knowing the types of products that sell well in your store as well as the taste and pricing expectations of your store's customers are key factors to consider. In this initial phase, the focus is on gathering as much data as possible to narrow the list of possible products. Focus on those that will likely generate income, complement the museum's mission or exhibitions, and fit within the museum's overall aesthetic and philosophy. Use your own sales reports to spotlight bestselling products and categories. It is also helpful to solicit input from employees, customers, and especially from the museum's curator to understand the viability of product ideas and concepts.

Once this research has been completed and an idea for a product has been chosen, the next phase is to select the artist or vendor who can bring your vision to fruition. Depending on the particular product, this process may require interviewing many different artists and vendors or only a few. While a Google search will probably give you many likely candidates, your best bet would be to start with artist councils or guilds, trade shows, and professional organizations, like the Museum Store Association. As with most interview processes, it is important to collect reviews and references on artists or vendors from peers or persons they've worked with. People creating a custom product will have different qualifications and criteria that they expect from an artist or vendor, but you should also look for artists and vendors that are easy to work with, flexible, and accessible. Considering that some manufacturing is done overseas, it is important to select a vendor who meets your needs and timelines. Overseas manufacturing can be less expensive but also comes with its own sets of challenges. High minimums and less quality control are a few.

After identifying the artist or vendor who can deliver on your vision, the next phase is negotiating the terms of engagement. Most artists or vendors will require you to purchase a minimum number of the products, but there are other terms that must be agreed upon. Some artists and vendors will have written policies or terms of engagement, while others will not. It is important to discuss the details to ensure that both parties are on the same page and that "surprises" will be minimal. I find at this stage it is helpful to develop a written timeline in collaboration with the chosen artist or vendor. This overall timeline should include deadlines and a contingency plan to navigate the unexpected. Working backward from your desired delivery date will keep everyone on track.

Anticipate much back and forth in the early weeks and months as you start the process and even after you have chosen your artist or vendor. You should ask your artist or vendor to produce a prototype to ensure that the parties are of the same mind when it comes to the level of quality, aesthetics, and dimensions of your product. It is important to discuss who will absorb the costs for these samples, how many will be produced, and how changes will be addressed. As with most business relationships, the terms and understandings of the parties should be reflected in written contracts or memorandums of agreement. Leave no detail to chance, as product development represents a large investment in time, money, and resources. In most instances, I have found that the process of developing a product, from concept to delivery, will typically take six to eight months.

At the prototype stage, I find it helpful to circle back to the curator, customers, and store's employees. Their feedback and will prove to be invaluable and offer you a fresh perspective—which is a very good thing to have if you have been working with a specific vision of the product for an extended period of time. This would be the time to make any changes.

While you are waiting for your custom product to arrive, start thinking about packaging, merchandising, and marketing. You might have already tackled packaging as you developed your product; if you did, congratulations! The artist or vendor might have suggestions, or you might have already considered how you would present it. If you haven't, you must determine if it needs a package at all. Some items, like jewelry, might work best in a jewelry case, without packaging. As the jewelry sells, it can be wrapped up in a nice gift box with ribbon. Other items might require packaging, like a puzzle, gadget, or home décor item. Packaging is a great way to share educational points on the item and its relation to the collection and use photography to help sell it. Packaging can also help protect the item, merchandise it, and store it.

Start thinking about your product launch. What will you do to let the world know that you have created something exciting, unique to your store, and new? Using social media can help you get your staff and customers excited about what is coming. Give them sneak peeks at the progress, share photos, and generate buzz about the product and launch. Develop a marketing strategy with your team and others in the museum. I find that the best advertising strategy is to generate a buzz through newsfeeds, social media, and word-of-mouth. Using professional photography, signage, and other in-store marketing materials will help promote awareness and highlight the item in the store.

Your wait is over and your custom product has finally arrived. Now what? Ensure that you inspect every one of your quantities to ensure quality control and that you are paying for what you wanted. Damages, quality issues, and any other "surprises" should be immediately reported to the vendor or artist. If you haven't already done so, determine prominent placement on your sales floor to highlight your new item. Your team should be educated about the new product so that they can generate excitement with customers. Share the artist's story, how it was created, the materials, and the relevance to the collection. Whenever possible, if an artist is involved in creating the product, work with him or her on a cohesive marketing strategy that involves an in-store launch. Customers, especially museum patrons, will appreciate connecting with the artist and learning about his or her inspiration, vision, and motivation. A trunk show can be a wonderful way for the artist to launch a product and generate great interest.

At the end of the project, it is important to celebrate your accomplishment, document the process, and note any changes that will improve the next project. Thank your team members and other shareholders. Each new product you develop will bring its own challenges and rewards, and each experience offers valuable lessons that can be used for the next project. With a little luck and practice, you can learn to develop new products that are profitable, pay homage to your museum's mission, and generate excitement among visitors!

RESOURCES

Borrus, Kathy S. "Marketing Crafts through Museum Stores." *Museum International* 40, no. 1 (1998): 22–27.

Chung, James, and Susie Wilkening. *Museums & Society 2034: Trends and Potential Futures.* Washington, DC: Center for the Future of Museums, 2008. Retrieved from aamus.org/upload/museums society2034.pdf.

Kelly, Robert F. "Culture as Commodity: The Marketing of Cultural Objects and Cultural Experiences." *ACR North American Advances* 1987.

Skinner, Sarah J., Robert B. Ekelund Jr., and John D. Jackson. "Art Museum Attendance, Public Funding, and the Business Cycle." *American Journal of Economics and Sociology* 68, no. 2 (2009): 491–516.

Theobald, Mary Miley. *Museum Store Management.* Nashville: AltaMira Press, 2000.

38

Expert Opinion: Aligning the Pittock Mansion Mission and Museum Store

Jennifer Gritt, Associate Director, Pittock Mansion

The Pittock Mansion is a historic house museum in Portland, Oregon, operated by the Pittock Mansion Society in collaboration with Portland Parks and Recreation. The mission of the Pittock Mansion Society is to inspire understanding and stewardship of Portland history through the Pittock Mansion, its collections, and its programs.

What does museum leadership expect from the museum store (for example, financial performance, visitor satisfaction, partnerships with other departments)?

As the associate director of a historic house museum, I'm currently the acting director for visitor services, museum store, and marketing. Because I'm leading the change efforts, redevelopment, and restructuring of all three departments, I'm in a position to shape the efforts of those departments and bring them together in the ways where it makes sense.

As for financial performance, the expectation at the start of the redevelopment of the museum store was to get the products aligned with the mission and museum experience, phase out irrelevant and underperforming inventory, increase turn, and bring in more custom products. The driving expectation is that the museum store should have something for everyone and that it continues the educational aspects of the museum experience.

The main goal right now is to get more members and locals to shop in the museum store and keep working on increasing dollars per person. We've increased sales by 26 percent over last fiscal year, and the store is generating more revenue for the organization than it ever has historically. The expectation from our board of directors is that we keep building on that momentum.

How do you determine the store's revenue and/or performance goals? What metrics or ratios do you monitor?

Right now, we are focused on dollars per person. Prior to joining Pittock Mansion in 2015, the organization was seeing a dramatic increase in visitation and admissions revenue and a dramatic decrease in museum store sales. This was mostly due in part to an imbalance of inventory, old and irrelevant inventory, too much inventory at the highest price point, and overall merchandising and look of the store.

As there was no "open to buy" when the redevelopment started in 2015, we had to generate sales and then reinvest that shot of revenue into inventory that was going to essentially "start a plate spinning." In the Mansion's case, it was the lack of notecards and paper products that caught my immediate attention. We increased the amount of inventory in the paper products department and saw an immediate increase not only in sales but dollars per person.

The initial month-to-month and fiscal year sales goals had to focus less on overall sales and more on increasing sales in certain departments while reducing the inventory imbalance in other departments. So whenever we had positive movements in either of those initiatives, it was a win. It's very important to deal with your problem inventory first and make sure you are addressing inventory-by-department imbalances. In our case, over 30 percent of our overall inventory on hand was jewelry, which generated roughly 4 percent of annual sales. We had too much jewelry on hand, which was a significant department imbalance.

As of fiscal year 2018, we've pretty much cycled out old and irrelevant inventory and can now start adding other metrics. Adding a margin goal to the increase in dollars per person metric lets us also make sure that we are achieving our sales growth in a healthy way—meaning we are bringing in relevant inventory that customers are paying full price for. Sales can be inflated with deep discount markdowns. So to focus on the margin will help museum store directors stay focused on the long-term goals and health.

For example, the first year of the redevelopment was all about getting rid of old, irrelevant, and high-priced inventory. Doing so increased overall sales but drove the margin down to 48 percent for the fiscal year. For the next fiscal year, the board of directors got excited about the sales (we set a new store sales record for the organization), which applied some pressure to increasing sales goals for the coming fiscal year.

Doubtful we were going to make the sales goals, I continued to focus on the departments and bringing in more "museum experience" relevant inventory as well as started developing several new custom products. From month to month, the store's sales were only coming in at roughly 2 percent higher than the year prior while the budget was projecting an 8 percent increase. But the margin was increasing and started to level out at 52 percent from month to month.

What this ended up demonstrating was that even though the overall sales weren't meeting their monthly targets, the museum store was actually generating more revenue for the organization than the fiscal year prior due to the increase in margin.

Who determines the prices for the store products? How are prices set?

As acting "director of retail" who is overseeing the redevelopment, I determine what inventory is brought in and what the price of that inventory will be. I start with a standard 50 percent markup. If the inventory is larger, heavier, and therefore incurs a higher freight charge, I take that into consideration and increase it to 52–53 percent markup depending on what it is.

For inventory that has a higher price point, I usually stay at 50 percent. For lower price point inventory, I monitor the turn rate and increase from 50 percent accordingly.

The other thing that determines price point is what is going on with the inventory the item is going to sit next to. If I brought in decorative matchboxes for $2.00 a box, but I'm selling a comparable item for $6.00, I'll price the matchboxes at $6.00 rather than $4.00. This is also key for custom products that you can usually get at a better wholesale cost and can maintain more of a 60–70 percent markup.

We also have member and volunteer discounts to consider. If I'm bringing in product attached to an exhibit where members will be more of a presence among the consumers, I'll factor that in to make sure I'm consistently getting at least 50 percent on the sale.

For books, however, I don't deviate from the title's listed price. While books usually don't have a great margin, they are an important part of the educational extension of the museum experience. Increased book presence is usually done in conjunction with increased custom products to balance out.

Overall, I usually focus the tendency for higher markups on lower priced items, custom goods, and comparable products. Higher-priced items usually stay at a 50 percent markup.

How do you select/develop products that are on brand and on mission?

Again, this is where setting up your departments to align with "categories of experience" within the museum and analyzing sales and performance by department can help. In our case, we have a dominant masculine storyline with the patriarch of the family who built and owned the Mansion. At the time when the store redevelopment occurred, the men's accessories department had two items in it that were at a price point of over $100. The buying plan for that department started with making sure we had items at three price point levels that tied either to some object of Henry Pittock's or some aspect of his life (for example, he was an avid hiker and outdoorsman).

For custom products, the goal right now is to have "logo" items available, but broaden the custom to include patterns or more abstract aspects of what visitors are seeing and experiencing. For us, we are just scratching the surface in custom development and are focusing efforts less on "logo" items or images of the historic house museum and more on the textures and patterns of the home.

Logo items or reproductions of art images on postcards, notecards, notepads, and scarfs are a typical custom goods approach, but our goal is to think beyond that and explore reproductions and replicas as well as creating inspired items that are unique but not necessarily screaming "Pittock Mansion!!"

One example is that we created a set of marble coasters (we have a marble staircase) with wall patterns that exist in the home. Depending on a customer's style, the coasters can be decorative and remind them of the experience and while at the same time is something they can use as decoration in their home. It's a beautiful decorative coaster that is only sold at our store.

What is the ratio of museum-developed products versus commercial products?

Approximately 35 percent of our current inventory is museum developed.

If the store is expected to draw customers outside of museum visitors, how does the store reach that audience?

I don't have any data on that as this upcoming fiscal year will be the first time we are going to be dedicating marketing efforts to the museum store. The biggest thing we will focus on in our marketing efforts is the uniqueness of our custom products, curated book selection, and educational items. Marketing efforts will include store connections—when possible—in press releases as well as print ads. We're also putting together a word-of-mouth campaign.

I'm also very careful about not carrying the same commercial items as other area "attractions" and popular shops so we really try to maintain the "unique" and "can't-get-it-anywhere-but-here" angle.

How do you balance mission with the commercial aspects of the store?

The educational component of museums, and then by extension museum stores, makes it a little easier to balance the commercial expectations with mission. Visitors want to keep the experience going and, in the museum store, they can touch and handle and feel similar objects to the ones they were not allowed to touch and feel in the museum. As long as the store's inventory is a relevant extension of the museum experience, the two go hand in hand.

I think another helpful approach in determining a mission-based retail experience is to align the store's departments with "categories" of experience, if you will. For the historic house museum, we have three experiences involving kitchens and dining rooms. What's going on in those rooms? What objects are in there? What is the interpretation? And then you can bring in products that line up with what visitors are experiencing as they walk through the museum.

If we set a goal to educate our audience about a specific topic and brought in a series of books about that topic that went on to sell well, we report that as a "win" in store sales. It's a measurement of both engagement and revenue—with a greater emphasis on engagement. Focusing on the former first tends to generate more positive numbers in the latter.

Beyond the Bottom Line

The True Worth of Museum Stores

Stuart Hata, Director of Retail Operations,
Fine Arts Museums of San Francisco, the
de Young, and Legion of Honor

Museum stores are an integral part of any museum, delivering a multitude of purposes for the institution to which they belong, from earning income and extending mission-related programs to visitor engagement and educational outreach. In addition, museum stores provide an appealing and satisfying experience for visitors that enriches their understanding of the institution they patronize while offering inspired appreciation beyond their visit. Therefore museum stores should be recognized as treasured destinations unto themselves and valued by their institution and stakeholders beyond the bottom line.

The success of a museum store depends not only on how much revenue it generates or how skillfully it operates but also on how well the store is integrated into the overall strategy of the institution and positioned for its audience. While revenue generation is a key measure of success, museum stores provide additional value by selling carefully "curated" merchandise that complements and represents their institutions to the general public and, through those sales, extend their institutions' educational mission to visitors. In addition, museum stores are key marketing vehicles that offer accessibility to the public and promote brand outreach beyond the walls of the museum. Stores that are considered a vital resource and component of their institution are empowered to succeed and prosper.

In recent years, there has been an unfortunate trend to simply monetize museum stores and treat them as solely revenue generators and prerequisite visitor amenities. Institutionally operated stores have been traded out for generic, cookie cutter retail operated by for-profit concessionaires, all in the interest of pure bottom line profits and reduced staffing and expense for institutions. The result is a greatly diminished and less meaningful shopping experience for visitors at outsourced museum stores and less potential for future revenue growth at institutions. However, independent museum stores are fighting back and challenging this purely bottom line mentality by advocating for their importance and value to their institutions.

ADVOCACY FOR MUSEUM STORES

A trusted ally and resource for all types of stores and their institutions is the Museum Store Association (MSA), a 501(c)(3) international organization based in the United States and founded in 1955 with the mission of advancing the nonprofit retail industry, its museum stores, and the success of the professionals engaged in it. In 2014, MSA released its official position regarding concessionaires operating museum stores:

MSA Position on For-Profit Retailing in Nonprofit Cultural Institutions
  After careful research and discussion, the MSA Board has established MSA's position on the for-profit retail industry's (concessionaires) presence inside nonprofit cultural institutions. Retailing that is first and foremost focused on profit may ignore the big picture of the institution, why it was founded, why it exists and the memories it has the potential to create for its patrons. Retail operations within a cultural institution that operate under the museum's charter can produce profit while supporting the institution's mission, and, most importantly, serve as a powerful extension of the institution's brand. Often the last experience a patron has inside a cultural institution—the final interaction with the brand—is during the museum store visit. If the institution abdicates this valuable opportunity to a retail entity whose commitment is not fully aligned with the institution's brand and vision, the value of the patron's final touch point is sorely diminished.

  The MSA Board's research concluded with the understanding that the goal of outsourced, profit-driven retailers is not, by definition, ideally aligned with the mission and goals of nonprofit cultural institutions. In addition, when a nonprofit institution turns over store operations to a for-profit retailer it loses an integral member of its management team—the store manager—whose job is to carry out the institution's mission and support the institution's financial objectives. Lastly, the Board found that the product lines and customer service provided by third-party, for-profit retailers operating in cultural institutions do not offer an effective connection to the institution, and therefore to its patrons. (Issued by the MSA Board of Directors, October 2014)

Additionally, to combat the trend in outsourcing, MSA delivers educational information and programs throughout the year culminating in an annual conference "MSA FORWARD" featuring networking, keynote speakers, and educational sessions by industry leaders and peers as well as a trade show highlighting the best vendors in the industry. MSA also undertakes a Non-Profit Retail Industry Study every few years to provide valuable benchmarks on store performance, financial data, operations and salary information, as well as best practices in marketing. The information contained in this report is an essential tool for comparing stores of similar revenue size and category and can assist in developing marketing strategies and guiding business decisions, such as maintaining an independently operated museum store.

INTERNATIONAL DIRECT-TO-CONSUMER CAMPAIGN

In November 2017, MSA launched a new international shopping and cultural campaign for consumers, Museum Store Sunday, that annually puts the spotlight on the unique, mission-related products found at independent museum stores worldwide. This annual event, timed to occur during the all-important Thanksgiving shopping weekend, invites holiday shoppers to *Be a Patron* by purchasing the quality gifts filled with inspiration and educational value found at museums and cultural institutions; their patronage will enable ongoing and future cultural appreciation and knowledge. Working in partnership with the United Kingdom's Association for Cultural Enterprises and the Museum Shops Association of Australia and New Zealand, MSA's Museum Store Sunday aims to be *the* global annual day to shop conscientiously and support museum stores and their missions around the world. By advocating for and encouraging high standards of curated products and professionalism, MSA helps museum stores and their nonprofit retail professionals better serve their institutions and the public.

GENERAL MUSEUM STORE OBJECTIVES

A museum store should deliver expected sales and contribution (earned income revenue) to the museum as well as serve as a vital educational resource that reflects the museum and serves the community. Revenues generated by museum stores go directly into the operating budgets of the parent organizations, providing economic sustainability for the museum and cultural engagement for the community. Following are general objectives that all museum stores should strive to attain.

Provide Earned Income

A museum store's top priority is to provide earned income for its institution. This is achieved through the careful management of inventory and resources, by selecting and producing mission-related merchandise with top gross margins, excellent customer service, attractive and compelling displays, and by implementing innovative marketing efforts and events. Strategies and physical store locations that capture optimum visitor traffic result in higher sales and profitability. Because most museum stores do not carry the full expenses of commercial retail, such as rent, utilities, security, insurance, and other overhead costs, the museum store should produce a net profit double that of commercial retail, generally between 10 and 20 percent of overall gross sales on an annual basis.

Reflect and Promote the Educational Mission of the Museum

The store and its merchandise should directly reflect the collection and programming of the museum in order to emphasize the museum store's unique focus and educational mission. The look, feel, and contents of the museum store should directly represent the brand and message of the institution. It must be immediately apparent to the museum visitor, upon entering, what the store is *about*. The merchandise of the store is its most important aspect and it must be carefully selected and developed, with focus on unique and special products of "museum quality" that connect them to the visitor's experience in the galleries. Store staff should be informed about the museum's collections and programs so they can share that knowledge with visitors and answer inquiries in a friendly and effective manner. Last, store presentation, marketing, and events should reflect collections and programs and tie these initiatives back to the institution.

Enhance the Visitor Experience

As one of the most popular and enjoyable experiences of a museum visit, the museum store offers visitors the opportunity to "take a piece of the museum" home with them to be inspired about what they viewed and further the learning encounter they experienced. The store should strive to be educational on all levels; it should be interesting and fun, a place of discovery, and should encourage the visitor to see and learn in new ways. If shopping at the store is a positive and delightful experience, this will help to define and solidify a positive image of the institution in the customer's mind and frame the overall experience in a very memorable way. Patrons will want to return to shop and will share their positive store experience with the community.

Effectively Service Their Markets

Museums traditionally have broad market bases; however, specialized institutions can cater to and appeal to specific markets. For most museums, those attending will range from school children to seniors, from college students to working professionals, from families to single adults. It is important that store management carefully plan purchases, programming, signage, and displays that capture the interest of each of the various market groups. With this approach, the store can ensure that the museum visit is meaningful and connected to its various patrons.

GENERAL MUSEUM STORE STRATEGIES

Operating a well-conceived museum store requires strategic planning and execution in order to adequately reflect the parent institution and achieve sustainable financial rewards. Following are some general strategies for achieving museum store objectives that can be applied to all types of institutions such as art, history, science/technology, performing arts, libraries, military, maritime, sports, music, zoos, aquariums, children, parks, cultures, and sports, to name a few.

Provide a Focused and Unique Merchandise Selection

The museum store can develop distinctive, quality products that further reinforce the value of the museum and its mission to its patrons. These products, based on the special aspects of the museum, such as its exhibitions, architecture, collection, and brand, provide unique and exclusive offerings to the store's customers and museum visitors. Smartly developed products provide top margins for increased profitability. Careful selection of additional unique and related merchandise will further convey the educational importance of the products for sale and distinguish the store from its competitors. By working with local artisans and selling their works, the store engages with local talent and shows its support for the community, creating overall goodwill that reflects positively on the institution.

Position the Store as a Premier Resource for Focused Products

Each museum store can position itself as the premier resource of focused product based on its institution specialty, area of expertise, and location. With this specialized approach, the museum store becomes a trusted and known resource for consumers and the museum's community. While the store may not have the selection and breadth of Big Box or chain stores, it can advantageously distinguish itself through its refined shopping experience and high-quality merchandise. The museum store can lay the claim of carrying "museum quality" products that set it apart from other stores in the world.

Run the Store as a Business in the Nonprofit Arena

The success of the store depends on its ability to be managed and operated as a business. While a museum store is considered part of a "nonprofit" enterprise, the store must act as a "for-profit" retailer in order to effectively compete within the general retail environment and deliver solid business results. Effective inventory management and controls, careful purchasing, and a smooth and efficient store operation involving exceptional customer service will provide the expected earned income revenues that the museum depends on for its operation. Coupled with these standard retail procedures are additional facets particular to museum stores that create a complex business—from continually sourcing unique merchandise assortments that reflect changing exhibitions and programs to serving diverse stakeholders, such as members, donors, staff, and the general public.

Regard the Museum Store as a Full-Fledged Department of the Museum

The museum store should be regarded as a respected and vital department of the museum like any other integral museum department. The store should not be considered simply as a museum and visitor amenity. The store is a key extension of the museum experience and serves a very important educational, representative, and financial role for the museum. Within the museum, the store should be an active participant in the decision-making process with other museum departments, the administration, and senior leadership. Departments that museum stores traditionally work closely with include publications, membership, development, curatorial, education, marketing and PR, design, and exhibitions. It is very important for the museum store to have a voice when it comes to the museum deciding on what exhibitions the museum will develop or host in order to assess revenue potential for the institution.

Develop Greater Visibility and Outreach via Marketing, Events, and Online Presence

Integration with the museum's marketing, audience engagement, and educational efforts will position the store as not only a great place to shop but also as an important educational resource to the community. Coordination of store identity, marketing, and branding in alignment with the institutional brand will promote and brand the store and museum consistently to the general public. As the public dependency on online tools and experiences grows each year, it is essential for the museum store to establish an online presence and visibility regardless of its size. Whether it is a simple image of the store with operating hours and description or a robust, state-of-the-art e-commerce business, the online existence of the store only further communicated the importance of the store and helps develop its audience and customer engagement beyond its physical location. Last, consistent promotion through email marketing and special store events such as artisan appearances and book signings provide customer engagement and encourage store loyalty.

Create a Museum Store Mission Statement for Its Stakeholders and Audience

It is imperative that each museum store should have its own store "mission statement" that is derived directly from the museum's mission statement. A store mission statement is crucial in guiding the store and its staff with merchandise selection, assortment, values, and purpose within the museum and its role in the greater community. The statement can also be broadcast directly to store customers with in-store signage, graphics, and online video statements that communicate how purchases from the

Figure 39.1   De Young Museum Store
Courtesy of the Fine Arts Museums of San Francisco

Figure 39.2   De Young Museum Store—Museum Store Sunday 2018
Courtesy of the Fine Arts Museums of San Francisco

Figure 39.3   De Young Museum Store Display Tables
Courtesy of the Fine Arts Museums of San Francisco

Figure 39.4   De Young Museum Store Decorative Arts and Art of Africa Displays
Courtesy of the Fine Arts Museums of San Francisco

museum store directly support the institution. A vibrant museum store also creates a tremendous sense of pride and celebration for the museum's primary stakeholders: staff, trustees, members, students, visitors, and its general audience within the cultural community.

In summary, a thoughtful and strategic approach to operating a museum store will result in a store filled with exceptional and unique quality products that directly reflect the institution. Patrons should find a well-run store with exceptional customer service provided by educated and engaging staff who can speak about the merchandise, museum, and its programs. Additional outreach beyond the walls of the museum store can be achieved through integrated and targeted marketing and an online presence that the public now expects.

Much more than a "gift shop" or "bookstore," not any store can call itself a "museum store." The products sold and the experiences museum stores present to visitors are singular and exclusive to each cultural institution. This wealth of diversity and distinction is what sets museum stores apart from any other retail store or shopping experience. Museums are here to stay and those that fully support and embrace their retail operations know that independently operated museum stores contribute to the success of their institutions by providing not only a valuable source of revenue but also, beyond the bottom line, their stores fulfill the institution's educational mission while serving its audiences and the community at large.

Section VII

THE FUTURE OF REVENUE

As we have seen with the data presented throughout this book, rates of change for revenue sources can be volatile and unpredictable. Changes in tax policy, donor preferences, and economic activity impact an institution's revenue and are outside the control of any individual institution. After the Great Recession of 2008, nonprofit organizations, like their for-profit counterparts, examined how their organizational structures and business practices might have to change in light of macroeconomic shifts.

In 2009, William Landes Foster, Peter Kim, and Barbara Christiansen published their landmark article "Ten Nonprofit Funding Models" in the *Stanford Social Innovation Review*. This article identifies and defines ten business models used by large nonprofit organizations in an attempt to create a vocabulary that "non-profit executives can use . . . to improve their fundraising and management."

Museums, historic sites, zoos, botanical gardens, and aquariums use the member motivator business model, which "connect[s] members (and donors) by offering or supporting the activities that they already seek." Leaders in member motivator organizations ask themselves:

- Will our members feel that the actions of the organization are directly benefiting them, even if the benefit is shared collectively?
- Do we have the ability to involve and manage our members in fundraising activities?
- Can we commit to staying in tune with, and faithful to, our core membership, even if it means turning down funding opportunities and not pursuing activities that fail to resonate with our members? (Foster, Kim, and Christiansen, 2009)

With their special public trust responsibilities and ethical considerations, the "members" of a museum should equate to the general public, in the context of the Foster article. Then the first and last questions reflect the museum community's discussions about inclusion, diversity, connectivity, authenticity, sustainability, and mission.

The American Association of Museums established the Center for the Future of Museums in 2008. The Center's blog and annual TrendsWatch report "[help] museums navigate the future . . . [by] understanding . . . the dynamic nature of our cultural,

275

political, and economic landscape" (Center for the Future of Museums n.d.). The Center's research can help institutions answer the earlier questions and understand the impact of ex-museum trends on museums, including revenue generating possibilities. Elizabeth Merritt, founding director of the Center, wrote about her experience co-teaching a workshop on brainstorming ways to generate income from natural history collections (Merritt 2017).

Of course, the Great Recession of 2008 did not instigate funding or revenue problems for museums. As Cary Carson reminds us, attendance downturns and financing issues have challenged museums for decades. In 2004, Carson wrote a memo to fellow executives at the Colonial Williamsburg Foundation "to challenge conventional wisdom and stretch people's imaginations." Carson imagined multimedia productions, consortiums, and personalized content that would compel the next generation of museum attendees (Carson 2008). Carson's theorizing has either been realized or is currently under consideration. Amy Drake and Allison Weiss describe how the Southern Oregon Historical Society suspended public operation in 2009 and then reinvented itself by incorporating Michael Frisch's "shared authority" concept—an approach that our final contributor, Rachel Boyle, has also implemented. All of our contributors have reminded us to continually reevaluate our methods and approaches in light of the ever-changing economic environment and of the new technologies that can improve our abilities to fulfil our missions.

CHAPTERS PREVIEW

Our final two authors, James Stevens, senior associate at ConsultEcon, Inc., and Rachel Boyle, PhD, public historian at Omnia History, close the book by asking institutions to reexamine their business models and to reevaluate their relationships with the public. James Stevens focuses on earned income as a means to counterbalance reductions in public and private contributed income. He shares examples of how institutions have used data, variable pricing, and partnerships with other arts and cultural institutions to diversify and expand earned income opportunities. Rachel Boyle provocatively challenges institutions to move toward a cooperative funding model, based on the award-winning Chrysler Village History Project. She argues that institutions should move away from chasing large grants or fundraising bequests and refocus on public stakeholders. By cultivating local, long-term relationships, an institution is better able to fulfill its mission and to operate within its budgetary means.

The variability and fluidity evidenced in the quantitative data shared throughout the book and in the strategic and tactical recommendations from our contributors show that both the past and the future are difficult to measure, analyze, and predict. What is the solution? The dialogue among professionals and an understanding of the quantitative data facilitated by this book offer a methodology for a continual and continuous discussion of museums and revenue.

RESOURCES

Carson, Cary. "The End of History Museums: What's Plan B?" *The Public Historian* 30, no. 4 (2008): 9–27.

Center for the Future of Museums. https://www.aam-us.org/programs/center-for-the-future-of-museums/.

Drake, Amy, and Alison Weiss. "History: Made by You: A New Approach from the Southern Oregon Historical Society." *Oregon Historical Quarterly* 113, no. 4 (Winter 2012): 584–95.

Landes Foster, William, Peter Kim, and Barbara Christiansen. "Ten Nonprofit Funding Models." *Stanford Social Innovation Review* 7, no. 2 (2009): 32–39.

Merritt, Elizabeth. "FutureProofing Museum Business Plans." *museum* 96, no. 3 (2017): 17–20.

40

Evolving the Business Model with a Comprehensive Earned Income Approach

James Stevens, Senior Associate, ConsultEcon, Inc.

INTRODUCTION

Out of economic necessity or strategic mandate, museums are sharpening their focus on admissions, redefining visitor experience, leveraging big data market research and pricing strategies, and evolving from exhibition-driven to program-driven organizations. Implications include redefining what attendance and engagement means, employing technology and data in new ways, and articulating a clear set of costs and benefits of new programs and facility investments that generate earned revenue and net income in a nonprofit governance structure.

MUSEUM BUSINESS MODELS

With the economic recession exposing the limitations of museum business models, museums have had to diversify their mix of revenue. Earned revenue in the recession became more important as contributors scaled back and endowments and endowment proceeds decreased. Regional impact studies of the arts and cultural industry, such as in Greater Philadelphia, demonstrate how the earned revenues as a proportion of total revenue for arts and cultural organizations as a whole increased in the years after the economic recession due to declines in the total amount of contributions and interest income from endowment and other investment funds (Culture across Communities 2015). In the past decade, many museums have increasingly focused on the amount of revenue and income they earn because public and private sources have changed and reduced funding. Earned revenue is one way to fill the gap left by reduced contributions. During the recession government and philanthropy shifted focus to other community needs. Museums have since had to buckle down and focus on the business of earning money.

Whether out of necessity or due to a new strategic plan, earning revenue and income can be difficult for a nonprofit museum to implement due to governance and organizational resistance. Incorporating profit-maximizing business practices in a nonprofit institution can be challenging. How does earning revenue and profit fit into

279

a museum's mission and institutional culture? Does leadership or staff have the internal capacity (or desire) to pursue earned revenue and profit, including both program-related revenue and unrelated business income? The path of least resistance for some organizations is to maintain the status quo. However, maintaining the status quo is often not a sustainable business model, especially over the long term. The economic recession necessitated museums to explore new revenue sources and sharpen their focus on making money.

This pivot arguably leads to more sustainable business models. It also necessitates the museum c-suite contain new business and program managers that challenge the traditional institutionalized curator and educator culture and push for museums to increased earned revenue. How curation and education translate into attendance, engagement, and impact is an ongoing topic of conversation in the museum industry. For those museums that embrace earned revenue, they have to operate like a business with a bottom line orientation. In part that means assessing the feasibility of new facilities, programs, and unrelated business activity by their ability to earn a return on investment. Ideally, facilities and programming maximize revenue and net income to support, sustain, and subsidize mission-driven programming. Increasingly, donors are viewing program investments through the lens of economic returns, as well as philanthropic goals, charitable purpose, or societal or other returns to the investment. While first costs for program development or capital funds for expansions or new facilities can be high, museums have to create business plans for earned revenue streams that are rooted in the market realities of their location, the scope and appeal of their product (that is, visitor experience, visitor engagement, collections, facilities), their competitive context, and the experience of comparable programs or projects.

Knowing the Marketplace

Museums need to know inside and out their local and regional marketplace of museums, cultural organizations, and entertainment offerings in order to accurately measure if they are keeping up. That marketplace makes up the cultural industry in their locality. Museums also need to know what their peer organizations in similarly situated markets, facilities, and interpretive focus are doing to attract new audiences, generate earned income, and achieve their missions. Annual updates are necessary to establish time series trends for attendance and pricing to inform analysis of a museum's operating context. Benchmarking museum operations to similar organizations and those in their local and regional marketplace over time helps organizations know how they compare to their peers and competition. Building the cultural industry through cooperative marketing and advocacy work is paramount to the long-term success of nonprofit cultural organizations, and regional and national data sources for relevant operating data are becoming more and more available through initiatives like DataArts. Understanding the museum's positioning in its local and cultural industry networks with a data-driven and consistent approach to market research is critical to effectively navigating the marketplace and to identifying the approaches essential to generating earned income.

Knowing Population Trends and Demographics

If the population in your local area and region is growing and your attendance is flat, your museum is losing market share. How stable a museum's attendance is year to year is dependent on the business decisions and related expenditures and how new and changing exhibitions, programming, and events are required to sustain attendance over time and build audiences. Museums are opening up and becoming more community-oriented facilities, hosting sometimes equal numbers of mission-related events as private functions to generate new income for operations. Broadening the scope of the museum's mission and institutionalizing appropriate business practice from a market-driven perspective has the potential to fund new growth in mission programming.

Engaging the Consumer

Testing consumer appeal through primary market research is often out of reach to cash-strapped nonprofits. Many museums cannot afford expensive visitor studies or market research programs. The promise of low-cost internet survey tools like survey-monkey.com enables any organization to create and deliver a survey. The evolving set of tools for data analysis cost a modest amount of money and are easily integrated into email and internet outreach. There exists a market opportunity for a simple low-cost ticketing application that if adopted broadly could have profound impacts on museums' ability to mobilize data and analytics for deeper insight into marketing and operations. Aggregating that data across the museum industry offers broader understanding of visitation patterns and benchmarking against peer institutions. Knowing existing audiences enables museums to refine methods of reaching existing audiences and to identify new audiences to target for future visitation and engagement.

Consumer Trends Impacting the Bottom Line

Leisure time is evolving. People have less leisure time and take fewer vacations. The US Travel Association has quantified the billions of dollars in vacation hours not used by the American workforce, which for the travel industry means lost travel spending on vacation. The museum industry is experiencing the same market forces as the travel industry, trying to get consumers to take a break from working or commuting or doing what it is they typically do and visit a museum. Media content has proliferated through the internet and mobile devices. Getting someone's attention is both easier and cheaper to do but harder to obtain in any meaningful way. Their options are endless at the touch of a button for a substantial majority of us. Museums are still sorting out how to bridge the digital and the real in a way that enhances their drawing power and on-site experience for increased earned revenues.

Exhibition Evolution

Admissions income is at the core of what many museums do and can be a large share of the revenue they earn. Many museums are evolving away from reliance exclusively on permanent exhibitions. Visitation to museums cannot be one and done, and repeatability requires freshness, currency, and relevancy in content. Museums are developing changing, temporary, and special exhibitions to drive repeat attendance. Education programs and events are increasing attendance too, although typically not at a scale of general admissions to exhibitions. Nonetheless, programs and events offer a deeper level of onsite engagement, promote repeat visitation, and appeal to a diverse array of niche audiences. Program- and event-driven admissions can be costly, especially if they are staff time intensive and disrupt regular museum operations. Understanding the operating costs and earned revenue potential of new program concepts, from implementation to operations, is imperative when planning for new exhibitions, programs, and events.

STEM and STEAM

Because public and private education goals have emphasized STEM (Science, Technology, Engineering, and Math) learning and STEAM (Science, Technology, Engineering, Art, and Math), all types of museums have increasingly incorporated STEAM topics into their exhibitions and their programming. Educational programming is often supported by contributions but can be leveraged to enhance visitor experience and indirectly support admissions income. For example, the Independence Seaport Museum in Philadelphia partners with Navy engineers and local schools on building submersible robots. It recently converted its storefront retail space to an accessible maker space that creates more activity (when in use) and conveys a more active and engaged visitor experience than the traditional history museum experience. These types of programmatic changes and new partnerships help to enhance educational mission through programming. In addition, the new programming leverages new facilities, the submersible test and training pool in the case of the Independence Seaport Museum, to improve the ticketed visitor experience.

Hybrid Museums

A recent trend reflected by a handful of new museums—science centers, natural history museums, and other educational attractions—is to incorporate more living collections to enhance the visitor experience and thereby increase attendance and revenue potential. These hybrid museums are an emerging model that incorporates science exhibits, aquarium, zoo, theaters, research and development programs, and other facility programs. Located in Golden Gate Park near the De Young Art Museum in San Francisco, the California Academy of Sciences opened in a 400,000-square-foot new museum in 2007 that features extensive science, aquarium, and living world experience. Since the academy's opening, other new science centers have been developed as hybrid museums. Opened in May 2017 with a total project cost of over $300 million, Frost Science in Miami is a 250,000-square-foot science center with major aquarium features. The Cleveland Natural History Museum opened a new wildlife center featuring the native flora and fauna of northeastern Ohio. A smaller example in North Carolina is the Greensboro Science Center. Its $32 million phased master plan included renovating the 65,000-square-foot science museum, adding a 22,000-square-foot aquarium, and renovating the 22-acre zoo.

Blended Content

Science centers are finding that living collections aquariums have science learning value and greater audience appeal, and so new museum developments like the California Academy of Sciences, Cleveland Natural History Museum, the Greensboro Science Center, and Frost Science in Miami are blurring the lines of visitor experience with blended science content that explores living systems more deeply in the visitor experience. Funders, such as the Pew Center for Arts and Heritage, have also emphasized interdisciplinary programming that pushes museums into different creative realms (for example, a library staging a play with a local theater company). For many museums, blending content can be as simple as producing a performance or offering a reception targeting adults and where alcohol is served on a Friday or Saturday night in a science museum that normally host hundreds of school children mornings during the week.

Admissions revenue is directly related to the scope and quality of product and visitor experience. Changing that is a function of creativity and willingness to explore blending content that has more audience appeal than the current existing museum product. Blending content is by no means a solution for all museums. The financial performance of new exhibitions with blended content and interdisciplinary programs may be questionable, and the long-term audience engagement is elusive in some instances. Museums hosting more performing arts do not necessarily engender more museum patronage.

Culture and Commerce

Mixing mission with commerce may hold more promise than trying to appeal to other cultural audience segments. Cross cultural promotion and marketing may only breed more competition among local cultural organizations chasing the disposable income of niche cultural audiences. Mass audiences seeking entertainment experiences are larger markets. Introducing commerce into cultural organizations may appeal to a broader swath of consumer segments including audiences not traditionally associated with cultural participation. Commercial activities that are associated with cultural activities may create just enough additional exposure on the cultural audience margins to build new audiences and ideally generate additional earned revenue.

Pricing Potential

Different types of museums have different levels of earned revenue potential from admissions due to the prices they are able to charge for their product. Zoos and aquariums, for example, charge higher ticket prices because of the visitor experience they offer. Therefore they typically earn a large portion of revenue from admissions. Science centers and children's museums also earn healthy revenue from admissions.

Having multiple venues, films, simulators, rides, and other upcharges enhances per capita revenue and has the potential to appeal to new and different audiences. Art museums rotate art from their collections to creating changing exhibitions. Traveling exhibitions and "blockbusters" are a reason for variable ticket pricing, which is influenced by popularity and audience appeal of art being shown. History museums typically have low admission pricing compared to other museums, and some, like Bullock Texas State History Museum, have added theaters for upcharges and designed lobbies and other facilities to host more event rentals for earned income that generates visitation that is not only traditional attendance model of earned income generation.

Dynamic Pricing

Indianapolis Zoo employed dynamic pricing technology that has enabled them to smooth daily onsite visitation, increase the number of memberships, and improve overall visitor satisfaction. Dynamic pricing is the practice of pricing items at a level determined by a particular customer's perceived ability to pay. Customers can pay a lot for a visit, and those customers who cannot afford to pay a lot or would prefer to pay less can get a bargain if they are willing to visit the zoo during nonpeak periods. Peak period visitors pay the highest rates, and because they pay before they visit, they do not feel that they are paying too much. By smoothing visitor demand throughout the day, week, and year, the Indianapolis Zoo experiences less crowding, which has improved customer satisfaction with the visitor experience (Indianapolis Zoo and Digonex 2015).

Going Free

Flying in the face of making more money through price discrimination, some historic sites and other publicly operated museums are free, so they earn no revenue from admissions. The Dallas Museum of Art and others like it are removing all financial barriers to admission by offering free admissions. This revenue loss has been offset in part by related increase in retail sales, memberships, and contributions. The Alamo and the Gateway Arch are examples of free attractions with high retail sales that help support mission-related operations. However, the setting and institutional context in these examples may be unique and any museum that wades into these waters needs to consider the implications on revenue of offering free admissions.

Keeping Up with Inflation

Museums are not focused their earned revenue streams if they are not raising ticket prices to keep up with inflation. Many museums have increased ticket prices at rates over and above the general increase in inflation over the past decade, and attendance levels have not necessarily suffered. The typical museum-going audience of higher-income households is not as price sensitive as museums might think. Museum audiences are willing to pay top dollar for a premium experience. And when philanthropy is involved, paying top dollar to a charity is worth the investment. The question on pricing is not just whether or not to increase prices, but whether or not to increase prices commensurate with the value of the experience that is offered. Museums offer changing exhibitions, programs, and special events to created sustained value that offers visitors a reason to visit and to return.

CONCLUSION

Ultimately, museums make strategic choices based on strategic planning within the context of their governance, history, leadership, and staff culture. Earning income can create more sustainable business models in museums. Earning income requires museums to be more bottom-line oriented. Museums will have to incorporate best practices in technology adoption and use to gain real-time, market-driven analytics to inform decision making about programming and earned revenue. Overall, as in any consumer service business, museum staff should be friendly, knowledgeable, and engaging. Human interactivity is still the most popular feature of museums despite the proliferation of technology. Stressed out visitor assistants and educators on the front lines are assured to translate to poor customer experience. Making sure exhibits are in working order and facilities are accessible, clean, and attractive is also paramount to visitor satisfaction. As museums become more program and event driven, having appropriate staff in place becomes increasingly important. Staff experience and creativity is a source of program development. It is management's responsibility to ensure that new programs are developed and tested responsibly using sound strategic, feasibility study, and business planning. Unlike grant-driven program development that is subject to the ongoing discretion of donors to continue to fund the program, generating earned revenue and net income is perhaps a more entrepreneurial way of developing museum programs that enables organizations to be more customer and audience responsive than they have been in the past.

BIBLIOGRAPHY

Culture across Communities. "An Eleven City Snapshot, Greater Philadelphia Cultural Alliance." October 2015. https://www.philaculture.org/research/2015-portfolio-culture-across-communities.
Indianapolis Zoo and Digonex. "Overcrowded Weekends and Under-Leveraged Wednesdays." Funworld. November 2015. https://www.digonex.com/wp-content/uploads/2015/11/Funworld-Nov-2015-Industry-Report.pdf.

41

Envisioning Shared Authority as an Alternative Economic Model for Cultural Organizations

Rachel Boyle, PhD, Public Historian, Omnia History

Consider the amount of time and energy your museum pours into securing and abiding by grants or navigating the restrictions of wealthy donors. Now imagine devoting the same resources to listening to, engaging with, and serving the local community. Fundamentally reorienting the economic and social relationship with public stakeholders holds tremendous potential to transform the ethical and financial realities of museum work. In the field of public history, shared authority means acknowledging the power of both scholars and the public to create history and meaning. Originally proposed by Michael Frisch in 1990 as a guiding concept for conducting oral histories, a generation of public historians is pushing to expand the application of shared authority not only to collaborative storytelling but also to shared social and economic endeavors (Frisch 1990). In other words, shared authority is not just good public history but also a sustainable financial model for cultural organizations.

In this chapter, I will begin by exploring the idea of shared authority and interrogating the meaning of the term "public stakeholders." Then I make a case for abandoning fundraising as part of a broader shift away from an institutional scarcity mentality. Finally, I will conclude by envisioning a cultural cooperative as an example of a future business model. Overall, I aim to balance big picture ideas and questions with concrete suggestions. Rather than advocate for a pure or infallible financial model, I suggest shared authority as a guiding principle that can begin to unite the economic and social imperatives of a cultural organization and even use museums as a tool to resist the inequalities of capitalism.

SHARED AUTHORITY AND STAKEHOLDERS

Through the lens of shared authority, producing a historical or cultural output is an inherently collaborative process among public stakeholders and the professional—whether oral historian, scholar, or museum worker. The category of public stakeholder risks being as nebulous as "community" or "audience" but importantly connotes a vested interest or shared goal. As a public historian, I often work with historical societies who broadly identify stakeholders according to a local geographic region such as

287

a neighborhood, town, or even state. Yet even then certain groups emerge as invested stakeholders, others are identified as important yet are never engaged, and still others are intentionally or unintentionally excluded. All cultural organizations should think seriously about who exactly they intend to serve, ideally driven by an institutional commitment to advancing equity and combatting oppression. Shared authority, then, positions cultural organizations to leverage institutional resources like knowledge, collections, skills, and space for the tangible social and economic benefit of stakeholders within a broader social mission.

Stakeholders are not defined by their ability to contribute money. Certainly monied stakeholders can play a valuable role; for example, funds from foundations and wealthy donors can accomplish high-impact work and supply the start-up money for self-contained or self-sustaining projects. Project-based work in turn can productively resist the problems characteristic of bureaucratized institutional work. However, I advocate rejecting the framework and mentality of fundraising to secure resources in favor of a financial approach rooted in shared authority.

ABANDON FUNDRAISING

If the many conversations I've had with cultural and nonprofit workers across the country are any indication, many of us have worked for an organization that has become dependent on short-term, high-dollar grants for basic operation over the long term. It might start with grant guidelines reshaping a project's scope; over time, institutional priorities may shift to accommodate the interests of philanthropists and foundations. Cultural organizations seeking grants can quickly become like a dog chasing its own tail, neglecting the needs and interests of the broader public who cannot immediately provide that high-dollar high.

This approach feeds a scarcity mentality that maintains the only way to develop resources is to appeal to those in power. An idea explored by business consultants, personal development writers, and spiritual leaders, the scarcity mindset articulates the pessimistic and defensive posture that inhibits mindful interaction, constructive collaboration, and innovative thinking. In *The Active Life*, Parker Palmer observes,

> The scarcity assumption pervades our institutional lives by putting the power in the hands of the few and keeping it there. Hierarchies are always rooted in the belief that power itself is, or ought to be, a scarce commodity, rooted in the belief that few people are qualified to hold power, or that few should be allowed to hold it, lest the threatening abundance of power, known as "democracy," comes to pass. From the teacher who grades on the curve to the administrator who rules by fiat, the control of the few over the many is rationalized by scarcity assumption. (Palmer 1990)

An abundance mentality offers the antidote to scarcity. For a cultural organization this means acknowledging the power, skills, and resources of everyone at the table and inviting more people to the table in the first place. Relying on a broad cross-section of diverse income stakeholders offers a route to financial abundance that looks radically different from fundraising.

Here are tangible steps to embrace the abundance mentality of economic shared authority:

- Listen to stakeholder needs and align organizational priorities accordingly
- Acknowledge resources beyond large sums of money, including stakeholder time, labor, and skills
- Believe that $10 from 100 people is just as important—and more sustainable in the long term—than $1,000 from one person
- Build long-term relationships among diverse stakeholders to develop a sustainable, growing revenue stream
- Structure a budget that operates within its means (tangibly backed by stakeholder buy-in) and does not require big, last-minute infusions to break even
- Forego flashy projects that might bring in the big foundation bucks but do not have any existing buy-in from the local community
- Appreciate stakeholders who contribute resources to an organization that reflects them and their needs

Overall, economic shared authority frames all institutional work as a joint endeavor with public stakeholders. Engagement expands beyond program or outreach departments and becomes intentionally integrated with resource development for the benefit of both the institution and its stakeholders.

CULTURAL COOPERATIVE

For emerging organizations or institutions ready for a complete transformation, the cooperative model goes beyond a rejection of fundraising and provides an alternative structural approach to cultural work. A cooperative applies shared authority to the economic foundation of an organization to resist dependency on wealthy donors, competitive grants, or unreliable government funding. Additionally, it creates a system that can endure the recurring upheavals of capitalism and empowers cultural organizations to intentionally foster equitable economic relationships with stakeholders.

As inspiration for this approach, the Chrysler Village History Project emerged as a perfect storm of passionate public historians and enthusiastic residents from the working-class neighborhood of Chrysler Village in the southwest corner of Chicago. I had the honor of convening and coordinating the group, who donated their time and resources to leverage the newly revealed history of the area for the benefit of the contemporary community. In August 2016, the three-year project culminated with the launching of a robust online oral history archive and a community festival featuring the unveiling of commemorative signage and a mural designed and painted by local elementary students. The project was a public historian's dream and received awards of distinction for its collaborative approach from the Association of State and Local History, the National Council of Public History, and the Midwest History Association. However, the project had an important limitation: the public historians involved could not sustain professional involvement with the community long-term without compensation. What would a Chrysler Village History Project look like that not only delivers tangible benefits to the community but also pays for the public historian's labor? Where should the money come from to fund cultural workers? What is the responsibility of the professional to their funders? Their community? Should the two be one the same?

As one answer to these questions, I propose a cultural cooperative that would consist of members who contribute money or labor in exchange for a defined role in determining what services are provided. For example, residents could dedicate their time to a planning committee or a business might donate a certain value worth of resources. To resist replicating problems identified in historical societies or museums, the cooperative's membership structure would need to be feasible and valuable to a cross-section of the community. Even then, the cooperative must make an intentional effort to collaborate with local institutions and networks connected to stakeholders with limited to no extra time or money.

All members would participate in the determination of services provided by the cooperative, whether an oral history project, community festival, or an afterschool program for youth to paint historical murals. A cultural cooperative could, pending membership priorities, pursue cultural tourism as a way to deliver tangible financial benefits to a working-class community. With residents as members, the cooperative offers a strategy to engage with the risky economics of cultural tourism while resisting gentrification. The cooperative approach also shifts away from a volunteer, internship, or other unpaid labor model by providing stakeholders with tangible services—and a say in those services—in exchange for time and labor.

The resources pooled by the cooperative cover not only services but also the cultural professional's income. As a result, a key component of the work of the cooperative employee is to powerfully demonstrate the distinct and tangible value of their work to the community. By continually fostering buy-in, the cooperative fundamentally roots the attention of the cultural worker to contemporary, local issues. The professional can—and should—still push the public to deal with contentious local issues of wealth disparity, racism, and sexism but constantly frames the work in response to the primary needs of the cooperative's membership.

Even maintaining and growing collections should be guided by the concerns of public stakeholders. If collections do not resonate with the needs of the local community and cultural workers are unable to effectively communicate their value, the cooperative should be open to deaccessioning collections or transferring materials elsewhere. This also creates an opportunity to think creatively about what community-centered collecting can look like in a cooperative setting. Collections, then, emerge as yet another area where internal organizational priorities should match those of public stakeholders.

Certainly, a cultural cooperative does not deliver a fully satisfying escape from the realities of capitalism. Questions remain about who funds the cooperative during the grueling early years of cultivating grassroots support before the organization is financially sustainable. Yet the concept of a cultural cooperative provocatively applies shared authority on an economic level to redirect organizational focus away from donors and bureaucracy and toward the tangible realities of local stakeholders.

Whether abandoning fundraising or building a cooperative, economic shared authority illuminates a path that integrates the social imperatives of museums and cultural organizations with the financial strategies that undergird them. The spirit of shared authority can be intuitively applied to the programmatic aspects of museum work, yet the economic realities of an organization's resources often prescribe the limits of what can be accomplished. Why not position public stakeholders as the arbiters of a museum's economic conditions? Public stakeholders then become collaborators at every stage of cultural work and empower an organization to enact a social mission through their economic relationships.

BIBLIOGRAPHY

Frisch, Michael. *A Shared Authority: Essays on the Craft and Meaning of Oral and Public History*. Albany: SUNY Press, 1990.

Palmer, Parker. *The Active Life: A Spirituality of Work, Creativity, and Caring*. San Francisco: Harper and Row, 1990.

Resource List

MUSEUM MANAGEMENT BOOKS

Chmelik, Samantha. *Museum Operations: A Handbook of Tools, Templates, and Models*. Lanham, MD: Rowman & Littlefield, 2017.

Genoways, Hugh H., and Lynne M. Ireland. *Museum Administration 2.0*. Revised by Cinnamon Catlin-Lugutko. Second edition. Lanham, MD: Rowman & Littlefield, 2017.

Manual of Museum Planning: Sustainable Space, Facilities, and Operations. Edited by Barry Lord, Gail Dexter Lord, and Lindsay Martin. Third edition. Lanham, MD: AltaMira Press, 2012.

Small Museum Toolkit. Edited by Cinnamon Catlin-Legutko and Stacy Klingler. Lanham, MD: AltaMira Press, 2012.

PROFESSIONAL ASSOCIATIONS—MUSEUM

American Alliance of Museums. http://www.aam-us.org.
American Association for Museum Volunteers. http://www.aamv.org.
American Association for State and Local History. http://www.aaslh.org.
American Museum Membership Conference. http://americanmuseummembership.org/.
American Public Gardens Association. http://www.publicgardens.org.
Association for Living History, Farm, and Agricultural Museums. http://www.alhfam.org.
Association of Art Museum Directors. https://http://www.aamd.org.
Association of Children's Museums. http://www.childrensmuseums.org.
Association of Nature Center Administrators. http://www.natctr.org.
Association of Science and Technology Centers. http://www.astc.org.
Association of Zoos and Aquariums. http://www.aza.org.
Institute of Museum and Library Services. http://www.imls.gov.
International Planetarium Society. http://www.ips-planetarium.org.
Museum-Ed: Connecting the Museum Educator Community. http://museum-ed.org.
Museum Store Association. https://www.museumstoreassociation.org
National Council on Public History. http://www.ncph.org.

PROFESSIONAL ASSOCIATIONS—OTHER

American Bar Association. http://www.americanbar.org/.
American Institute of Certified Public Accountants. http://www.aicpa.org.
Association of Fundraising Professionals. http://www.afpnet.org.
Boardsource: Exceptional Governance Practices for Nonprofit Boards. https://boardsource.org.
Center for Nonprofit Management. http://www.cnm.org.
Foundation Center: Tools and Resources for Philanthropy and the Social Sector. http://foun
dationcenter.org.

DATA RESOURCES

American Association for State and Local History. Visitors Count!—Visitor Research Pro-
gram. http://tools.aaslh.org/visitors-count/.
Association of Art Museum Directors. "Art by the Numbers." https://aamd.org/our-members/
from-the-field.
BoardSource. *Museum Board Leadership 2017: A National Report*. Washington, DC: Board-
Source, 2017. https://www.aam-us.org/wp-content/uploads/2018/01/eyizzp-download-the
-report.pdf.
Center for the Future of Museums. "Trendswatch." http://www.aam-us.org/resources/
center-for-the-future-of-museums/projects-and-reports/trendswatch.
Culture Track by LaPlaca Cohen. https://culturetrack.com/.
DMA: Data and Marketing Association. https://thedma.org/.
Dun and Bradstreet Credit and Risk Products. http://www.dnb.com/products/finance-credit
-risk.html.
Guidestar Nonprofit Reports and Form 990s. http://www.guidestar.org.
Humanities Indicators—American Academy of Arts and Sciences. https://humanitiesindicators
.org/content/indicatordoc.aspx?i=101.
Institute of Museum and Library Services Data Collection. https://www.imls.gov/research-tools/
data-collection.
Institute of Museum and Library Services. Museum Universe Data File. https://data.imls.gov/
Museum-Universe-Data-File/Museum-Universe-Data-File-FY-2015-Q3/ku5e-zr2b.
Know Your Own Bone blog by Colleen Dilenschneider. https://www.colleendilen.com/.
MarketResearch.com. http://www.marketresearch.com.
NCCS: National Center for Charitable Statistics. https://nccs.urban.org.
NCCS Data Archive. https://nccs-data.urban.org/data.php?ds=core.
Pew Research Center: Polling and Demographic Research. http://www.pewresearch.org.
US Census Bureau Data. http://www.census.gov/data/data-tools.html.
US Census Bureau: Statistics of US Businesses. https://www.census.gov/programs-surveys/
susb.html.
US Trends in Arts Attendance and Literary Reading—National Endowment for the Arts.
https://www.arts.gov/publications.

IMPACT FACTORS

Alleyne, Shirley Brown. "Making Programs Self-Sustaining at a Small Historic House Museum." *The Journal of Museum Education* 35, no. 2 (2010): 201–5.

Grzanowski, Cindy. "The Art and Science of Pricing: Maximizing Earned Revenue for the Performing Arts." *Arts Insights* 18, no. 1 (2018): 1–3.

Lucas, Stacey. "Variable Pricing—Increase Revenue While Capturing Data." Audience Roundtable Blog, May 14, 2018. https://www.audiencebuildingroundtable.org/knowledge base-group/2018/05/14/2018-5-14-variable-pricing-increase-revenue-while-capturing-data.

Professional Pricing Society Resource Center. https://pricingsociety.com/resource-center/.

Stafne, Marcos. "Integrating Service and Experience: When Education Meets Admissions." *The Journal of Museum Education* 35, no. 3, part 2 (Fall 2010): 257–65.

PASSIVE INCOME RESOURCES

Budak, Susan E., and Susan N. Gary. "Legal and Accounting Challenges of Underwater Endowment Funds." *Prob. & Prop.* (January/February 2010): 24.

Endowment Fund Investment Policies Sample—Montana Nonprofit Association. https://www.mtnonprofit.org/wp-content/themes/association-child/docs/Files/Org-Dev/Principles_and_Practices/MNA_Sample_Docs/Sample-Investment-Policy-1.pdf.

Gary, Susan N. "Charities, Endowments, and Donor Intent: The Uniform Management of Institutional Funds Act." *Georgia L. Rev.* (2007): 41.

Uniform Prudent Management of Institutional Funds Act. http://www.uniformlaws.org/Act.aspx?title=Prudent%20Management%20of%20Institutional%20Funds%20Act.

FUNDRAISING RESOURCES

The 2016 U.S. Trust ® Study of High Net Worth Philanthropy. New York: US Trust Philanthropic Solutions and Family Office Group, 2016.

American Alliance of Museums. "Financial Stability. Standards Regarding Financial Stability. Standards Regarding Developing and Managing Business and Individual Donor Support." http://ww2.aam-us.org/resources/ethics-standards-and-best-practices/financial-stability.

American Alliance of Museums. "Museums as Economic Engines: A National Report." 2017. https://www.aam-us.org/2018/01/19/museums-as-economic-engines/.

Association for Fundraising Professionals. "Resource Center Toolkits and Resources." http://www.afpnet.org/ResourceCenter/content.cfm?ItemNumber=3136.

Association for Fundraising Professionals Fundraising Effectiveness Project. http://afpfep.org/reports/download/.

Association of Donor Relations Professionals. *Donor Relations and Stewardship Defined.* http://www.adrp.net/assets/documents/adrpdefinitionsexpanded.pdf.

Avalon Consulting Group. "Avalon Cultural Coalition Benchmarking Presentation." Available upon request from info@avalonconsulting.net.

Barden, Pamela. "12 Principles of Fundraising." NonProfitPRO, May 1, 2013. http://www.nonprofitpro.com/article/12-principles-fundraising/all/.

Barry, Frank, Lawrence Henze, David Lamb, and Catherine Swank. *Cultivating Lifelong Donors: Stewardship and the Fundraising Pyramid.* Edited by Heather Friedrichs Lyman and Lindsey Houston Salmony. Charleston: Blackbaud. 2010.

Blackbaud Institute for Philanthropic Impact. "2017 Charitable Giving Report." https://institute .blackbaud.com/asset/2017-charitable-giving-report/.

Bloomerang. "A Guide to Donor Engagement." https://bloomerang.co/engagement.

BoardSource. "Measuring Fundraising Effectiveness: Why Cost of Fundraising Isn't Enough." https://boardsource.org/news/2017/02/measuring-fundraising-effectiveness-2/.

CASE Sample Contact Report. https://www.case.org/Publications_and_Products/Fundrais ing_Fundamentals_Intro/Fundraising_Fundamentals_section_10/Fundraising_Fundamen tals_section_102.html.

Classy. https://www.classy.org/blog/.

Craver, Roger M. *Retention Fundraising: The New Art and Science of Keeping Your Donors for Life.* Medfield, MA: Emerson and Church, 2015.

Culwell, A. C., and H. McLean Grant. "The Giving Code." https://www.openimpact.io/ giving-code.

Developing Major Gifts. https://philanthropy.iupui.edu/professional-development/courses-seminars/the-fund-raising-school/developing-major-gifts.html.

Donahue, Roberta L., and Caitlin Deranek Stewart. "Special Events." In *Achieving Excellence in Fundraising*, fourth edition, edited by Eugene R. Tempel, Timothy L. Seiler, and Dwight Burlingame, 417–21. Hoboken, NJ: John Wiley & Sons, Inc., 2016.

donorCentrics. https://www.blackbaud.com/target-analytics/donorcentrics.

The Fundraising Effectiveness Project, AFP Association of Fundraising Professionals. http:// afpfep.org/about/.

Gainpaulsingh, Mena. *Top 10 Donor Stewardship "Rules" to Ensure that Your Fundraising Thrives.* http://www.afpnet.org/ResourceCenter/ArticleDetail.cfm?ItemNumber=42279.

Garecht, Joe. *Beginner's Guide to Donor Cultivation.* The Fundraising Authority http://www .thefundraisingauthority.com/donor-cultivation/guide-to-donor-cultivation/.

Giving USA: The Annual Report on Philanthropy for the Year 2016. Chicago: Giving USA Foundation, 2017.

Grace, K. S. *Beyond Fundraising: New Strategies for Nonprofit Innovation and Investment.* New York: John Wiley & Sons, Inc., 1997.

Havens, J. J., and P. G. Schervish. "Millionaires and the Millennium: New Estimates of the Forthcoming Wealth Transfer and the Prospects for a Golden Age of Philanthropy." http:// www.bc.edu/content/dam/files/research_sites/cwp/pdf/m_m.pdf.

Havens, J. J., and P. G. Schervish. "Why the $41 Trillion Wealth Transfer Estimate Is Still Valid: A Review of Challenges and Questions." *The Journal of Gift Planning* (January 2003). http://www.bc.edu/content/dam/files/research_sites/cwp/pdf/41trillionreview1.pdf.

Hillinger, T. J. "Measuring Acquisition's Long-Term Impact." Avalon Consulting Group's *FYI* (blog). https://www.avalonconsulting.net/blog/measuring-acquisitions-long-term-impact/.

Hillinger, T. J. "Your Second Gift Rate Is Talking. Are You Listening?" Avalon Consulting Group's *FYI* (blog). https://www.avalonconsulting.net/blog/your-second-gift-rate-is-talking -are-you-listening/.

Indiana University Lilly Family School of Philanthropy. "Giving USA 2017: The Annual Report on Philanthropy for the Year 2016." https://givingusa.org/tag/giving-usa-2017/.

Indiegogo: The Largest Global Crowdfunding and Fundraising Site Online. http://www.indi-egogo.com.

The James Irvine Foundation (with AEA Consultants). "Critical Issues Facing the Arts in Cali-fornia: A Working Paper from the James Irvine Foundation." September 2006.

Johnson, Grossnickle, and Associates Resources for Nonprofits. http://www.jgacounsel.com/resources.

Joslyn, Heather. "4% Growth in Giving Is a Possibility This Year—But Impossible to Say Because of Tax Law." *The Chronicle of Philanthropy*, February 13, 2018. http://www.philanthropy.com/article/Giving-in-2018-Could-Grow-4-/242533.

Kent Dove Sample Script. http://majorgivingnow.org/downloads/pdf/dove.pdf.

Kerr, Kerri. "Where Is the Acquisition Variable in the Retention Equation?" Avalon Consulting Group's *FYI* (blog). https://www.avalonconsulting.net/blog/wheres-the-acquisition-variable-in-the-retention-equation/.

Kickstarter: The World's Largest Funding Platform for Creative Projects. https://www.kickstarter.com.

Kihlstedt, Andrea, and Andy Robinson. "Cycle of Fundraising." In *Train Your Board (and Everyone Else) to Raise Money*. Medfield, MA: Emerson and Church, 2014.

LaRose, Jimmy. "What Tax Reform Means for Charity: More Money, Money, Money." https://insidecharity.org/2018/01/09/what-tax-ref-rm-means-for-charity/.

Levis, Bill, Manager, Fundraising Effectiveness Project; Ben Miller, DonorTrends; and Cathy Williams, Association of Fundraising Professionals. Contributions by Caity Craver, DonorTrends, and Jim Greenfield, ACFRE. "2018 Fundraising Effectiveness Survey Report, A Project of the Growth in Giving Initiative." April 12, 2018. http://afpfep.org/reports/.

Lockshin, Vanessa Chase. http://www.thestorytellingnonprofit.com/blog/21-ideas-to-refresh-your-donor-stewardship/.

Love, Jay. *Donor Retention*. https://bloomerang.co/?s=donor+retention.

Love, Jay. *Follow the Donor Bill of Rights for Donor Retention Success*. https://bloomerang.co/blog/follow-the-donor-bill-of-rights-for-donor-retention-success/.

M+R. "Benchmarks 2018." https://mrbenchmarks.com/.

MacLaughlin, Steve, Chuck Longfield, Angelea Vellake, and Erin Duff. "Charitable Giving Report: How Fundraising Performed in 2017." Edited by Olivia Franzese. Blackbaud Institute. https://institute.blackbaud.com/asset/2017-charitable-giving-report/.

McCrea, Jennifer, Jeffrey C. Walker, and Karl Weber. *The Generosity Network*. New York: Penguin Random House Company, 2013.

Million Dollar Ready: Assessing Institutional Factors that Lead to Transformational Gifts. Indianapolis: Johnson, Grossnickle, and Associates and the Lilly Family School of Philanthropy at Indiana University–Purdue University Indianapolis, 2013.

National Council of Nonprofits. *Tax Cuts and Jobs Act, H.R. 1 Nonprofit Analysis of the Final Tax Law*, Tax Cuts and Jobs Act of 2017, Public Law 115-409. December 22, 2017. Updated February 22, 2018.

Network for Good. https://www.networkforgood.com/non-profit-fundraising-resources/.

Network for Good. *6 Keys to Donor Retention*. https://www.networkforgood.com/nonprofitblog/6-keys-donor-retention/.

Network for Good. *How to Get Donations, 14 Reasons People Give*. https://www.networkforgood.com/nonprofitblog/how-to-get-donations-14-reasons-why-people-donate/.

Penny, N. "Are Museums Too Preoccupied with Visitor Numbers? *Apollo Magazine*, April 23, 2018. https://www.apollo-magazine.com/are-museums-too-preoccupied-by-visitor-numbers/. Accessed May 2018.

Qgiv. *Donor Stewardship: Create Lifelong Donors in 10 Steps*. https://www.qgiv.com/blog/donor-stewardship-guide/.

Ralser, Tom. *ROI for Nonprofits: The New Key to Sustainability*. Hoboken, NJ: John Wiley & Sons, Inc., 2007.

Seymour, Harold J., *Designs for Fund-Raising.* Second edition. Rockville, MD: Fund Raising Institute, a Division of the Taft Group, 1988.

Shefska, Zach, *Metrics 101: Donor & Donation Retention.* The Fundraising Report Card. November 2, 2016. https://fundraisingreportcard.com/donor-and-donation-retention/.

Supporting Advancement Sample Contact Report. http://www.supportingadvancement.com/forms/sample_forms/trinity_contact_report.htm.

Tempel, E. R., T. L. Seiler, and D. F. Burlingame, ed. *Hank Rosso's Achieving Excellence in Fund Raising.* Second edition. San Francisco, CA: Jossey-Bass Publishers, 2003.

Tempel, Eugene R., Timothy L. Seiler, and Dwight Burlingame, eds. *Achieving Excellence in Fundraising.* Hoboken, NJ: John Wiley & Sons, Inc., 2016.

Top 75 Fundraising Websites and Blogs to Follow in 2018. https://blog.feedspot.com/50-must-read-fundraising-blogs-you-should-be-reading/.

Wagner, Lilya. *Careers in Fundraising.* San Francisco, CA: Jossey-Bass, 2001.

Weinstein, Stanley. *The Complete Guide to Fundraising Management.* San Francisco, CA: Wiley, 2002.

Williams, Karla A., ACFRE. *Donor Focused Strategies for Annual Giving.* Edited by James P. Gelatt. Aspen's Fund Raising Series for the Twenty-First Century: Gaithersburg, MD: Aspen Publishers, Inc., 1997.

GRANT RESOURCES

Brophy, S. S. *Is Your Museum Grant Ready: Assessing Your Organization's Potential for Funding.* American Association for State and Local History Book Series. Lanham, MD: AltaMira Press, 2005.

The Chronicle of Philanthropy. https://www.philanthropy.com.

Cilella, S. G., Jr. *Fundraising for Small Museums: In Good Times and Bad.* American Association for State and Local History Book Series. Lanham, MD: AltaMira Press, 2011.

Collections Assessment for Preservation Program (CAP), Institute of Museum and Library Services. https://www.imls.gov/grants/available/collections-assessment-preservation-program-cap.

Federation of State Humanities Councils/Council Programs. http://www.statehumanities.org/program/.

The Foundation Center's Philanthropy News Digest. https://philanthropynewsdigest.org.

The Foundation Directory Online. https://fconline.foundationcenter.org.

GrantStation. https://grantstation.com.

Hruska, B. "Oh Just Write a Grant and Fix the Building: Landing Grants to Support Your Institution." In *Small Museum Tool Kit 2: Financial Resource Development and Management,* edited by C. Catlin-Legutko and S. Klingler, 57–80. American Association for State and Local History Book Series. Lanham, MD: AltaMira Press, 2012.

Institute of Museum and Library Services. www.imls.gov.

National Assembly of State Arts Agencies/About State Arts Agencies. https://nasaa-arts.org/state-arts-agencies/.

National Endowment for the Arts. www.nea.gov.

National Endowment for the Humanities. www.neh.gov.

National Endowment for the Humanities/Preservation Assistance Grants for Smaller Institutions. https://www.neh.gov/grants/preservation/preservation-assistance-grants-smaller-institutions.

National Park Service/Certified Local Government Program. https://www.nps.gov/clg/.

National Science Foundation. www.nsf.gov.

National Trust for Historic Preservation. www.preservationnation.org.

Ohio Arts Council/Grants. http://www.oac.ohio.gov/grants.

Ohio Facilities Construction Commission. http://ofcc.ohio.gov/Services-Programs/Cultural-Facilities-Grant-Program.

Ohio History Connection/Ohio History Fund. https://www.ohiohistory.org/historyfund.

Ohio History Connection/State Historic Preservation Office/Certified Local Government Program. https://www.ohiohistory.org/preserve/state-historic-preservation-office/clg.

Ohio Humanities/Grants. http://www.ohiohumanities.org/grants/.

Preservation Assistance Grants for Smaller Institutions, National Endowment of the Humanities. https://www.neh.gov/grants/preservation/preservation-assistance-grants-smaller-institutions.

State Library of Ohio/Library Services and Technology Act (LSTA) grants. https://library.ohio.gov/services-for-libraries/lsta-grants/.

Tarr, G. A. "Laboratories of Democracy?" Paper prepared for Rutgers University, Camden, Center for State Constitutional Studies. https://statecon.camden.rutgers.edu/sites/statecon/files/publications/lab.pdf.

Verhoff, A. "History Fund Recipient: Fayette County Historical Society." *The Local Historian* 33, no. 4 (September/October 2017): 5–6. https://www.ohiohistory.org/OHC/media/OHC-Media/Fayette-Co-Hist-Soc_HF_LH_Sept-Oct2017.pdf.

EARNED INCOME RESOURCES

American Alliance of Museums. *Annual Condition of Museums and the Economy.* Washington, DC: AAM, 2013.

Andoniadis, Andrew. *Museum Retailing: A Handbook of Strategies for Success.* Edinburgh: Museums Etc., 2010.

Bailey, Martin. "V&A to Scrap Academic Reproduction Fees." *The Art Newspaper*, November 30, 2006.

Bohlen, Celestine. "Retrenching Guggenheim Closes Hall in Las Vegas." *New York Times*, December 24, 2002.

Borrus, Kathy S. "Marketing Crafts through Museum Stores." *Museum International* 40, no. 1 (1998): 22–27.

Canadian Heritage Information Network. "Like Light through a Prism: Analyzing Commercial Markets for Cultural Heritage Content." Public Works and Government Services Canada, Ottawa, 1999.

Chung, James, and Susie Wilkening. *Museums & Society 2034: Trends and Potential Futures.* Washington, DC: Center for the Future of Museums, 2008. aamus.org/upload/museumssociety2034.pdf.

Greenlee, J. S., and J. M. Trussel. "Predicting the Financial Vulnerability of Charitable Organizations." *Nonprofit & Management Leadership* 2, no. 10 (Winter 2000): 199–210.

Haight, Andrew, and Rebecca Reilly. *Case Study: Museum Cafes: Integrating Food, Money, and Mission.* St. Louis: American Alliance of Museums Conference, 2017.

Hamma, Kenneth J. "Public Domain Art in the Age of Easier Mechanical Reproducibility." *D-Lib Magazine* 11, no. 11 (November 2005). http://www.dlib.org/dlib/november05/hamma/11hamma.html.

Jennings, Marilee, and Wendy Weiden. *Food as Discovery: Curating a Culinary Experience for Mission Alignment—A Case Study of* FoodShed *at Children's Museum of San Jose.* San Jose: Children's Museum of San Jose, 2016. https://www.cdm.org/wp-content/uploads/2016/10/FoodShed-Case-Study-Final.pdf.

Kelly, Robert F. "Culture as Commodity: The Marketing of Cultural Objects and Cultural Experiences." *ACR North American Advances* 1987.

Manask, Arthur M., and Robert D. Schwarz. *Restaurants, Catering and Facility Rentals: Maximizing Earned Income*. Edinburgh: Museums Etc., 2012.

Museum of Modern Art Oral History Program. "Interview with Kirk Varnedoe by Sharon Zane." November 28, 2001. https://www.moma.org/momaorg/shared/pdfs/docs/learn/archives/transcript_varnedoe.pdf.

Museum Store Association, ed. *Museum Store: The Manager's Guide: Basic Guidelines for the New Museum Store Manager*. Fourth edition. New York: Rutledge, 2016.

Oster, S. M., C. W. Massarsky, and S. L. Beinhacker, eds. *Generating and Sustaining Nonprofit Earned Income: A Guide to Successful Enterprise Strategies*. San Francisco, CA: Jossey-Bass, 2004.

Pantalony, Rina Elster. "Managing Intellectual Property for Museums." World Intellectual Property Organization, 2013. http://www.wipo.int/copyright/en/museums_ip/.

Robinson, A., with contribution from Jennifer Lehman and Terry Miller. *Selling Social Change (Without Selling Out): Earned Income Strategies for Nonprofits*. San Francisco, CA: Jossey-Bass, 2002.

Scott, Tom. "We're Making the Most of Our Image Collection." *The Art Newspaper* 27, no. 300 (April 2018).

Skinner, Sarah J., Robert B. Ekelund Jr., and John D. Jackson. "Art Museum Attendance, Public Funding, and the Business Cycle." *American Journal of Economics and Sociology* 68, no. 2 (2009): 491–516.

Tanner, Simon. "Reproduction Charging Models & Rights Policy for Digital Images in American Art Museums: A Mellon Foundation Funded Study. https://kclpure.kcl.ac.uk/portal/en/publications/reproduction-charging-models--rights-policy-for-digital-images-in-american-art-museums(95d04077-f8ec-4094-b8c1-d585c6b16d9b).html.

Theobald, Mary Miley. *Museum Store Management*. Second Edition. Nashville, TN: Rowman & Littlefield Publishers, 2000.

Tomkins, Calvin. "The Modernist: Kirk Varnedoe, the Museum of Modern Art and the Tradition of the New." *New Yorker Magazine*, November 5, 2001.

Tomsho, Robert. "Columbia University to Close Fathom.com E-Learning Service." *Wall Street Journal*, January 6, 2003.

Weil, Stephen E. *Making Museums Matter*. Washington, DC: Smithsonian Institution, 2002.

Young, Anne M., ed. 2015. *Rights & Reproductions: The Handbook for Cultural Institutions*. Indianapolis, IN: American Alliance of Museums. (Second edition to be published in 2019.)

THE FUTURE OF REVENUE

Carson, Cary. "The End of History Museums: What's Plan B?" *The Public Historian* 30, no. 4 (2008): 9–27.

Center for the Future of Museums. https://www.aam-us.org/programs/center-for-the-future-of-museums/.

Culture across Communities. "An Eleven City Snapshot, Greater Philadelphia Cultural Alliance." October 2015. https://www.philaculture.org/research/2015-portfolio-culture-across-communities.

Drake, Amy, and Alison Weiss. "History: Made by You: A New Approach from the Southern Oregon Historical Society." *Oregon Historical Quarterly* 113, no. 4 (Winter 2012): 584–95.

Frisch, Michael. *A Shared Authority: Essays on the Craft and Meaning of Oral and Public History*. Albany: SUNY Press, 1990.

Indianapolis Zoo and Digonex. "Overcrowded Weekends and Under-Leveraged Wednesdays." Funworld. November 2015. https://www.digonex.com/wp-content/uploads/2015/11/Funworld-Nov-2015-Industry-Report.pdf.

Landes Foster, William, Peter Kim, and Barbara Christiansen. "Ten Nonprofit Funding Models." *Stanford Social Innovation Review* 7, no. 2 (2009): 32–39.

Merritt, Elizabeth. "FutureProofing Museum Business Plans." *Museum* 96, no. 3 (2017): 17–20.

Palmer, Parker. *The Active Life: A Spirituality of Work, Creativity, and Caring*. San Francisco: Harper and Row, 1990.

Index

About the Editor

Samantha Chmelik, public historian at Preston Argus, LLC, uses her background in operations management, benchmarking, and strategic planning to help cultural and history organizations implement their missions. She has worked and volunteered at libraries, museums, and nonprofit organizations for two decades. She is the author of *Museum Operations: A Handbook of Tools, Templates, and Models* and *Museum and Historic Site Management: A Case Study Approach*, both published by Rowman & Littlefield.

About the Contributors

Blue Anderson is the manager of visitor services for the Columbia River Maritime Museum in Astoria, Oregon, and began her museum store career in 2001 at the San Bernardino County Museum. Blue is a member of the board of directors for the Museum Store Association and is a past president of the Pacific Northwest Chapter. She is also a member of the Board Governance Committee and MSA's Education Advisory Group. She has a bachelor's degree from Butte College.

Tim Ardillo, CFRE, is a consultant with Johnson, Grossnickle, and Associates (JGA). With a development career that spans more than twenty years, Tim has a breadth of fundraising experience across a variety of nonprofit sectors leading efforts ranging from annual fund development, major and planned giving, and campaigns. Before joining JGA in 2014, he served as director of institutional advancement for the Indianapolis Zoo, where he also served as campaign director and led the zoo to the successful completion of a more than $34 million capital campaign and the launch of a $10 million endowment campaign. Tim also led successful campaigns and conducted major gift work while serving as the development director for the Arc of Indiana and in a similar role for the Ronald McDonald House of Indiana. As regional campaign director and then deputy executive director of the Delta Sigma Phi National Headquarters, Tim garnered philanthropic support from alumni for a $5.5 million capital campaign through personal cultivation, solicitation, and stewardship of major donors. Tim volunteers his time with the Association of Fundraising Professionals–Indiana Chapter, having served as president, past president, governance chairman, and program chair. He also serves as the vice president of the board for the Indiana Educational Scholarship Fund. He holds a bachelor's degree in public relations and marketing from the University of Louisiana, Monroe.

Marie Berlin, director of the Young at Art Institute and Community Initiatives, has over fifteen years of experience in museums and nonprofit organizations. She specializes in arts and educational endeavors. Marie creates dynamic programs, exhibits, festivals, and content for children and families. She as bachelor's degree in art and art education from Luther College.

Kristin Bertrand is the director of development at the San José Museum of Art, where she leads the museum's development, membership, and facility rental programs. Before joining the San José Museum of Art in 2015, Bertrand served at Ballet San José as acting director of development, annual giving manager, development officer, and school administrative director. Bertrand is also a founding board member of the Rawson Project Contemporary Ballet and holds a bachelor's degree in English from Rollins College.

Rachel Boyle is a public historian, curator, and consultant whose research focuses on gender, violence, and urban culture. She holds her PhD in US and public history from Loyola University and has worked with the Minnesota Historical Society, the Rogers Park/West Ridge Historical Society, and the Newberry Library. Dr. Boyle also spearheaded the Chrysler Village History Project, which received awards from the American Association of State and Local History, the National Council on Public History, and the Midwestern History Association. Dr. Boyle is the co-founder of Omnia History, a public history collaborative committed to using the past to promote social change in the present.

Megan Bryant is the director of collections and interpretation of the Sixth Floor Museum at Dealey Plaza. Megan began her career at the museum over twenty years ago. Beginning as the museum's first registrar, she has continued in collections management systems and practices. She has a master's degree in anthropology and museum studies from the University of Denver and a bachelor's degree in anthropology from Grinnell College.

Nicholas D'Addezio, director of marketing, is responsible for market strategy and supporting revenue lines at Longwood Gardens. In this role, he manages Longwood's advertising; develops target audiences, segmentation, and promotions; manages digital marketing; and oversees the membership division. Prior to his start at Longwood, D'Addezio worked for fifteen years in various sales and marketing roles in the education technology industry. He has a bachelor's degree in business administration from LaSalle University and an MBA with a focus in marketing from Drexel University.

Melissa Dietrich, associate director of membership, is responsible for overall program management to increase participation and retention, as well as enhance members' experiences. Prior to joining the Longwood team, she honed her skills at global hospitality firms: Brinker International and ARAMARK. Dietrich is active among membership colleagues through the American Public Gardens Association (APGA). Recently she was elected as chair of the APGA's Development and Membership Community, which provides a framework for fundraising and membership professionals in the public garden industry. She has a bachelor's degree in food service management from Johnson and Wales University.

Christa Dyer has worked in retail for over sixteen years but entered the nonprofit world of retail six years ago. Originally from Las Vegas, Nevada, she studied business administration and management at the University of Nevada, Las Vegas. Previously Christa oversaw visitor services and retail operations for Discovery Children's Museum in Las Vegas before moving to San Antonio, Texas, to help open the DoSeum, San Antonio's Museum for Kids, as their director of operations. Christa is the previous president of the SW Chapter of the Museum Store Association and currently serves on the editorial board for *Museums and More Magazine*. She is a first-year recipient of 40 Under 40 for the gift industry in America, awarded in 2017 by Great American Publishing. Christa is nationally recognized for her museum retail successes in multiple national publications (*Museums and More Magazine, Hand to Hand Magazine-Association of Children's Museums*, and other publications). Most recently, Christa has moved to Nashville, Tennessee, and is the director of retail for the Country Music Hall of Fame and Museum. Christa holds a large passion for museum operations but is a powerhouse when it comes to museum retail as she has a wealth of knowledge for buying, merchandising, store design, store operations, and more.

Susan N. Gary, the Orlando J. and Marian H. Hollis Professor of Law at the University of Oregon School of Law, served as the reporter for UPMIFA. She received her bachelor's degree from Yale University and her JD from Columbia University. Before entering academia, she practiced with Mayer, Brown, and Platt in Chicago and with DeBandt, van Hecke, and Lagae in Brussels. Professor Gary teaches trusts and estates, estate planning, nonprofit organizations, and an undergraduate course on law and families. She has written and spoken about the regulation of charities, fiduciary duties including the prudent investor standard, the definition of family for inheritance purposes, donor intent in connection with restricted charitable gifts, and the use of mediation to manage conflict in the estate planning context. Professor Gary is an academic fellow and former regent of the American College of Trust and Estate Counsel, the preeminent US organization for estate planning lawyers and academics, and is a member of the steering committee of the Intentional Endowments Network. She has served as a trustee on the University of Oregon Board of Trustees, on the Council of the Real Property, Trust and Estate Section of the American Bar Association, and on the advisory board of the NYU National Center on Philanthropy and the Law. She has held leadership positions in three sections (trusts and estates, elder law, and nonprofits) of the Association of American Law Schools.

David M. Grabitske holds a doctorate in business administration and a passion for the history enterprise. He has held most positions in history organizations from intern through CEO during the past nearly thirty years and currently serves as site manager of the Landmark Inn State Historic Site in Castroville, Texas, for the Texas Historical Commission.

Jennifer Gritt is the associate director of the Pittock Mansion in Portland Oregon. Ms. Gritt oversees visitor services, museum store, and marketing in addition to her deputy director and strategic planning responsibilities. Prior to the Pittock Mansion, she served as Operations Manager for the Portland Japanese Garden. She is the President of the Pacific Northwest Chapter of the Museum Store Association and has presented at the association's annual conference. Ms. Gritt leverages her over fifteen years combined professional experience in frontline management, staff training and support, customer service, marketing, and writing to facilitate collaborative and forward-thinking environments.

Michael Guajardo is the director of retail operations for the Virginia Museum of Fine Arts in Richmond, Virginia. VMFA ranks as one of the top comprehensive art museums in the United States and its permanent collection encompasses more than thirty-three thousand works of art spanning five thousand years of world history. Michael brings over twenty years of retail experience, having worked in multiple capacities with such retail giants as the Bombay Company, Pier One Imports, and Federated Department Stores. His special talents and strengths encompass operations, sales analysis, team building, product development, and merchandising. Michael enjoys and embraces the opportunity to work and interact with members of the business and museum communities.

Stuart Hata, a veteran museum store retailer for over twenty-nine years, is the director of retail operations for the Fine Arts Museums of San Francisco, the de Young, and Legion of Honor. He is responsible for driving a multimillion dollar business and oversees merchandising, store operations, warehousing, product development, retail marketing, licensing, wholesale, and the online FAMSF store (shop.famsf.org). Stuart has presented on various museum store topics at conferences for the Museum Store Association, American Alliance of Museums, National Museum Publishing Seminar, Western Museums Association, California Association of Museums, Association for Cultural Enterprises UK, and the Museum Shops Association of Australia and New Zealand. He currently serves as the chair of MSA's Marketing and Communications Committee, a member of the MSA Finance and Advocacy Committees, and was the 2016/2017 president of the MSA board of directors.

Jennifer Hayden is the director of PR and marketing at the National Museum of Nuclear Science and History. Jennifer creates and manages the marketing strategies for exhibitions, events, programs, and campaigns for the museum and the international celebration for Nuclear Science Week. She is a member of the Young Professionals of Albuquerque, the New Mexico American Marketing Association, and the Young Leaders Society of United Way of Central New Mexico and sits on the Board of Directors for CLNKids. She has a bachelor's degree in marketing and public relations from Texas Tech University.

Rennae J. Healey has a master's of science degree in historic preservation from Eastern Michigan University and for the past decade has been working in Michigan museums. Ms. Healey has a collection management background but has worked closely with event rentals at the Ford Piquette Avenue Plant for the past two years.

Sara Kennedy is the events manager at the Crocker Art Museum in Sacramento, California. She has spent the past fourteen years planning fundraisers, private events, conferences, and weddings. She began her event planning career at the Nevada Museum of Art in 2004. Her museum and arts administration work includes the Nevada Discovery Museum, Wilbur D. May Museum, and the Nevada Arts Council. She has also worked as a wedding planner both as a freelancer and at a hotel and spa. Sara specializes in social event planning including weddings. She was voted Best Wedding Planner in Northern Nevada in 2014. Sara grew up with artist parents and spent her childhood visiting museums and is thrilled to have a career as an event planner at a museum. As an accomplished photographer, her work has been exhibited in several galleries and museums throughout Nevada and California.

Kimberly A. Kenney became curator of the McKinley Presidential Library and Museum in October 2001 and was promoted to assistant director in 2017. She is the author of six books: *Canton: A Journey Through Time, Canton's West Lawn Cemetery, Canton's Pioneers in Flight, Canton Entertainment, Interpreting Anniversaries and Milestones at Museums and Historic Sites*, and *Through the Lens: The Photography of Frank Dick*. Her work has appeared in *The Public Historian, White House History, The Repository, The Boston Globe, Aviation History*, and the literary magazine *Mused*. She has appeared on *The Daily Show, First Ladies: Influence & Images*, and *Mysteries at the Museum*. Her program "The 1918 Influenza Pandemic" was featured on C-SPAN's series *American History TV*. She graduated summa cum laude from Wells College in Aurora, New York, with a major in American history and minor in creative writing, where she became a member of Phi Beta Kappa. She earned her Master of Arts degree in history museum studies at the Cooperstown Graduate Program.

Faith Brown Kerr is a freelance writer and editor specializing in direct response marketing and fundraising communications. She previously served as director of marketing at the Democratic National Committee and associate director of development for membership at NARAL.

Alyssa Kopf is the vice president of strategic services for the Denver Foundation. Alyssa leads the Denver Foundation's approach to performance management, human resources, organizational culture, and branding and marketing. Alyssa is the former CEO of Community Shares of Colorado, earned her MBA from the Daniels School of Business at the University of Denver, and was selected as a Bonfils-Stanton Livingston Fellow.

Nicole Krom, membership and outreach manager at Longwood Gardens, has more than ten years of experience in the nonprofit field. She spearheads membership strategies, communications, and events, as well as acting as the liaison for Longwood's community partner programs. Imagining and executing new ideas are her passion, and her recent focus has been on visitor experience in cultural institutions, leading Nicole to create the Visitor Experience Group. She also serves as president of the Museum Council of Greater Philadelphia. She graduated with a master's degree in museum education from the University of the Arts and a bachelor's degree in art history from Villanova University.

Holly Piper Lang has more than ten years of professional experience in grants management and is currently the primary grants officer for an art museum in San Diego as well as the owner of Holly Piper Grant Writing Services. With experience securing local and national grants of $5,000 to $250,000+ for diverse organizations such as the Aquarium of the Pacific, Fleet Science Center, and the San Diego Architectural Foundation, she has had the pleasure of working with, and for, various worthy causes. Holly received her bachelor's degree in history and MBA from the University of Redlands. She also holds certificates in nonprofit management and nonprofit marketing from San Diego State University.

Tracy Lawler is president of JGL Food Service Consultants. JGL is a food service consultancy based in Princeton, New Jersey, with offices in New York and Los Angeles. The company specializes in working with cultural institutions and has worked with more than one hundred museums and fifty performing arts centers across the United States. JGL's services include assessments, feasibility studies for expansions, and RFP process. Learn more at www.jglconsultants.com. Tracy can be reached at Tracy@jglconsultants.com or (732) 274-1694.

James G. Leventhal, deputy director and chief development officer at the Museum of the African Diaspora in San Francisco, is a museum leader who has been in the field as an arts professional for over thirty years with significant experience in all elements of high-impact museum work from education, marketing, collections digitization, and organizational development to fundraising. James last served as the director of development at the San José Museum of Art. In the Bay Area, James has also worked at the Exploratorium (director of development), the Contemporary Jewish Museum (deputy director, development), the Judah L. Magnes Museum (director of development and marketing), and the Fine Arts Museum of San Francisco during the tail end of the Campaign for the new de Young.

Martin Levine is a principal at Levine Partners Consulting focusing on aligning organizational purpose with operational reality for small/midsize nonprofit organizations. He is a regular contributor to *Nonprofit Quarterly*. Prior to forming Levine Partners, Marty served as CEO of JCC Chicago, creating a purpose-driven organization, continuously realigning service and management systems to responsively and effectively fulfill JCC Chicago's mission. He has published articles on organizational change and has presented at numerous conferences. A native of New York City, Marty attended CCNY (BS) and Columbia University (MSW). Marty has chaired and served on nonprofit boards and has volunteered with numerous organizations.

Cari Maslow is the associate vice president, engagement, at Carnegie Museums of Pittsburgh. She has more than twenty-five years of experience in nonprofit management and has worked in the arts, social services, and education, holding roles in development, marketing, information systems, and financial management. In her current role, she oversees the membership, mid-level giving, prospect strategy, research, and donor relations programs, as well as the financial management and operation of a sixty-person advancement and community engagement department. She holds a master's degree from the H. John Heinz III College at Carnegie Mellon University and a bachelor's degree from Boston University.

Tonya Matthews is a thought leader in science, technology, engineering, and math (STEM) education and informal learning, community engagement, and organizational equity and inclusion. She is currently a principal equity and executive strategy consultant. Her diverse background includes academic and professional work as a scientist, educator, community volunteer, and award-winning writer/poet. Dr. Matthews served as the first president and CEO of the Michigan Science Center, a hands-on STEM museum and led the organization to reclaim the legacy of science centers in Detroit and become a STEM hub for the state of Michigan. Prior to this role, Matthews was vice president of museums at the Cincinnati Museum Center, leading the research, education, and engagement footprint of the three museum, three research center complex. She is also founder of the STEMinista Project, a multipronged collective impact initiative to inspire the interest of girls and retention of women in STEM careers. Matthews currently serves on the National Academy of Sciences Board on Science Education and as vice chair of the National Assessment Governing Board, overseeing the design of the Nation's Report Card. Matthews is graduate of Duke University and received her doctorate in biomedical engineering from Johns Hopkins University.

Heather McClenahan is the recently retired executive director of the Los Alamos Historical Society. Heather had served as executive director since 2011 and oversaw the renovation and expansion of the museum. She has a master's degree in US history from the University of South Florida and bachelor's degrees in journalism and political science from Drake University.

Julie McDearmon serves as the director of institutional advancement at the Indianapolis Zoo. She has been with the zoo for more than four years and manages the operations of a comprehensive fundraising program. Her current role allows her to work in a field she is truly passionate about: animal conservation. Julie has been in nonprofit fundraising for seventeen years and has broad fundraising experience that includes annual fund management, budgeting, staff and volunteer management, major gifts, moves management, donor and board relations, grant writing, donor stewardship, special events, database management, planned giving, and capital campaigns. She is an Indianapolis native and during her tenure in development has worked at the Indiana University Lilly Family School of Philanthropy, Indiana University School of Nursing, Lambda Chi Alpha Educational Foundation, Jameson Camp, and Nursing Home Ombudsman Agency in Lexington, Kentucky. Julie currently serves on the board of directors of the Association of Fundraising Professionals–Indiana Chapter, is a member of the Association of Zoos and Aquariums Advancement Committee, and is a certified fundraising executive through CFRE International. Julie received her bachelor's degree in business management from the Kelley School of Business at Indiana University. In 2016, she was named one of *Indianapolis Business Journal*'s Forty Under 40.

Valerie Newell, managing director of Mariner Wealth Advisors, has over twenty years of experience in serving on nonprofits boards as a trustee and as an advisor managing the endowments of nonprofit organizations. She is an emeritus trustee and past chair of the board of trustees at the Cincinnati Art Museum, the Museum Center at Union Terminal, and the University of Cincinnati Foundation. She is also a trustee of the Bowling Green State University Foundation, Summit Country Day Foundation, and the Junior League of Cincinnati Endowment Fund. Ms. Newell is an expert in fiduciary responsibility, UPMIFA, and investment management. She was ranked #3 in 2018 and #4 in 2017 on *Barron's* list of Top 100 Women Financial Advisors. She was #14 on *Barron's* 2017 list of Top 100 Independent Wealth Advisors and ranked #1 Wealth Advisor in Ohio by *Barron's* in 2018, 2017, and 2016 while serving as chairman of RiverPoint Capital Management.

Rina Elster Pantalony is a Canadian copyright lawyer, having spent more than twenty-five years working with cultural heritage institutions in Canada and the United States on matters concerning the digital reproduction and distribution of collections and related materials. For over ten years, she was faculty in the Moving Image Archive Preservation Program in the Department of Cinema Studies, Tisch School of the Arts, New York University, where she taught graduate courses in copyright law. Additionally, she chairs the Legal Affairs Committee of the International Council of Museums and is published by the World Intellectual Property Organization as an expert in intellectual property management for cultural heritage institutions. Ms. Elster Pantalony was appointed director of Copyright Advisory Services, Columbia University, in the fall of 2014.

Allison Porter is the president of Avalon Consulting Group, a full-service direct marketing fundraising agency. Since 1997, Avalon has helped clients raise millions of dollars to achieve their visions for a better world while building relationships with people who share their passion and support their important causes. Avalon has a long record of helping clients grow membership and fundraising programs that motivate supporters to contribute to arts and culture. Clients include the John F. Kennedy Center for the Performing Arts, Friends of the Smithsonian, National Museum of the American Indian, National Museum of African American History and Culture, American Film Institute, National Air and Space Museum, Wolf Trap Foundation for the Performing Arts, and American Air Museum in Britain.

Kelly Purdy is the deputy vice president of the Philanthropic Services Group for the Denver Foundation. Kelly leads the foundation's planned giving program, works with donor-advised fund clients on their philanthropic goals, leads the foundation's arts and environmental affinity groups, and oversees strategic operations and systems efficiency within the fundraising department. She has a master's degree in nonprofit management from Regis University and a bachelor's degree in political science and international affairs from the University of Colorado.

Michelle Gallagher Roberts received her bachelor of science degree from Central Washington University and graduated from the University of Denver with a master's degree in anthropology and a specialization in museums studies. For over twelve years she was the head of registration and collections at the New Mexico Museum of Art (Santa Fe, New Mexico). Working in museums since 1997, she has worked in all aspects of registration, collections management, and exhibitions. She is a contributing author on several books related to museums, including *Basic Condition Reporting: A Handbook* and *Rights & Reproductions: The Handbook for Cultural Institutions.* Currently, Michelle is the deputy director at the New Mexico Museum of Art.

Gina Rogak, the director of special events at the Whitney Museum of American Art, has spent twenty years working in or consulting for museum special events. At the Whitney, Gina is responsible for generating revenue of more than $7 million annually through fundraising events and facility rentals, as well as planning and executing all exhibition openings events, including five Whitney Biennials since 2008.

Beverly Sakauye has been chief development officer at the National Civil Rights Museum at the Lorraine Motel, Memphis, Tennessee, since July 2009. Part of the senior management team, she is responsible for overall resource development strategies. She led the campaign that raised $28 million for its first major renovation and established its endowment fund (now at $8 million) with a National Endowment for the Humanities Challenge Grant. Her thirty-plus year career has been dedicated to diverse nonprofits concentrating on development and management in Chicago, New Orleans, and Memphis, where she helped to open the Ogden Museum of Southern Art at the University of New Orleans in 2003 as associate director. She also served as an adjunct instructor on development strategies for the arts administration graduate program at the University of New Orleans. She earned a bachelor's degree from Roosevelt University in sociology 1980, is a member of the Association for Fundraising Professionals, and has made national presentations and served on various grant review panels.

Sara Schultz has a bachelor's degree in public history and a master's degree in sociocultural studies of education from Western Michigan University. She has worked at the Ford Piquette Avenue Plant since 2014 and has coordinated many rentals at the museum, ranging from intimate weddings to events for Fortune 500 companies.

Suzette A. Sherman, president of the Sherman Consulting Group, has extensive management and consulting experience in marketing, fundraising, membership, guest services, and business development, including seventeen years in leadership roles for museums. Her expertise lies in helping cultural organizations establish business models that cultivate loyalty among visitors, members, and donors and generate sustainable revenue streams. Suzette serves the marketing, membership, fundraising, audience research, visitor experience, and business development needs of museums, public gardens, zoos, aquariums, and other cultural attractions. She has also taught the fundamentals of museum fundraising course for Johns Hopkins University's Museum Studies Master of Arts program and served on multiple American Alliance of Museum committees. She received an MBA from University of Minnesota and a bachelor's degree in business from Marquette University, and is a Leadership Philadelphia Fellow.

Gary N. Smith is the president and Texas history program officer of the Summerlee Foundation. Mr. Smith has worked for many years in the Texas history community, serving as executive director of the Dallas Heritage Village for eighteen years and the McFaddin-Ward House (Beaumont) for ten years. He is a past president of the Texas Association of Museums and taught museum administration courses as an adjunct faculty member at Baylor University for ten years.

James Stevens is an economic planner and management consultant with more than a decade of experience working with museum and community leaders to evaluate the earned revenue potential of new programs, plans, facility developments, and public-private partnerships. Based in Pennsylvania and Massachusetts, James is a senior associate at ConsultEcon, Inc., a national and international economic research and management consulting firm that specializes in development and business planning for museums, cultural and community projects, recreational and visitor attractions, tourism, economic development, and mixed-use real estate. James's professional experience includes positions in marketing communications, product development, and community development. James has a master's degree in city planning from the Massachusetts Institute of Technology and a bachelor's degree in history from Cornell University. He is regular presenter at national and regional industry conferences and is a member of the American Alliance of Museums, the Mid-Atlantic Association of Museums, the American Association of State and Local History, the American Planning Association, and the Urban Land Institute, among other professional and industry associations.

Andrew J. Verhoff is the coordinator of the Ohio History Fund, a competitive matching grant program of the Ohio History Connection. The Ohio History Fund's charter administrator, he has led teams that have made sixty-three grants totaling nearly $600,000 between the start of the program in 2012 and 2018. He also co-coordinates the Ohio Historical Markers program, collaborating with local historians to add more than three hundred markers to the state's landscape between 2009 and 2018. He was the coordinator of local history services at the Ohio History Connection from 2009 to 2014 and managed two of its museums in Marietta, Ohio, from 2003 to 2009. A native of Ottawa, Ohio, he holds a bachelor's degree in history from Ohio University in Athens and master's degree in public history from Indiana University, Indianapolis.

Margaret Walker has been the assistant curator at the Vanderbilt University Fine Arts Gallery since 2014, where she has independently curated exhibitions on World War I propaganda posters and the American print revival and has co-curated several more. She holds degrees in history and art history from Princeton University and the University of Edinburgh, respectively, at both places focusing on the arts during World War I. She has published articles with *History Today* and *Nashville Arts Magazine* on a variety of topics. In 2016, Margaret was chosen by the Cystic Fibrosis Foundation as one of Nashville's "30 Under 30." A fun fact about Margaret is that she recently completed a travel project and blog titled *The European Tour of Tennessee* (http://eurostaycation.tumblr.com).

Lily Williams is a development specialist with more than thirty years of broad-based fundraising experience, encompassing major gifts, membership, annual fund, and grant writing. Specializing in creative fundraising solutions for arts and culture organizations, Lily has raised money for numerous prominent museums, including the Philadelphia Museum of Art, the Barnes Foundation, and the Fabric Workshop and Museum. She is also a freelance writer and former newspaper columnist. Lily lives and works in Philadelphia.

Zinia Willits is the director of collections and operations at the Gibbes Museum of Art in Charleston, South Carolina. She received her master's degree in public history from the University of South Carolina and has worked at the Gibbes since 2003, where she manages the museum's permanent collection and oversees all museum operations as well as logistics for its active exhibition and loan programs. Prior to working at the Gibbes, Ms. Willits served as registrar for the Augusta Museum of History and assistant registrar for the Michael C. Carlos Museum at Emory University. Ms. Willits is the vice president of the Southeastern Museums Conference and a member of the executive council and program committee. She was appointed to the 2018 American Alliance of Museums National Program Committee and serves as a peer reviewer for the Museum Assessment Program in the area of collections stewardship. She has presented sessions on registration and collections management at state, regional, and national conferences and has expertise in the areas of collections management, exhibit planning and design, storage planning, grant writing, and facilities management.

ROUNDTABLE PARTICIPANTS

Christina Arseneau, Director, Niles History Center
Dorothy Asher, Director, Lizzadro Museum of Lapidary Art
Thaisa Bell, School Programs Manager, Nashville Zoo
Barbara Hogue, Executive Director, Christ Church Preservation Trust
Lauren Malloy, Program Director, Historic Congressional Cemetery